Mastering 3D Graphics

Digital Botany and Creepy Insects

Bill Fleming

Wiley Computer Publishing

John Wiley & Sons, Inc.
NEW YORK · CHICHESTER · WEINHEIM · BRISBANE · SINGAPORE · TORONTO

Publisher: Robert Ipsen

Editor: Cary Sullivan

Managing Editor: Brian Snapp

Associate New Media Editor: Brian Snapp

Text Design & Composition: Pronto Design & Production, Inc.

Library of Congress Cataloging-in-Publication Data:

Fleming, Bill, 1969–
    Mastering 3D graphics : digital botany and creepy insects / Bill fleming.
p.   cm.
    "Wiley computer publishing."
    ISBN 0-471-38089-X (paper/CD-ROM : alk. paper)
    1. Computer graphics. 2. Three-dimensional display systems. 3. Botany in art. 4. Insects
      in art. 1. Title.
T385 F59216 2000
006.6'93-dc21   99-053031

Printed in the United States of America.

10 9 8 7 6 5 4 3 2 1

CONTENTS

Contributor Biographies   vii

Introduction   ix

Part One: Digital Botany   1

Chapter 1: Creating Natural Environments   3

    Christmas Comes Early   11
      Creating the Branches   13
      Creating the Pine Needles   18
    Dressing the Tree   23
    Wrap Up   31

Chapter 2: Creating Plants and Flowers (LightWave)   33

    When to Use Greenery   33
    Gathering Your Reference Material   35
    The Modeling   35
      Creating the Stamen   39
      Creating the Stem   40
      Creating the Leaves   40
      Creating the Bud   40
    Creating the Textures   43
      Creating the Bud Texture   45
    Applying the Textures   47
    The Assembly   49
    Wrap Up   49

Chapter 3: A Bouquet from an Alien Friend (3D Studio MAX)   53

    Reference Material: Homework First   53
    Choosing the Color Palette   54

The Concept   55
    Analysis of a Plant Arrangement   56

Modeling the First Plant   58
    Applying UVW Mapping   61

Creating a Template for Texture Painting   63

Creating the Materials   66
    The First Base Material   66
    The Structure of the Final Material   66
    Creating the Texture and Mask for Bud2   67
    Creating the Final Multi/Sub-Object Material   71

Secondary Plants   72

Lighting and Final Touch   75

Wrap Up   78

Chapter 4: Tackling a Thorny Challenge (trueSpace)   79

A Prickly Problem   80

A Cactus for Music Lovers   87

Nobody Knows My Saguaro   90

The Mystery Cactus   92

Now for Something Completely Different   94

Adding the Final Touch   96

Wrap Up   97

Chapter 5: The Entrance . . . A Study on Digital Botany (Strata StudioPro)   99

The Tools   100

The Entrance, What's Up with That?   101

Tutorial 1: The Tree   102
    Texturing the Tree   110

Tutorial 2: Grasses   113

Tutorial 3: The Hillside   121

Tutorial 4: Water and Algae   126

Tutorial 5: Building the Scene and Inserting a Camera   131

Tutorial 6: Lighting   135

Wrap Up   145

Chapter 6: Surfacing: Half the Battle (Photoshop)   147

Wrap Up   166

Part Two: Creepy Insects   **167**

Chapter 7: What's Under the Fridge? Part 1: The Model (LightWave)   **169**

  Creating the Roach   172
    Modeling the Body   179
    Building the Leg Protrusion   182
    Creating the Second Body Segment   185
    Modeling the Third Body Segment   188
    Creating the Shoulder Segment   192
    Creating the Head   193
    Modeling the Body Armor   200
    Creating the Head Armor   201

  Wrap Up   206

**Chapter 8: What's Under the Fridge? Part 2: The Surfacing
(Photoshop and LightWave)**   **207**

  Insect Surfacing   207

  Defining Surfaces   210

  Creating Painting Templates   212

  Painting the Image Maps   214

  Surfacing the Roach   226

  Wrap Up   229

Chapter 9: When Dragons Ruled the Skies (3D Studio MAX)   **231**

  The Setup   231

  Modeling the Dragonfly   234

  Modeling the Head   237

  Creating the Legs   239

  Modeling the Wings   242

  Surfacing the Dragonfly   243
    Mapping the Wings   243
    Mapping The Eyes   244
    Mapping the Body   247
    Mapping the Tail   248
    Mapping the Legs   249

  Wrap Up   251

Chapter 10: Stag Party (trueSpace)   **253**

  Modeling the Head   254

  Creating the Thorax   263

Making the Abdomen   264

Adding the Legs   269

Surfacing Bailey   272

Wrap Up   274

Chapter 11: The Postman Butterfly Caterpillar (Strata Studio Pro)   275

Modeling and Organization   276

The Main Body Section   276
   Applying the Bones   280
   Creating the Tail   283

The Head   286

The Legs   290

Creating the Spines   294

Additional Scene Elements   298

Lighting   300

Wrap Up   301

What's on the CD-ROM   303

Index   307

I'd like to thank Darris Dobbs, Chris MacDonald, Eni Oken, Jerry Potts, and Frank Vitale for their contributions to this book. They are truly some of the most talented 3D artists I know and quite exceptional tutorial authors. I'm honored to work with them and have them as contributors to this book.

Below you'll find their biographies. Please take a moment to get to know them better by visiting their Web sites. And definitely e-mail them to let them know how you liked their tutorials. Feedback is the only way we can ensure we provide you with the best tutorials that cover the topics you desire.

Darris Dobbs

Darris Dobbs is the co-owner and art director of HieroglyFX Design. HieroglyFX is a small animation and graphics studio, best known for character design and photorealistic modeling of creatures both real and imagined. He is also the co-author of TrueSpace 3&4 Creature Creations and Animating Facial Features and Expressions. He earned a bachelor's degree in Animal Science from Kansas State University and has spent many years handling a variety of animals professionally. Darris credits this hands-on experience for his ability to create lifelike digital characters. His clients include filmmakers, documentary producers, game creators, and Web designers. He writes extensively on the subjects of 3D Graphics and the use of Visual Effects in film. Darris lives with his family and a house full of pets in the Wichita, Kansas area. His e-mail address is hieroglyfx@aol.com. His Web site is located at http://members.aol.com/hieroglyfx.

Chris MacDonald

Chris MacDonald is a freelance artist and a junior in high school living in Fredericksburg, Virginia. He is currently working in conjunction with Team Komodo and Komodo Comics on the new 3D comic book, Platinum. Chris is an avid LightWave user specializing in environmental photorealism such as botany, terrain, and man-made structures. He can be reached at busha@aol.com.

Eni Oken

Eni Oken is a freelance 3D artist based in Los Angeles. As an architect with 11 years of experience in computer graphics, she has participated in the creation of 3D art (both realtime and pre-rendered) for numerous interactive projects, such as games, Web sites, virtual worlds, and multimedia. Well known companies include Activision, Sierra On-line, L-Squared, and others. She has received several awards for her work, including the 1997 and 1998 3D Design Big Kahuna. She is also the author of three books and several magazine articles that cover topics related to computer graphics. To see more of Eni's work, please go to www.oken3d.com.

Jerry Potts

Jerry Potts has been working with 3D Studio Max and PhotoShop for some-time now. He's a freelance artist with formal art training at Illinois State University. Jerry is currently making background renders for an educational game called Haunted Math for Developing Mind Software. More of his work can be seen at www.geocities.com/SoHo/Studios/1038. You can contact Jerry at jpotts@fgi.net.

Frank Vitale

Frank Vitale has been at the digital art thing for about 10 years. Based in Scottsdale, Arizona, he works freelance from his home on projects in film, broadcast, CD-ROM games, print, and Web development. He is available to answer your questions and welcomes any comments you might have. Frank is also a regular teacher for Strata, Inc. Have a look at the texture tab in StudioPro 2.5. The texture collection under the "StonesThrow" Tab was created by Frank for the 2.5 release. You can contact Frank at vitalef@home.com or visit his Web site at www.vitalef.com.

Welcome to the first compilation book of the popular tutorial Web site—Mastering 3D Graphics (www.mastering3dgraphics.com). In this book we have compiled the tutorials from our first two issues, which cover digital botany and creepy insects. Of course, we didn't have enough room in the book for all the tutorials from the Web site, since our monthly volume is enormous, but we did provide all the tutorials for both issues on the companion CD-ROM.

Between the book and CD-ROM, you'll have more than 1,000 pages of tutorials to pour through, covering 12 popular 3D programs. A complete list of the tutorials and programs covered can be seen at the end of the book in the "What's on the CD-ROM" section.

So why did we choose digital botany and creepy insects for our first compilation book? Well, it's simple really. These two topics are both quite complex and very rarely covered. It can be difficult to find any quality training resources as it is but then if you do manage you'll likely find nothing covering digital botany and creepy insects. We had a great deal of demand for both of these topics at Mastering 3D Graphics, so we decided they would make a perfect duo for our first compilation book. When you are finished with this book you'll be able to create your own natural 3D world and populate it with a variety of creepy insects, making this a turnkey book for developing natural wonders.

I hope you enjoy this book. Be sure to visit the Mastering 3D Graphics Web site at www.mastering3dgraphics.com to see more great tutorials written by the authors of this book and many more talented 3D artists.

Overview of the Book and Technology

New technology is steadily being developed, which expands the capabilities of 3D products. Even the most basic 3D programs posses many of the essential tools for creating amazing 3D images. Although the capabilities of 3D programs will continue to grow, the principles of 3D graphics will always remain constant. This book covers many techniques and technologies for creating 3D images. These techniques are not fixed to any one specific program. They can be used with nearly any 3D program on the market. Of course, we cover specific programs in the tutorials, but that doesn't mean the tools and techniques are unique to that program. Nearly every 3D program today has all the tools and power you'll need to create dazzling digital botany and creepy insects.

If you use any of the following programs, you should read this book: LightWave, 3D Studio MAX, 3D Studio, Strata Studio Pro, ElectricImage, RayDream, true-Space, Animation:Master, Soft/FX, Bryce, Rhinoceros 3D, and Cinema 4D. All of these programs are covered between the book and CD-ROM.

How This Book Is Organized

This book is divided into two parts. The first part deals with developing 3D digital botany, and the second part covers creating creepy insects. In each part, you'll find a general chapter, covering the basic concepts of the topic, and then you'll be presented with detailed tutorials for LightWave, 3D Studio Max, trueSpace, Strata Studio Pro, and Photoshop. You don't have to read one part to understand another, nor do you need to read each chapter, although I recommend it, since many of the tools and techniques are common among 3D programs. If your preferred program isn't covered in the book, don't worry. You'll probably find a tutorial for it on the companion CD-ROM, which features tutorials for several other 3D programs, a list of which can be found at the end of the book in the "What's' on the CD-ROM" section.

Part One: Digital Botany

This part covers the premiere issue of Mastering 3D Graphics-Digital Botany. One of the most challenging projects you can undertake is the task of creating a natural world in 3D. Digital botany has long been one of the most elusive aspects of the 3D business. Although there are many terrain-generation programs, none really offer you the detail and flexibility needed to create plants and environments you can view in close detail, while still appearing realistic. You are also limited to whatever plants and terrain they have. In this part, we'll explore techniques for creating your own natural, and in some cases, alien wonders.

Chapter 1: Creating Natural Environments

This chapter deals with the principles of creating photorealistic digital botany and natural settings. It's a primer of observation and detail. Nothing defines photorealism more than detail. Speaking of detail, I couldn't resist throwing in a tutorial on creating a photorealistic pine tree-manually. I know what you're thinking. Is this guy nuts? Well, yes, I am but trust me, creating the pine tree is actually a great deal easier than you might imagine, and it opens the door to many more possibilities.

Chapter 2: Creating Plants and Flowers (LightWave)

Chris MacDonald, someone who I consider to be a true digital botanist and master of 3D plant life, shows you how to create a very realistic lily in Light-Wave. Chris shows you every step, in great detail, to making a realistic plant, including how to add the natural chaos many artists forget to address.

Chapter 3: A Bouquet from an Alien Friend (3D Studio Max)

Eni Oken, one of my favorite digital artists, takes you to another world of botany-literally. In this chapter Eni shows you how to create a very intriguing alien world setting, complete with weird and wacky plants. Not only does she cover the modeling and surfacing but also the principles of staging and light-ing. It's truly a marvelous tutorial for anyone using 3D Studio Max.

Chapter 4: Tackling a Thorny Challenge (trueSpace)

Darris Dobbs, the mercenary of 3D graphics, and by far the most accomplished trueSpace artist I know, shows you how to populate a digital garden with four several species of cacti and an Aloe plant. Skin care is an important aspect of 3D graphics, you know.

Chapter 5: The Entrance . . . A Study on Digital Botany (Strata Studio Pro)

Frank Vitale, the master of Strata Studio Pro, takes you on a very detailed exploration of digital botany. He shows you how to build a Goblin pond in grand fashion, complete with grassy hillside, a gnarled old tree, and fungus on the water. Frank uses many simple yet powerful techniques that will save you countless hours and headaches.

Chapter 6: Surfacing: Half the Battle (Photoshop)

Frank Vitale shows you the trick of his trade. As one of the leading 3D texture artists, Frank has climbed many mountains in pursuit of the best techniques for re-creating reality in his textures. In this tutorial, Frank shows you how to paint very realistic flower and leaf textures in Photoshop.

Part Two: Creepy Insects

Nothing is more frightening than an insect. Let's face it, there's something about these weird little critters that gets under our skin. For example, the Giant Centipede in North America is eight inches long and eats small animals like mice! That's just too freaky. Insects are a source of terror and wonder, so they make a perfect topic for 3D tutorials. They have such a high level of detail, which makes them a solid foundation builder. If you can master insects you can model just about any creature.

In this part of the book we'll explore many tutorials for creating some cute and sometimes eerie insects. We will cover both modeling and surfacing techniques in great detail.

Chapter 7: What's Under the Fridge? Part 1: The Model (LightWave)

In this chapter we'll explore, in painstaking detail, the process of creating a very detailed photorealistic Madagascar Hissing Cockroach. You might say I got a bit carried away with the tutorial, but my motto is "The more detail the better!" With more than100 figures, you'll find this tutorial to be quite an undertaking, but the result will be well worth the time invested.

Chapter 8: What's Under the Fridge? Part 2: The Surfacing (Photoshop and LightWave)

Modeling an insect is a challenge, but that challenge doesn't end with the model. Surfacing the insect can be a challenge as well. These little critters have plenty of subtle, and sometimes not so subtle, details. It's important to include all the details in our surfacing is we want the bug to appear realistic. This chapter covers a very detailed exploration of creating textures for the Madagascar Hissing Cockroach we modeled in Chapter 7, "What's Under the Fridge? Part 1."

Chapter 9: When Dragons Ruled the Skies (3D Studio Max)

Jerry Potts, a wonderful 3D Studio Max artist, shows you how to create a dragonfly in detail. Jerry covers everything from the modeling to the texturing. The good news is that he uses no plug-ins. Everything is created using the core tools of 3D Studio Max, particularly my favorite modeling tool, MeshSmooth.

Chapter 10: Stag Party (trueSpace)

Darris Dobbs does it again with another incredible tutorial. This time he shows you how to create a photorealistic Stag Beetle in trueSpace. You'll be amazed at some of the techniques he covers, including how he used simple, procedural textures to give the beetle a truly realistic paint job.

Chapter 11: The Postman Butterfly Caterpillar (Strata Studio Pro)

Frank Vitale shows you how to create a marvelously detailed and creepy Postman caterpillar. He covers the modeling and surfacing of this critter, but also goes into detail on using Bones, lighting, and staging. It's a wonderful tutorial for Strata Studio Pro users or anyone who is interested in creating a realistic insect.

What's on the CD-ROM

In this appendix you'll find details about the support files for the tutorials covered in the book. You'll also find two full issues of the Mastering 3D Graphics Web site on the CD, featuring another 20 tutorials not covered in the book!

Who Should Read this Book

This book is for any 3D artist who wants to create digital botany or creepy insects. In fact, it goes far beyond simply these two topics. The techniques and principles discussed in this book can be applied to a wide variety of topics. For example, if you want to create an awesome alien creature, then you'll find the techniques covered in "Part Two: Creepy Insects" invaluable. Most alien creatures found in feature films and television are based upon insects. Let's face it, nothing is creepier than an insect—or more alien, for that matter.

This book is about more than plants and insects, it's about furthering the art of 3D graphics and expanding our boundaries.

If you fall into any of the categories below you should read this book:

Seeking a career in 3D. If you are seeking a career in 3D graphics, this book is a must. Although there are literally thousands of 3D artists seeking work, only a handful are capable of generating solid 3D graphics. A proficiency in creating digital botany and creepy insects puts you at the top of the stack of resumes in the major studios. You should read the book cover-to-cover because it will give you a distinct advantage in the job market.

Multimedia/games. If you are in the multimedia or game industry you are well acquainted with 3D graphics. 3D effects have permeated every aspect of your industry. Where it was once acceptable to use 2D or low-quality 3D graphics, it is now required that you create detailed and often photorealistic effects. Competition is fierce, forcing you to keep improving the quality of your 3D graphics. In this book, you'll discover hundreds of techniques for wowing your customers and clients with awesome 3D graphics.

Film/broadcast. No industry is more particular about the quality of 3D work than yours. Every form of visual media is being saturated with 3D graphics, whether it's needed or not. From virtual sets to animated stunt characters, 3D effects have become a part of nearly every film and broadcast production. Traditional special effects are being replaced with digital effects. This book will provide you with the knowledge to create virtual digital botany photorealistic sets and, of course, those awesome alien creatures to populate the sets.

Print media. Computer graphics have taken your industry by storm. More 3D graphics are popping up in print media every day. Your industry is probably the most challenging when it comes to 3D graphics. Unlike the film industry, where most things move by you too fast to really get a good look, your work lies there motionless so even the smallest flaw can stand out like a beacon. This book will show you countless techniques for creating eye-popping 3D images that will keep your viewers glued to the page.

3D modelers. You are the foundation of every 3D image. It all starts with modeling. If you want to know the secrets of making detailed models, you should dive right into this book. You'll discover dozens of proven techniques for adding incredible detail to your models.

3D texture artists. There is no more important element of 3D graphics than textures. You are saddled with the responsibility of creating the eye candy. It's up to you to create realistic textures that make the model photoreal. You've mastered the painting technique, but now you want to learn the elements that make a texture realistic. You should skip ahead to Chapter 6, "Surfacing—Half the Battle," and Chapter 8, "What's Under the Fridge? Part 2," where you'll learn how to add subtle nuances to your texture to make then undeniably realistic.

Hobbyists. You've been experimenting with 3D and you really want to do something spectacular. Let's face it, you want to show the world what you're capable of doing. You want to leave them dumbfounded when they look at your 3D images. Well, you're only 400 pages away from doing just that!

Whether you are an amateur or a professional, you will benefit from reading this book. In short, if you are a 3D artist who's interested in creating digital botany or insects, read this book!

Tools You Will Need

You will, of course, need a 3D program to take advantage of the information this book has to offer. This book and accompanying CD-ROM cover the following programs:

- 3D Studio Max

- Animation:Master

- Bryce

- Cinema 4D

- Electric Image

- LightWave

- RayDream Studio

- Rhinoceros 3D

- Soft F/X

- Strata Studio Pro

- trueSpace

Of course, any 3D program is fine, since the principles and techniques are not limited to any one program. You will require a working knowledge of the modeling, surfacing, staging, and lighting aspects of your 3D program to grasp the concepts in this book. While this book covers a great deal of detail, it doesn't repeat anything you'll find in your user manual, such as tool descriptions and locations.

You will also need a painting program such as Photoshop. This is an important tool when creating the different types of image maps. Of course, the techniques and tools covered in Photoshop can be applied to most painting programs, including Fractal Painter, Corel's Photopaint, and Paint Shop Pro.

What's on the CD-ROM

The companion CD-ROM contains all the support files for the tutorials in the book and three full issues of the Mastering 3D Graphics Web site. Take a look at the "What's on the CD-ROM" section at the end of the book for more detailed information and a list of all the tutorials.

Getting Started

Photorealistic 3D can be the hardest thing you'll ever accomplish if you don't understand the techniques and principles. Fortunately, you currently have these techniques and principles at your fingertips. After reading this book you'll find photorealistic 3D to be one of the easiest endeavors you've undertaken. You are only 400 pages away from knowing everything you'll need to create stunning photorealistic 3D images. What are you waiting for? Dive in!

PART ONE

Digital Botany

Natural environments are one of the most challenging scenes to create in 3D. It's not due to their complexity but rather the nature of their complexity (no pun intended). Nature is entirely organic, so there are no linear lines and flat edges—well not many, anyway. This makes the task of modeling and surfacing natural objects significantly more complicated than industrial objects.

Of course, an industrial scene is actually far more complex to recreate than natural worlds. Industrial scenes are littered with chaos. There are countless small details on the streets, such as fire hydrants, chainlink fences, Dumpsters, cigarette butts, bottle caps, and the weeds that grow in the pavement cracks. This type of chaos doesn't exist in nature. Yes, there are plenty of plants, rocks, and trees in nature, but when you think about it that's really all there is. We don't see the aging and corrosion of industrial worlds, nor do we see the litter, well, we shouldn't.

Instead, we have organic chaos and plenty of it. Natural worlds are filled with plant life, which makes them challenging to recreate. You see we can get away with a scene looking relatively planned in an industrial world because everything is manufactured, but in nature nothing can appear planned, or the image will be unrealistic. Therefore, to create photorealistic natural worlds, we have to use complete chaos to ensure it doesn't look manufactured. This means we have to be very detailed in our staging and surfacing. Of course, we still need to apply some order to natural worlds to make them appear natural. Although nature is chaotic, it's also ordered. Yes, it's a tricky line we walk when creating natural worlds, but it's primarily all about observation.

In this part we'll be exploring how to create 3D digital botany in LightWave, 3D Studio Max, trueSpace, and Strata Studio Pro.

Although we didn't have the space to cover all 3D programs in the book, you will find equally detailed digital botany tutorials for Ray Dream Studio, Soft F/X Pro, Vue d'Esprit, Tree Professional, and Rhinoceros 3D on the companion CD-ROM. See the "What's on the CD-ROM" section of the book for a detailed listing of the CD contents.

CHAPTER 1

Creating Natural Environments

Bill Fleming

N atural worlds are very detailed, but their details are really limited to plants, trees, and rocks. Of course, there is also the dirt and water, but when you think about it, nature is really just a whole lot of a few objects. A forest is littered with trees. Although there may be several types of trees, it's the volume that creates the chaos. Of course, the trees in a forest represent the buildings of an industrial scene. They support the scene but they really don't carry the weight of the chaos and detail. It's the details on the ground level that create the chaos of natural settings, much as the details of city streets make an industrial scene realistic. Nature's weeds, rocks, twigs, and leaves are analogous to the garbage and clutter we see on city streets. There are tree stumps rather than fire hydrants, and bushes rather than mail boxes and newspaper stands. Of course, natural scenes are much more cluttered than industrial scenes. We don't see city streets covered in trash, at least not in most cities. Although the clutter of city streets is more detailed, the volume of clutter in nature is much greater, making natural environments very resource abusive.

Although a natural environment presents challenges due to the volume of organic details, the wilderness doesn't have an abundance of surfaces to get dirty and worn. We're not going to see a lot of grease, grime, rust, and oil in nature, nor will we see a great deal of garbage—well, hopefully, we won't. Natural worlds are usually relatively clean. Although they are covered in dirt, they don't have rusty, corroded, and grungy surfaces. We don't see bushes covered in dirt stains. The leaves may be dusty, but they aren't covered in grime. Of course, some places in nature, such as swamps and bogs, which are covered in fungus and other sticky things we prefer not to experience first-hand, are quite grimy, but these are usually isolated cases. For the most part, nature is free of grunge.

The first step in creating natural worlds is to observe the wilderness around us. We need to identify the key details that make a natural world believable. Certain details will make the natural scenes we create appear startlingly real-istic. It's really all about attention to detail and observation. I recommend before you begin to create your natural worlds you explore the wilderness around you and take plenty of pictures. If you live in the city and don't have access to natural settings, I suggest you spend a great deal of time watching the Nature Channel on television or visiting the local library or parks. If you try to re-create natural settings from memory, you're going to miss those criti-cal little details that make the scene undeniably realistic. You really need to immerse yourself in the environment to capture the small details such as peb-bles, ground cover, and twigs.

To get a better idea of the details we need to concentrate on when developing photorealistic natural worlds, let's take a look at an image of a natural 3D set-ting. Figure 1.1 shows an example of a complex natural environment.

Here we have a shot of the Unfathomable Crag from the Great Goblin Gaunt-let. Grumpy, the lead character of Goblin lore, is seen on a hunt for Shiny Things. Shiny Things are the currency of Goblins. Anything shiny has signifi-cant value, particularly metals, gems, and ores. This particular scene shows the fringe of the Rain Forest where it meets the Enchanted Desert. The Unfath-omable Crag is a major icon in Goblin legend.

It's rumored that a young boy and girl Goblin were running though the forest when they fell into the crag. Goblins are very resilient, so they didn't die in the fall, but the crag is miles deep and they couldn't climb out. They were forced to live out their lives in caves deep below the Earth's crust. Well, the Goblin sweethearts eventually had children, and their community grew larger with each generation. There is now a whole community of Crag Dwellers, and they are said to feed upon the unfortunate Goblins who fall in the Crag. It's told you can hear the screams of the Crag Goblins at night, which are meant to lure unsuspecting Goblins closer to the crag so they will fall in.

Of course, the legend is only partially true. Yes, the sweetheart Goblins did fall in the crag, and their family grew, but they don't eat the Goblins who fall into the crag. The new Goblins simply join the other unfortunate Goblins who feed upon insects and crawfish from a freshwater spring. It's actually quite nice in the Crag, a bit dark, but generally a pleasant place. The screams heard at night are actually sounds of celebration coming from the Goblins partying in the

Figure 1.1   A photorealistic natural setting.

Crag. Of course, the Crag Goblins don't want this to be known because then there would be hoards of Goblins leaping into the Crag to join the party, and there just isn't that much space, so they let the legend continue.

As you can see, the environment looks very realistic. It's riddled with the detail and chaos we expect to see in a natural world. We have random trees, scattered bushes and weeds, a chaotic ground cover, and dirt littered with rocks and twigs. It's actually a very detailed scene, yet there are really only a few types of objects in the scene. We have a tree, rock, clover ground cover, Guzloader (a prehistoric plant) plant, and dirt. If this were a city street scene, we would have far too few objects to make it appear realistic, but for a natural scene we have plenty of objects. The key is to have several of each object in the scene. In fact, let's take a closer look at the details to get a better idea of their importance. Take a look at the callouts in Figure 1.2.

A. **Fringe grass.** One of the most common elements we see in natural settings is grass growing around the fringe of permanent objects. This is a very simple element to create (we'll get to the how-to later in this chapter), but it adds a tremendous amount of chaos and detail to the scene. The simple

Figure 1.2 A closer look at the details.

grass has been wrapped around the rock, trees, and even the Crag to make the image appear more natural and chaotic. Grass is one of the most important tools for creating natural realities. It's the most common element in natural settings. It comes in a wide variety of visual forms and is extremely easy to create.

B. **Ground cover.** Ground cover is a staple in most natural settings. While it may not always be thick and abundant, there is most certainly some form of ground cover. It's necessary for the survival of surrounding plants because it traps the moisture of the soil so it won't evaporate, thereby retaining the precious water needed by the surrounding plants. About the only place you won't find a ground cover is a desert, and even deserts have ground covers, just very stark ones since the soil is very dry. The ground cover in this image is a perfect example of how Nature creates her ground covers. Notice how it's not an even coverage. The clover has dense and barren spots randomly through the image. This is important for making the ground cover believable. Let's face it, ground covers are only consistently dense in industrial worlds. The grass covering our front yards and parks is very dense because we engineered it that way. A grassy field in reality is very thin and not evenly distributed. The wind isn't terribly particular about where it blows the seeds. If you want to create convincing ground cover, you need to have spots where the density varies dramatically.

In addition to random density of ground cover, you should also add plenty of random chaos to the size and rotation of the ground cover details. The clover in this image was made chaotic by applying a fractal noise displacement. You should always add chaos to your ground cover so it doesn't look too perfect.

C. **Random rocks.** Nature is full of random rocks. They are perfect elements to accent your natural settings because they are easy to create in abundance. They are also easy to surface because they don't have very many details. Now, typically a rock like the one in Figure 1.2 would be dirty from being buried in dirt, but this rock is clean because it's exposed to the natural elements such as rain and wind. It's been washed clean over the years by the elements and will eventually fall below when the dirt is eroded away. Of course, this is likely to reduce the Goblin population below when it hits one of them on the head.

D. **Bare spots.** Although the ground is covered with short moss, it also has numerous bare spots, which are critical for photorealism. Nothing grows with consistency in nature. There will always be dense and light spots of ground cover or any other plant life, such as trees. There will always be a clearing in a forest, since trees cannot grow with an even distribution in nature. In this image the moss texture is random, covering much of the ground but exposing random areas to make it more natural. To enhance the effect of the natural chaos, small pebbles have been added to the bare spots to break up the dirt texture. We can assume that some pebbles will be visible in the bare areas where the dirt has eroded away from exposure to the elements.

E. **Roots.** Roots aren't a staple of most natural settings, but they do add some nice detail and are fairly easy to create. Your scenes may not have a crag in them, but you should experiment with placing surface roots in the scene to add some chaos.

F. **Random weeds.** Nature is littered with random weeds, and they are seen in every natural setting on the planet. Your natural settings should always include an abundance of weeds. You should also provide a variety of weeds in your natural worlds. Figure 1.2 is a very tight shot with a big hole in the middle, so it has but one type of weed, a dandelion. If there were more surface area, it would probably have a variety of weeds, including ragweed, foxweed, and crabgrass.

G. **Plant placement.** The placement of plants is critical in a natural setting. Although the placement in our gardens and parks has nothing to do with the available water, in nature, major growth occurs near the water supply.

Plants need plenty of water, so they will grow where the supply is most abundant. That doesn't mean they grow only near bodies of water, but it does mean they need to grow in fertile soil, which means the soil needs to retain moisture. Plants in nature will grow near permanent objects and ground covers where the soil is rich with moisture. In this image the Guzloader plants are growing near the clover ground cover and the rock, which both help retain moisture in the soil.

As you can see, there really aren't too many details to photorealistic natural settings—there is just a large abundance of a few details. It's really all about where they are placed and their volume of distribution. If you want your natural settings to appear photorealistic, you need to provide a few simple elements, a randomly dense ground cover, random weeds, and the occasional rock and twig. The formula is really that simple. The key is to provide a good variety of weeds and chaos, and if possible a number of different kinds of ground cover of varied height. The image in Figure 1.2 has two different kinds of ground cover, moss and clover. The moss is a very low bump-mapped ground cover, and the clover is a higher, physical mesh ground cover. The combination of these two ground covers fills out the scene nicely. You don't

Figure 1.3 The sparse ground cover of a desert.

want a great deal of dirt showing unless you are creating a desert like the one shown in Figure 1.3.

Here we have a shot of the Enchanted Goblin Desert after a Goblin has walked through it and dropped a bead of sweat on the ground. The dirt in the desert is enchanted by the bones of the Great Mystics, who came to Earth in hopes of finding intelligent life to help propagate their dying race. Unfortunately, all they found was a civilization of dinosaurs and goofy Goblins. After thousands of years one of the Mystics died, so the other Mystics buried him on the Goblin Island. The Mystics had great powers, and their bones are magical. When the bones are placed in the dirt, they enchant the dirt for miles. Since Goblin Island is only 20 miles across, nearly half the island is enchanted by the Mystic's bones, and many inanimate objects have been brought to life, including mushrooms, stones, and even tubers, all of which can be seen in the color insert of this book.

Well, when water is dropped on the Enchanted Desert, it animates the dirt, creating Mud Goblins. These Mud Goblins are quite loud and obnoxious. The normal Goblins hate them because they are way too friendly, running around saying hello to everyone in sight. The Mud Goblins live only as long as there is enough moisture to keep the dirt wet, so when they are created they make a mad dash for the bordering rain forest. Of course, they rarely make it because they usually run in the wrong direction. The desert floor is littered with mounds of dirt that were former Mud Goblins. While they don't look like much from ground level, from the air they resemble mud corpses strewn about on a battlefield.

It takes quite a bit of dirt, typically several gallons, to create a Mud Goblin. So what happens when only a bead of sweat hits the desert dirt? It creates a Desert Wart, which is a tiny Goblin like the one seen in Figure 1.3. It's basically just a bump on the desert floor that is only a quarter inch in diameter. When it sprinkles rain in the desert thousands of these little guys are created, which can be very annoying since they are quite loud. The rule of thumb is don't, at any cost, drop any water on the desert floor. It's a punishable crime in the Goblin kingdom.

Take a close look at Figure 1.3, and you'll notice the ground is clearly visible with a light dispersion of grass and the occasional weed. There isn't much precipitation in the desert, so it's very barren. By contrast, a forest holds a great deal of moisture, so you want the ground to be thick with ground cover and weeds as shown in Figure 1.4.

Before you start developing your environment, be sure to consider the amount of rainfall and the general climate of your world. These factors determine the density of foliage we can expect to see in the scene. A rain forest has

Figure 1.4   Dense ground cover of a forest.

tremendous rainfall, so it's very thick with botany, while a desert has very little rainfall, so it's barren save for the occasional plant, and it's typically a dead plant. If you use the rainfall as the basis for the density of the botany, you can't go wrong.

The key to successfully creating organic worlds is to focus on the small details. It's all about observation. It's a matter of exploring the natural world and mimicking the details you see. Besides, a walk in the wilderness can be a nice break from frying your eyes with monitor radiation. Before you begin to create your 3D natural worlds, you should spend plenty of time exploring the natural environments around you to get a feel for the details you should include. Don't forget to bring your camera and something to sketch small details with, and be sure to make a list of the small elements you see. Don't be in such a hurry that you overlook that little mushroom peeking out from under a leaf or those random twigs under the canopy of a pine tree. Remember the more detail you add, the more realistic the image becomes.Speaking of detail, why don't we try our hand at one of the most obnoxiously detailed digital botany elements you can create—a pine tree.

Christmas Comes Early

Merry Christmas! Okay, you're probably not reading this book at Christmas, but I thought we'd have a little fun creating some 3D Christmas magic. One of the most complex and detailed digital botany objects we can create is a photo-realistic pine tree. Although many programs create 3D trees, they all seem to have the bad habit of placing the leaves and pine needles away from the branches. Nothing is more unrealistic than leaves floating away from the branches. But we really don't want to manually create a forest, do we? Well, not the whole forest anyway.

When building a digital forest it won't matter much if your leaves float away from the branches because most of the trees are in the background, too far away to see the errors. But if you want a tree in the foreground, you need to make sure that the leaves connect to the branches if you are truly seeking photorealism. One of the images I had wanted to create when I first started doing 3D graphics was a nice, warm Christmas image with a truly realistic pine tree. Of course, this is a bit of a challenge given the limitations of today's 3D programs, but I found that if I approached the tree the same way my family handled their Christmas tree, it would be rather easy.

For as long as I can remember, we had an artificial tree for Christmas. Every year my father would pull out the custom crate he manufactured for our tree, and we'd spend the day doing what took Mother Nature years—building a pine tree. The tree had a trunk with a ring of holes around it every six inches where the branches would be placed. It occurred to me that if I approached my 3D pine tree in the same fashion, I could achieve the same results, and just as fast. Of course, my 3D pine tree would be a serious memory hog, but with the power of today's computers it's not really all that bad. So, I began the process of manufacturing a 3D pine tree.

The basic idea was to manufacture a simple trunk object, and then create a series of branches in varying sizes, which would be cloned and placed around the tree. Because the shape of the tree tapers toward the top, the branches would have to be shorter with each step closer to the tip of the tree, just like my family's artificial tree. Well, I found the process and resulting pine tree to be very rewarding. It didn't take much time at all to create a rather realistic pine tree, which you can see in Figure 1.5.

As you can see, the effect is quite convincing. Those countless 3D pine needles really lend credibility to the photorealism of the tree. Of course, I also spent a great deal of time on the decorations and packages, but the tree is what anchors the photorealism of the scene because it has too much detail to be 3D. Remember, the more detail we add the more realistic the models become.

Figure 1.5 A digital Christmas tree.

Viewers cannot believe someone would go through the trouble of replicating every detail of a pine tree in 3D. It's just plain mind-boggling for most people, although we will soon see that it's really not that difficult to build the tree.

In the following tutorial we will construct a 3D pine tree. We won't be decorating it, since it would take an entire book to describe the process of making the ornaments and packages, but I'm sure you will have no trouble decorating your tree. Besides, we all have different taste when it comes to decorating Christmas trees. This tutorial is performed in LightWave, but it can be done in any 3D program. The process of modeling the tree is relatively simple and uses no "advanced" technology, so it doesn't matter if you are using POV-RAY or Soft-Image. You can perform the tutorial in nearly any 3D program on the market.

The tree we're going to create is supposed to be a Christmas tree, so it will be relatively well pruned to fit the classic cone shape of a Christmas tree. To make the tree more natural and wild, you would simply need to extend the occasional branch to add irregularity. Drooping a few branches would also be a good idea. Our tree is also going to be a bit sparse. It has nice gaps between the branches for hanging ornaments. While this would also occur naturally, our gaps will be more consistent so decorating will be a little easier. We do have some liberties given that we're creating the tree ourselves.

Okay, let's get cracking on our pine tree.

EXERCISE: CREATING A 3D PINE TREE

1. The first step is to build the trunk. We'll start with a Plane with six segments as seen in Figure 1.6.

2. We start with a plane instead of a disc because we are going to subdivide the trunk to smooth it, and four-point polygons are much better and more reliable than a disc with many points. To shape the plane, drag the points into an irregular disc shape as seen in Figure 1.7.

3. Next we need to grow the trunk by extruding it with 20 segments as seen in Figure 1.8.

4. Now we'll add a natural taper to the tree. Taper the tree trunk until the top is a quarter of the diameter of the base, as shown in Figure 1.9.

5. The trunk is starting to take shape, but before we call it a wrap we'll need to add chaos to the shape. Using the Magnet tool, add irregularity to the trunk shape by pushing and pulling the trunk in several places, as seen in Figure 1.10.

6. Finally, give the object a surface called "trunk," and then subdivide the mesh and save it as "trunk."

The next step is to create the branches around the tree.

Creating the Branches

The branches are going to be relatively low-resolution. There is no need to create highly detailed branches since they will be heavily obscured by the pine needles. The key here is to keep the polygon count to a minimum.

EXERCISE: MODELING THE BRANCHES

1. We'll start by creating the largest branch at the bottom, and then modify it to create the other smaller branches near the top. To begin the branch, create a plane with two segments and taper the points on both sides as seen in Figure 1.11.

2. Now position the plane in the middle of the trunk, about 1 foot up from the bottom. Then scale the plane so it's a quarter of the width of the trunk.

3. Next, extrude the plane with 12 segments, about 2 feet out from the trunk as shown in Figure 1.12.

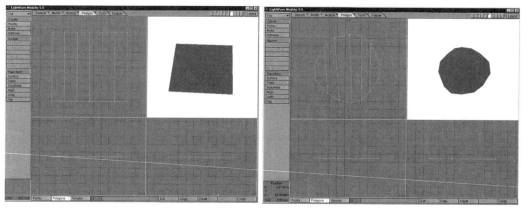

Figure 1.6   The trunk plane.   **Figure 1.7**   Shaping the plane.

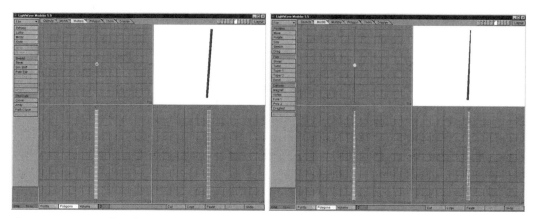

Figure 1.8   Extruding the trunk.   **Figure 1.9**   Tapering the trunk.

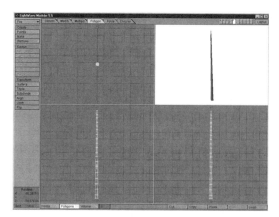

Figure 1.10   Shaping the trunk.

4. Use the magnet tool to add irregularities to the shape of the branch, as shown in Figure 1.13.

5. Now we need to add the extensions for the twigs we'll be creating later. Zoom in to the eighth segment of the branch in your y-axis viewport. Just behind the row of points on the bottom, split the polygon to create a smaller segment as shown in Figure 1.14.

6. Next, select the three polygons on the right of this segment, extrude them slightly, and then drag the points so you have a flat end as seen in Figure 1.15.

7. Now extrude the polygons out three more segments, and shape the extension as shown in Figure 1.16.

8. Finally, split the polygons directly in front of the extension as seen in Figure 1.17.

9. This will strengthen the mesh in this location so the subdivision doesn't round out the leading edge of the extension. Repeat the last four steps to add two more extensions on the branch, and then subdivide the mesh to smooth it as shown in Figure 1.18.

10. Great, we're making progress now. Now give the object a surface named "Branch," and then save it as "Branch_01" The next step is to make the twigs that attach to the ends of our branch extensions. Start by making a disc with five points, as shown in Figure 1.19.

11. Now extrude the plane with six segments, and position the segments as seen in Figure 1.20.

12. Notice how there are two small segments in the middle of the twig. This is where we will add extensions. Zoom in on these segments, and then select the two polygons on the right of the first segment. Extrude them, and then flatten the tip and drag the points to create a rounded shape, as shown in Figure 1.21.

13. Now extrude the extension tip two more times, and position the segments as shown in Figure 1.22.

14. Add another extension to the left side using the next segment, as demonstrated in Figure 1.23.

15. Now for the final extensions, we'll split the tip of the twig into two extensions. Zoom in to the tip of the twig, and then extrude the tip with two segments and rotate the new segments as shown in Figure 1.24.

16. That completes the first extension. The second extension is added by selecting the two polygons on the left of the short segment, extruding them, and then shaping the end to be round as seen in Figure 1.25.

17. Now give this object a surface named "Twig."

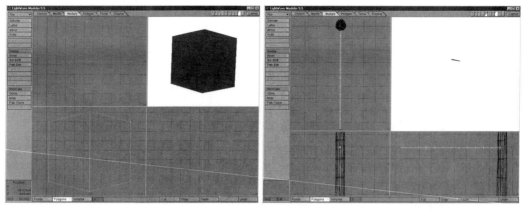

Figure 1.11   The branch plane.

Figure 1.12   Extruding the branch.

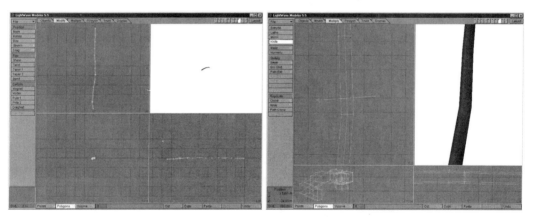

Figure 1.13   The irregularly shaped branch.

Figure 1.14   Creating a small segment.

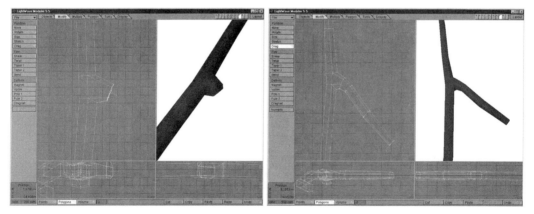

Figure 1.15   Starting the extension.

Figure 1.16   Completing the extension.

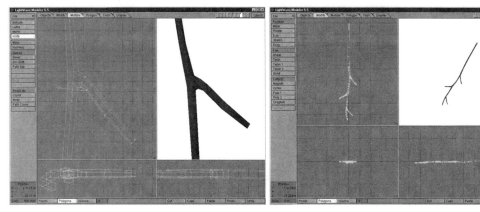

Figure 1.17 Splitting the branch.   **Figure 1.18** The completed branch.

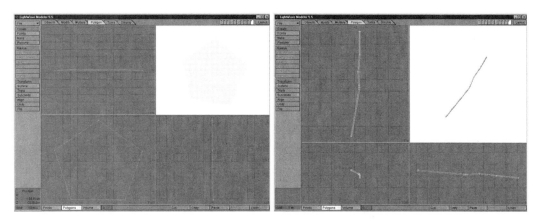

Figure 1.19 The twig plane.   **Figure 1.20** Extruding and shaping the twig.

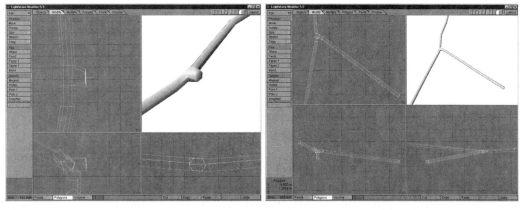

Figure 1.21 Starting the extension.   **Figure 1.22** Completing the extension.

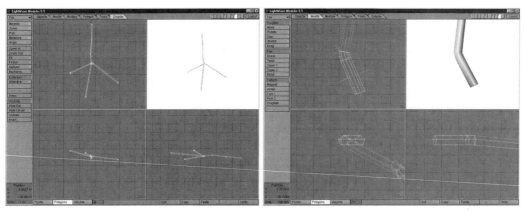

Figure 1.23 Adding another extension. **Figure 1.24** Adding the first extension.

18. The last step in completing the twig is to add tips to the ends of the extension. These tips are a little nub of a different texture than the twig. It's a small detail that really lends credibility to the realism of the tree. To create the nub, create a five-point disc and extrude it one segment. Then pull the two middle points of the tip outward a bit to round the tip as seen in Figure 1.26.

19. Great, now give the nib a new surface called "Nib," and place it at the end of one extension. Then, clone it three times, and place the clones at the ends of the remaining extensions as shown in Figure 1.27.

20. We're just about done with the branch now. The last step is to position the twig at the end of the first branch extension we created. You'll probably need to scale it up or down to fit properly. The diameter of the twig should be half that of the branch extension.

21. Now clone the twig three times, and position the clones at the ends of the remaining branch extension, as seen in Figure 1.28.

Well, that does it for the branch construction. The only remaining step is to add all those tiny little needles, which may seem a bit daunting but is actually quite simple. In fact, let's dive right in and get started.

Creating the Pine Needles

We'll need thousands of pine needles to make the tree photorealistic, but don't let that boggle your mind. We will actually create only a few pine needles and then make liberal use of object cloning to fill out the tree. Let's take a look at how the pine needles are created.

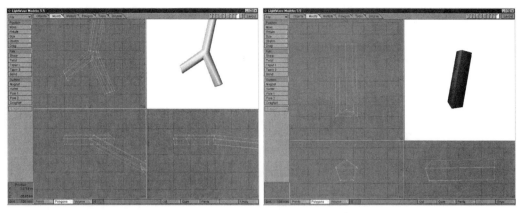

Figure 1.25 The second extension.   **Figure 1.26** The completed nib.

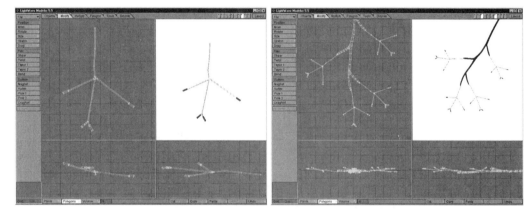

Figure 1.27 The cloned nibs.   **Figure 1.28** Positioned twigs.

EXERCISE: CREATING THE PINE NEEDLES

1. Our first step is to create one pine needle. Start by making a plane with two segments and shaping it as shown in Figure 1.29.

2. Merge the two polygons together to make one. This will cut the polygon count of your tree in half, which will really expedite your rendering time.

3. Now give the object a surface called "Pine Needle," and then position the pine needle at the end of your twig object as seen in Figure 1.30.

4. Clone the pine needle eight times, and position the clones randomly around the twig as seen in Figure 1.31.

5. Now group the pine needles together and name the group "Small Needles." This is the basic pine needle group we are going to clone several times to create a much larger pine needle group to fill out the branches.

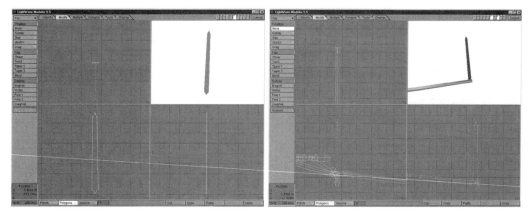

Figure 1.29 Creating the pine needle.   **Figure 1.30** Positioning the needle.

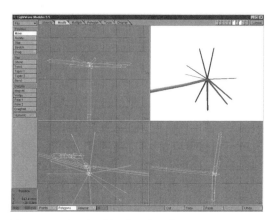

Figure 1.31 Positioning the clones.

6. Make nine clones of this group, and position them slightly apart, rotating them a bit each time to create chaos. The new cluster of pine needles should resemble Figure 1.32.

7. We're starting to get somewhere now. The next step is to group these new pine needles together in a group called "Large Needles," and then clone them four times and position them over the rest of the twig as shown in Figure 1.33.

8. It looks great doesn't it? You can see how cloning a group of pine needles really expedites the process of filling out the twig. Of course, your pine needles may overhang the twig ends, so you'll need to delete all the needles that are floating in space.

9. Now that we have completed the main pine needles, we're ready for the really cool detail. On the end of a pine tree twig you'll find the nib with a

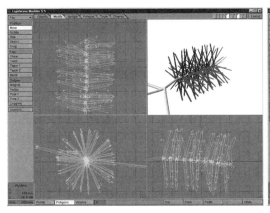

Figure 1.32 The larger pine needle cluster.

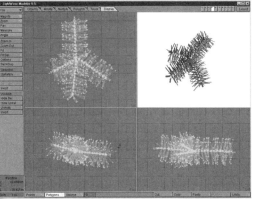

Figure 1.33 Completing the twig pine nee-

cluster of lighter-tone pine needles around it like a feather duster. Creating these pine needles will really add to the photorealism of our tree. To create this cluster, copy one pine needle from the twig, change its surface name to "Nib Needle," and then position it on one of the nubs. Then make 19 clones around the nub to create the cluster shown in Figure 1.34.

10. Group these pine needles, and name the group "Nib Needles." Clone this group and place the clones around each of the remaining nibs to complete the twig shown in Figure 1.35.

11. There are two ways to complete the rest of the twigs on the branch. We could group the pine needles, clone them, and try to position them over the existing twigs, but that would be a little complicated. It makes more sense to group the twig and needles, clone it, place the clones over the existing twigs, and then delete the old twigs. That way, we simply need to position the twig, not the needles.

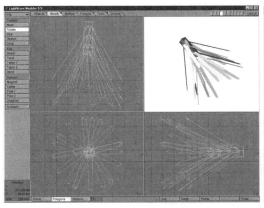

Figure 1.34 The nib pine needles.

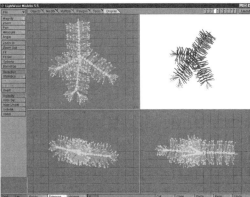

Figure 1.35 The completed twig.

12. Once we are finished with the twigs we need to move on to the branch, which is rather simple. First, make a clone of any "Large Needle" group, and then delete every other ring of pine needles. We don't want the branch to have nearly as many pine needles as the twigs, or the tree will be too fuzzy.

13. Name this new group of polygons "Branch Needles," and then position it at the base of the branch. Finally, clone the group as many times as it takes to fill out the branch, deleting any excess pine needles. Your finished branch should resemble Figure 1.36.

14. Well, that looks pretty darn good. We now have a nicely detailed pine tree branch. Of course, it's a bit rigid and flat, which is quite unnatural as you can see in Figure 1.37.

15. A pine tree branch should bend toward the tip from the weight of the branch and needles. For this reason we need to bend the branch a bit, and then rotate it upward to reflect the natural position and shape seen in Figure 1.38.

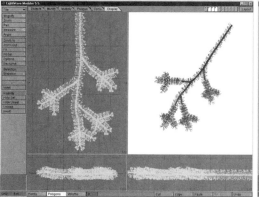

Figure 1.36 The completed branch.

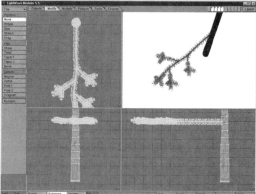

Figure 1.37 The unnatural shape of the branch.

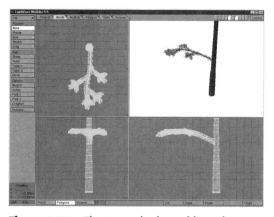

Figure 1.38 The properly shaped branch.

Okay, the branch is truly complete now, and here's where the magic begins. We're going to clone this branch around the tree to fill out the tree, but we certainly don't want to clone the branches one at a time because that would take a lot of effort. Instead, we'll make groups of branches that are cloned. Let's take a look at how this is accomplished.

Dressing the Tree

In reality the branches of an artificial tree are placed on the tree one at a time, making the task a bit time-consuming and labor intensive. Fortunately, in the 3D world we can expedite this process by creating groups of branches that are cloned around the tree, which will save us a great deal of time and headaches. Let's take a look at how we construct our pine tree.

EXERCISE: BUILDING THE TREE

1. The first step is to group our branch and give it a new group name called "Branch." Now the fun begins.

2. Make two clones of this branch and place them slightly above each other. Move the top two branches inward toward the trunk a bit to create a taper to the tree, and then delete the portion of the branch that penetrates the trunk.

3. Now rotate the top branch to the left a bit and the bottom branch to the right. Then rotate the bottom branch clockwise a bit, the middle branch counterclockwise, and the top branch clockwise to create a staggered pattern as you see in Figure 1.39.

4. You can see how the branches are now chaotically staggered, which makes them appear more natural. This is very important. We don't want

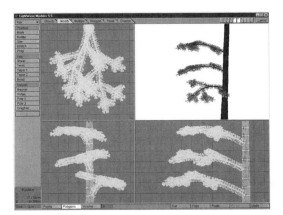

Figure 1.39 The staggered branch group.

the branches to appear too uniform, or the tree will look artificial in spite of our detailed pine needles.

5. Now save this group as a new object named "BranchesLevel_01a." The "a" is rather important because we're going to be making another set of level-one branches later to add chaos to the tree.

6. Now load the "Trunk" and "BranchesLevel_01a" objects into your rendering program.

7. Make five clones of the branch object, and place them even around the trunk as seen in Figure 1.40.

   You can see how the tree is starting to fill out, but it's not dense enough yet. We still need to add six more branches to this level of the tree, but first we need to create a new branch object so the tree doesn't appear too uniform. Fortunately, this is very easy to accomplish.

8. In your modeling program, load the "BranchesLevel_01a" object. Then reverse the rotation of each branch group so the lower branch is now rotated counterclockwise, the middle clockwise, and the top counterclockwise, as shown in Figure 1.41.

9. Save the objects as "BranchesLevel_01b," and load it into your rendering program.

10. Position the "BranchesLevel_01b" object between two of the current branch groups and make five clones around the tree, each between the other groups to fill out the base of the tree, as seen in Figure 1.42 and 1.43.

11. As you can see, the tree has bulked up nicely at the base, and it didn't take any time at all. Now would be a great time to test the look of our tree, but first we should texture it. In the Chapter01 folder of the companion CD-

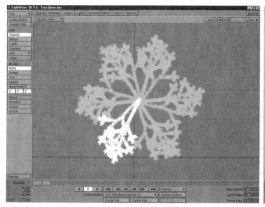

Figure 1.40 Positioning the clones.

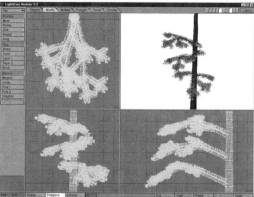

Figure 1.41 Reversing the rotation.

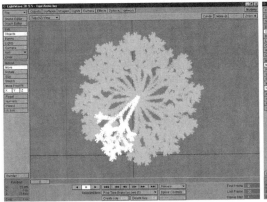 

Figure 1.42 The newly added branches, top view. **Figure 1.43** The newly added branches, camera view.

ROM you'll find two image maps, "PineNeedles.jpg" and "TreeBark.jpg." Load both into your rendering program.

12. Apply the "TreeBark.jpg" image to your "Trunk" surface as a cylindrical map on the Color channel. Make sure the texture tiles five times vertically so you don't stretch the image too far. Then apply the same image to the Bump channel with 100% Bump Value. Now set Specularity to 5%, and if you have Diffusion, set it to 75%.

13. Now copy this surface to the "Branch" surface. Change the texture-mapping method to Cubic for both the Color and Bump channels. Set the texture size so its dimensions are square and it repeats at least 10 times in all directions.

14. Now select the "Pine Needle" surface and apply the "PineNeedles.jpg" image as a cubic map on the Color channel. Make sure the texture tiles 10 times in all directions, and then apply the same image to the Bump channel with 100% Bump Value. Set Specularity to 35% and Diffusion (if you have it)to 80%.

15. Copy this surface to the "Nib Needles" surface. Keep all the settings the same but change the surface color to RGB 255, 255, 0 and set the Color channel image map Opacity to 85%, allowing a bit of the underlying yellow to show through. Using a base color and opacity for the image map saves us the need for another image map. All we want to do is yellow the nib needles a bit.

16. Copy this surface to the "Twig" surface, and keep the settings. We want slightly yellowed twigs.

17. Finally, copy this same surface to the "Nib" surface, but this time change the underlying color to RGB 85, 58, 31, so the nib is slightly brown.

18. Well, that does it for the surfacing. Now add a light to your scene, and do a test render of your tree and branches. Your results should resemble Figure 1.44.

19. The tree looks a little bare, but the branches are definitely very realistic. You can see how this is going to be a marvelous pine tree when we are finished. Speaking of finishing, let's tackle the rest of the branches.

20. The rest of the branches are done in the same fashion as before. Take the "BranchesLevel_01a" object, move it up and inward on the trunk, and then delete the parts that go beyond the other side of the trunk to create a new branch group. Save the new object as "BranchesLevel_02a."

21. Load the "BranchesLevel_02a" object, rearrange the branches, and create the "BranchesLevel_02b" object.

22. Load these objects into your rendering program and clone them around the tree as you did with the first two groups of branches.

23. Repeat this process a third time to create the final groups of branches so you have a complete row of branches running up the side of the trunk, as seen in Figure 1.45.

Here we see all the branch groups lined up along the trunk. Notice the irregularity in their position and shape. This is important if you want

Figure 1.44   A test render of the branches.

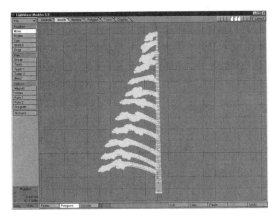

Figure 1.45   The completed branch groups.

your tree to appear natural. Figure 1.46 shows how all these branches appear when rendered.

24. Now that looks like a photorealistic pine tree! Well, except for the missing top, which we'll tackle right now.

25. The top is rather simple. It's basically a clump of twigs. We'll start the top by creating a little vertical branch. Create an eight-point disc and extrude

Figure 1.46   A test render of the branches.

it with 12 segments. Taper it to the top, and using the Magnet tool, bend the branch a bit as shown in Figure 1.47.

26. Place a "Twig" group at the top of the branch as seen in Figure 1.48.

27. Copy some pine needles to the branch as seen in Figure 1.49.

28. Remember to thin out the pine needles by removing every other ring. Now for the final touch clone six "twig" groups in a ring and arrange them chaotically as shown in Figure 1.50.

29. Now place them at the base of the branch as seen in Figure 1.51.

30. Great, the tree topper is now complete. All that remains is to save it as "TreeTop" and load it into your scene. Place the "TreeTop" object at the top of the tree and do a test render. Your image should resemble Figure 1.52.

Now that's a photorealistic pine tree! And it really didn't take much time or effort to create. Your tree is now ready to be decorated and added to a Christmas scene. Or, if you prefer, you can add chaos to the tree and add it to an outdoor scene.

If you plan to use the tree in distant shots you can get away with reducing the pine needle count. You can also render a nice high-resolution image of the tree with an Alpha channel and use the image as a texture map on a flat plane to populate a forest, which is a great memory-saving trick. This way you can custom manufacture a forest to meet your needs, rather than relying on a photograph, which may not suit your needs.

You can even make a few adjustments to create several different tree image maps for your forest, changing the shape and coloration of the tree. It's always a good idea to use a little trickery to save on system resources. The last thing we want to do is make more work for ourselves.

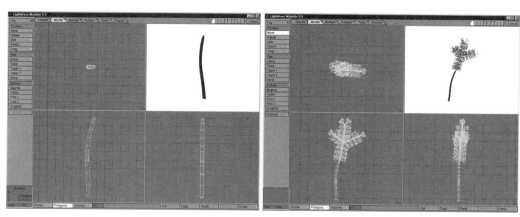

Figure 1.47 The tree top branch.   **Figure 1.48** The tree top twig.

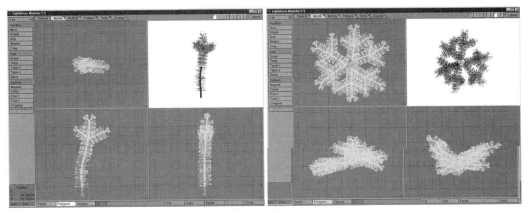

Figure 1.49 Putting pine needles on the branch.

Figure 1.50 Cloning the twigs.

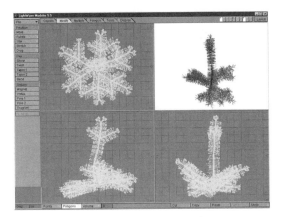

Figure 1.51 Adding the twigs to the tree top.

Speaking of more work, now that you have a wide variety of pine tree branches, you can make all kinds of great objects, like the Christmas wreath seen in Figure 1.53.

The same twigs I used in the tree were applied to this Christmas wreath. I simply cloned them around a center point to create the circular wreath. Then I created a few cool 3D objects like apples and pinecones. I topped it off with a bright bow and a few Christmas lights for character. Of course, I also changed the color to be more of a Blue Spruce.

One good thing about taking the time to manufacture your own digital botany is the reusable parts you'll end up with. Once you've created a few trees, bushes, and leaves, you'll have most of the elements you'll need to manufac-

Figure 1.52 The completed tree render.

Figure 1.53 A 3D Christmas wreath.

ture a complete forest simply by changing the arrangement, color, and size of the parts.

Wrap Up

Well, that was a bit more of a chapter than I had originally expected. We started off on the fundamentals of digital botany and ended up creating a seriously detailed pine tree. The good news is the same technique for creating the pine tree can be used on many other types of trees and bushes, including maple trees.

The process for creating a leafy tree is slightly different. Instead of applying all the leaves in the model, you create small leaf clusters, surface them with detailed leaf textures, and then apply the clusters to the ends of the branches and twigs in your rendering program. This allows you to add a very nicely detailed texture to the leaves and position them randomly on the tree. If you were to create the leaves as part of the original tree model, you'd have a heck of a time surfacing them because they will be at all angles and there would be way too many of them. The last thing you want to do is use a repeating simple, undetailed texture for leaves of trees in the foreground. It just kills the photo-realism of your image.

Oh yes, another great way to add leaves to a tree is to use a morph target. Basically, you create a big pile of leaves, one on top of another. Yes, they are all stacked up in one huge pile. This makes it possible to surface all of them with a single image map. After you surface the leaves, you go back into your modeling program and position them around the tree, changing their rotation and shape so they don't all appear the same. Maybe you curl a few and droop several others downward. Then you save the posed leaves as a morph target and morph your textured leaves to the posed leaves. It's a very effective technique for creating a highly detailed foreground tree object, and it's very easy to do.

Well, that's enough rambling from me, now it's time to hear from the other *Mastering 3D Graphics* authors, so turn the page and get ready to create some very cool digital botany in your favorite program. Remember, if your program isn't covered, you'll probably find a detailed tutorial for it on the CD-ROM.

Creating Plants and Flowers (LightWave)

Chris MacDonald

I can't tell you how many times I've been asked "How did you make those flowers?" or "Can you tell me how to model a good plant?" This is probably for a couple of reasons. First, when an image contains plants and/or flowers that are pleasing to the eye, they immediately stand out since it is still somewhat uncommon to find photorealistic greenery in images. Second, I also think that creating plants is still pretty daunting for a lot of people when they see tons of little leaves and all of the parts that make up a flower or a plant.

In this chapter, I hope to demonstrate how easy it is to create detailed flowers and plants that will add a great deal to an image (assuming the image calls for them, of course). The tutorial in this chapter requires a thorough familiarity with the tools in LightWave and Photoshop.

When to Use Greenery

The most common place to find greenery is going to be outside. One would be hard pressed to go anywhere outside and not see some sort of vegetation, whether it is the giant oak tree in your backyard or the nagging weeds growing in the cracks of the sidewalk. For the most part, an outdoor image that doesn't contain some sort of greenery is probably going to look like it's missing something. So we know that most outdoor scenes need greenery, but what about indoor scenes?

Now, obviously you're not going to place a big pot of flowers on the console of your intergalactic space cruiser. However, there are many other places in life where various kinds of plants or flowers can be found. Take a typical office building, for example. The first thing that comes to mind probably isn't the fake tree sitting in the corner. However, if you take a look at 75% of the office buildings in America, you're most likely going to find some sort of foliage or flora. The reason for this is that plants and flowers give indoor environments a much more pleasant atmosphere. In a 3D image, they greatly reduce the perfect, sterile look commonly found in many indoor scenes. They also add tremendous photorealistic credibility to the scene.

Take a look at Figure 2.1. This is a good example of how plants add life to a scene and really increase the overall realism of the image.

Plants and flowers can add a lot to an image, so a good 3D artist shouldn't be afraid to include them anywhere they would be found in reality. Okay, enough with the lecture, let's make some flowers!

Figure 2.1   Example of plants in a scene.

Gathering Your Reference Material

The first basic rule of modeling anything found in life is to have its real-world counterpart available for study (or at least a picture of it). Since we'll be creating lilies in this tutorial, a picture will suffice. Take a look at the reference image in Figure 2.2.

Notice the way that the petals are curved. Also look at the arrangement of the leaves along the stem. They appear to be staggered down the stem almost all the way down to the very bottom. We're going to alter our lily slightly so the flowers and buds will not be angled downwards as they are in the picture.

Now let's move on to the fun part—modeling!

The Modeling

We'll be doing things a little differently in this tutorial than you are probably used to. Instead of assembling everything in Modeler, we'll only be modeling the parts. Then we'll load them into Layout, surface them, clone them as necessary, and assemble the actual objects. By doing it this way, we can accurately apply tex-

Figure 2.2   Reference image.

ture maps and still be able to load the entire lily object into a scene as many times as we want by using the Load From Scene command in the Objects panel.

EXERCISE: CREATING THE FLOWER

1. Let's open up Modeler and turn on the OpenGL Smooth Shaded preview. I have my units set to Metric, so for this tutorial you'll want to do the same. The first thing that we'll create will be the actual flower. If you had actually scanned in various views of lilies or sketched out your own, you could load it in as a background image. But for this tutorial, we'll just wing it.

2. Drag out a rectangular box in the top view that's about 800mm long on the z-axis and roughly 250 mm wide on the x-axis. Before you hit Enter to create the box, open up the numeric options, and give it two segments along the z-axis. All right, now hit OK and make the box.

3. Now, in the Surfaces panel, turn on Double-sided, since we'll need to be able to view this from all directions. Then subdivide the box using the Faceted setting. Now select each row of points starting at the top working down and resize them along the x-axis until you get a shape similar to the pre-Metaformed petal in Figure 2.3.

4. This next part is a little tricky, so pay close attention. First, switch to Meta-NURBS mode and Metaform the petal one time. Now we will give the petal some shape. You can see in Figure 2.4 that the petal has five columns of points running along the z-axis; the two outer columns, the one middle column, and the two columns in-between.

5. Select the middle column of points that runs down the center of the petal and drag it down a little bit on the y-axis. This will be the center crease of the petal. Now deselect those points and select the outside column of

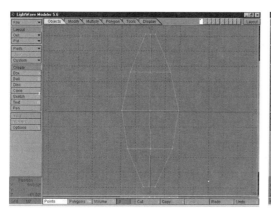

Figure 2.3   The petal before Metaforming and reshaping.

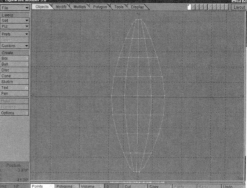

Figure 2.4   The five columns of points.

points on each side of the petal and drag them down slightly further than the center column. At this point, the face view should look like a squashed M, as shown in Figure 2.5.

6. Now rearrange the two columns of "in-between" points in the top view so that they are closer together toward the base of the petal and further apart up toward the tip. Figure 2.6 shows my results using the Taper 2 tool. The point in doing this is to accentuate the center crease near the base of the petal, while making it less pronounced toward the tip. If you like, you may now adjust the points toward the tip of the petal so it ends in a tiny droop. Be careful not to get too crazy with the droop, though, because now we're going to add a bend to the entire petal so that it has a nice arch to it.

7. Before we bend it, save the unfinished model as "metapetal.lwo." We will use this basic shape later on when we make the leaves. Now we're ready to use the Bend tool. Check the settings first just to make sure that the sense is set to positive. In your face view, apply about a 45° bend to it. This gives the petal a nice flowing curve to it, just as it would have in nature. Rotate the petal so that it's relatively parallel to the y plane. The easiest way to do this is to numerically rotate it 22.5° along the x-axis. The petal needs to be in this position so that when we go to texture it, we'll be able to apply a detailed planar image map on the y-axis. Also align the base of the petal with the origin (the intersection of all three axes) in all views. This is done so that when the model is saved, the pivot point will be at the base of the petal for accurate rotation in Layout. See Figure 2.7 for a visual on this.

8. Now, simply freeze the MetaNURBS object with a patch division of four. Okay, looking at our petal now, it looks a little too smooth. The key is to add a bit of randomness to the petal surface. The easiest way to do this is

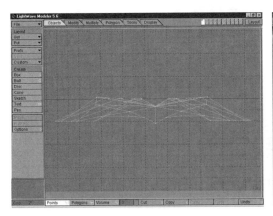

Figure 2.5   Petal in face view.

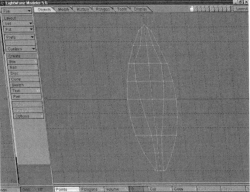

Figure 2.6   Tweaking the shape of the petal.

to apply Jitter. I applied 5 mm of Gaussian Jitter on the y-axis, but feel free to experiment. After Jittering, Metaform the petal once to smooth it all out. Now that we've Jittered it, the final step in modeling the petal is to bend the petal one more time. Bend it 60°, and then rotate it 30° to get it parallel again, as seen in Figure 2.8.

9. Actually, I lied. There's one more step. We need to Triple the polygons so we don't get any nonplanar errors when rendering the flowers in Layout. Before we finish up the flower, save the single petal as "petal.lwo." We will use this object later on in Photoshop to create the petal texture. Now that we have our basic petal, clone it five times around the origin to create the whole flower (see Figure 2.9).

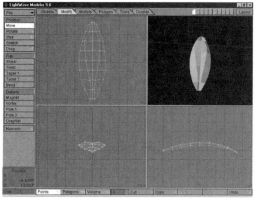

Figure 2.7 Applying the first bend.

Figure 2.8 Final petal, bent and aligned with origin.

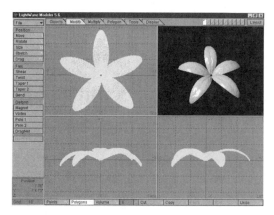

Figure 2.9 Petal cloned five times around origin.

10. You might want to vary the pitch of each so that they don't intersect. Be sure to assign a proper surface name to this object. I'm going to call it "Petal_P_Y" since I'll be applying a planar image map on the y-axis. Make sure that you turn on Smoothing. Actually, from now on, Smoothing will need to be turned on for every surface that we will make.

11. Now that we have our first object modeled, we're going to want to save it in a directory called something like "lily." This will be where we'll save all our objects. Go ahead and save the flower as "flower.lwo." Leave the flower in the first layer of Modeler and open up a second layer.

Creating the Stamen

12. Now we'll model the stamen that will end up in the middle of the flower. This is very simple; just create a cylinder (more like a pipe) with its height along the y-axis. Resize it as necessary to form a thin straw-like tube. Name this surface "Pollentube." We'll be able to get away with using a procedural texture for this object so its orientation really isn't necessary in the surface name.

13. Create a small elliptical sphere stretched along the y-axis, and place it on the top of the shoot. Surface the sphere as "Pollensphere." Bend the whole object a little bit in the top view and rotate it so that it appears to be "growing" out of the y plane. Now clone the stamen four or five times and give each clone a slightly different rotation. Put the petal that is in layer 1 into the background and resize the stamen so that it's sized relative to the petal, just as you saw in Figure 2.10. Paste the stamen into layer 1 and resave the flower.

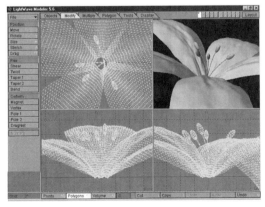

Figure 2.10 Adding the stamen.

Creating the Stem

14. Before we can add much more to the lily, we need to have a stem. Instead of using a cylinder, we'll use a box with MetaNURBS so that we have more control over the shape. Create a long stem-like box along the y-axis. Make the box roughly three meters tall and about 50 mm wide on both the x- and the z-axes. Once again, before you hit Enter, give the box eight segments on the y-axis. Go ahead and create the box, and then switch to MetaNURBS mode.

15. Looking at our reference image, we can see that there is a slight bulge in the stem at the top just before it reaches the flower. Since we're using MetaNURBS, we can easily stretch out the top-most segment of the stem to achieve this effect. After you get the top the way you like, freeze it and align the base of the stem with the origin point in all views. Now apply a small amount of bend (as seen in Figure 2.11), say, 15° or so, and surface the stem as "Stembig_Cyl_Y."

16. Then save it as "stembig.lwo." We called it "stembig" because we now need to scale it down to roughly one third the size of the original, surface it as "Stemsmall_Cyl_Y" and save it as "stemsmall.lwo." This smaller stem will allow us to add more flowers sprouting off of the main stem.

Creating the Leaves

17. Our next step is to create the leaves. Load the model that we saved before called "metapetal.lwo." This will be our basic leaf shape. First, drag the point at the tip of the leaf out so that the leaf comes to more of a point than the petal did. Finish adjusting the other points around the tip so that the leaf tapers off to that end point and roughly matches Figure 2.12.

18. The second major difference between the petal and the leaf is the width. The leaf is clearly much more slender, so scale the leaf along the x-axis until it's roughly half the width of the petal. Now it's starting to look more like a leaf. Resize the entire leaf until its length is about 1.2 meters. Then apply a little Bend to the leaf in the face view, rotate it until it's parallel, freeze the MetaNURBS object at the desired level of detail, and voilà—a leaf (see Figure 2.13). Surface it as "leaf_P_Y" with Double-sided turned on, and save it as "leaf.lwo."

Creating the Bud

19. Okay, now we have one more object to model, the bud. This is the easiest object to model. Create a rectangular box about 350 mm long on the y-axis

and 75 mm wide on the x- and z-axes. Metaform the box once, and select the nine points at the bottom. Squash them down along the y-axis so that the bottom of the bud has a concentration of points toward the bottom. Figure 2.14 illustrates this step.

20. Now Metaform the bud two more times, and create a cylinder with 16 sides and 16 segments that's 500 mm tall and slightly smaller in circumference than the stem we made before. Give it a bend of around 20° and line it up with the bottom of the bud so that it looks like a tail coming out of the bottom and align the bottom of the bud stem with the origin in all views, as in Figure 2.15. Surface the bud as "Bud_Cyl_Y" and the stem as 'budstem_Cyl_Y' and save the whole thing as "bud.lwo." See? I told you it was easy.

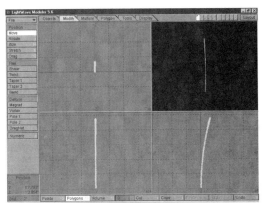

Figure 2.11   Bending the stem.

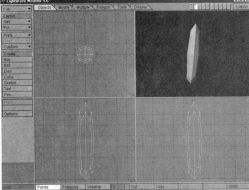

Figure 2.12   Accentuating the leaf tip.

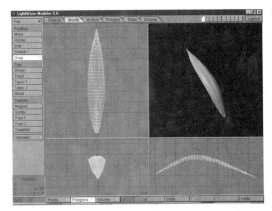

Figure 2.13   Final leaf model.

Figure 2.14   Squashing the points down along the y-axis.

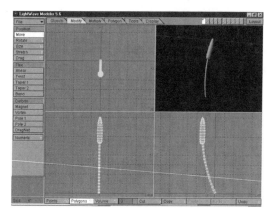

Figure 2.15 Bud with stem.

21. That's about it as far as the modeling portion of this tutorial goes. If all went well, you should have five objects like those in Figure 2.16.

So now we have these five pieces of a lily. "What do we do with them?" you ask. Why, we texture them, of course! Obviously, texturing is one of the most important aspects of creating a 3D image, so be sure to take your time in this section.

Figure 2.16 The five parts of the lily.

Creating the Textures

We'll begin with the flower. Load "petal.lwo" into Modeler if it's not already there and drag out the top view so that it encompasses the whole screen. Zoom in on the object now using the Fit All command. You should now be looking at a really big petal from the top. If you have screen capture software you can use it now, otherwise just hit the Print Screen key on your keyboard. This copies the current image on the screen to the Clipboard.

Here is where we need Photoshop or any other image-editing program that has "layers." I'll be using version 4.0.

EXERCISE: CREATING THE FLOWER TEXTURES

1. Open Photoshop and create a new document. The default size for the document should be whatever your screen resolution is because that is the size of the image currently on the Clipboard.

2. Now hit OK, and then paste the image from the Clipboard into the document. Using the Crop tool, crop the document so that the petal fills the whole image. I find that using the Guides to outline the shape of the box before drawing the selection makes this process much easier. See Figure 2.17 for a visual of this step.

Figure 2.17 Cropping the screen capture of the flower.

3. Now we can have some fun. Create a second layer on top of the wireframe image. Set the transparency of the new layer to around 80%. This allows us to see through the layer that we're painting on so that we can use the wireframe as a guide without actually painting onto it. Depending upon your equipment, you could either use the Photoshop tools to create the image map, or you could actually scan in a petal of some sort and apply that to the image. It's up to you. I opted to paint my lily by hand with an orange hue. We won't be covering the actual painting techniques in this chapter, but you will find a very detailed digital botany painting tutorial in Chapter 6, "Surfacing: Half the Battle," by Frank Vitale.

4. You can find my petal texture in the Chapter02 folder on the companion CD-ROM. It's called "Petal.jpg." You can paste this image in your template file or create your own. Either way, when you are finished, save it as a PSD file, but don't flatten it.

5. Now, go back into Modeler, load the "flower.lwo" object, zoom in on it, take a screen shot, and paste it into a new Photoshop document. Crop it around the flower just as we did with the petal. Now, open the petal document, select the second layer that contains the petal image, and copy it. Paste it into the new document on top of the wireframe flower. You can see in Figure 2.18 that only the petal was pasted, not the background wireframe of the petal. That's why we didn't flatten the image earlier.

6. The rest is easy. Just resize the new layer so that it fits one of the petals and line it up. Clone the layer four more times and use the Transform Layer tools to align each of the five layers with the petals. Make sure that all the layers are now set to 100% opacity and merge the petal layers

Figure 2.18   Petal pasted into layered document.

together. The easiest way to do this is to link them together via the Layers window and then choose Merge Linked. At this point, you might have to do some cloning and touching up here and there to get it just right. Copy the flower layer and paste it into a new, clean white document, flatten it, and save it as "petal.jpg." (See Figure 2.19.) Phew—you'll be happy to know that the hardest part is behind us.

7. Okay, now repeat steps 15–17 for the leaf, except this time at the end of step 17, copy the layer with the leaf texture on it and paste it into a new document, flatten it, and save it. Figure 2.20 shows you what I came up with.

This texture is also in the Chapter02 folder on the CD-ROM, under the name "Leaf.jpg." Now save your texture as "leaf.jpg."

Now for the bud.

Creating the Bud Texture

This is a little trickier to do but only because we're creating a cylindrical map rather than a planar map.

EXERCISE: CREATING THE BUD TEXTURE

1. The first two steps are the same as for the two planar maps that we just created. Get a screen capture of the bud in the face view, and crop the document to fit it. Be sure that you crop the image around only the bud, not the stem.

Figure 2.19 The final petal texture.

2. Here is where it changes. Paint the side of the bud just as you would paint the leaf or the petal. You can paint your own or load my bud texture from the Chapter02 folder on the CD-ROM. It's called "BudStart.jpg."

3. Once you're finished, copy it to the Clipboard and click on New to open a new document. Once again, the default size of the document should automatically be whatever the size of the image on the Clipboard is. Leave the height the way it is, but double the width.

4. Create the new document, and paste the image into it. Align the image with one side of the document. You can see that because we doubled the width, there is room for another copy of the image.

5. Duplicate the layer or simply paste the image into the document again and flip this new layer horizontally and line it up with the other side of the document. What you should end up with is two identical images mirrored next to one another, as seen in Figure 2.21.

6. Now flatten the image, and if there is a visible seam in the middle where the two layers were connected, paint it out with the Clone tool. Then save the image as "bud.jpg."

We should now have three textures: the petal texture, the leaf texture, and the bud texture. We'll be able to use them for the color textures and for the bump maps. Well, we're finally ready to put it all together in Layout, so let's go!

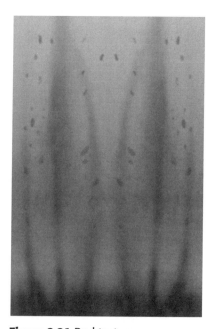

Figure 2.20   The leaf texture.   **Figure 2.21** Bud texture.

Applying the Textures

Open Layout and load the five parts of the flower:

- petal.lwo
- leaf.lwo
- bud.lwo
- stembig.lwo
- stemsmall.lwo

Don't worry if they overlap. We will position them later. Now load in the three image maps that we just created:

- Petal.jpg
- Leaf.jpg
- Bud.jpg

We'll texture the petal first.

EXERCISE: SURFACING THE FLOWER

1. Apply the "petal.jpg" image to the "Petal_P_Y" surface as a planar map on the y-axis, just as the surface name indicates. Choose "Automatic Sizing" and turn off Texture Anti-aliasing. Apply the same image as a planar bump map on the y-axis with the same options. Give the bump map an amplitude of about 100%. As far as the rest of the settings go, I chose what I thought looked best, but you can certainly adjust the surface attributes to your liking. Although these settings are optional, keep in mind the fact that most plants and even petals have some sort of specularity to their surface, which you should be sure to include on your flowers.

    - Luminosity = 0.0%
    - Diffuse Level = 80%
    - Specular Level = 15%
    - Color Highlights = Checked
    - Glossiness = Medium
    - Reflectivity = 0%
    - Transparency = 0%

2. We'll do the same for the leaf. Apply its texture map ("leaf.jpg") in the same manner. The only settings I changed are the other surfacing attributes:

- Luminosity = 0.0%
- Diffuse Level = 90%
- Specular Level = 15%
- Color Highlights = UnChecked
- Glossiness = Medium
- Reflectivity = 0%
- Transparency = 0%

3. For the bud, just apply the "bud.jpg" image as a cylindrical map on the y-axis. Select "Auto-sizing," turn off texture anti-aliasing, and if you like, apply it as a bump map as well. The rest of the surface settings for the bud are identical to those of the petal.

4. The three stem surfaces ("Budstem_Cyl_Y," "Stembig_Cyl_Y," and "Stemsmall_Cyl_Y") can all be surfaced with the leaf color texture. Simply apply it as a cylindrical map along the y-axis. You can also use the leaf's surfacing attributes for the stems. Easy, eh?

5. Okay, last but certainly not least, is the stamen. The "stamen" surface is easy.

- Surface Color = 240,150,40
- Luminosity = 0.0%
- Diffuse Level = 90%
- Specular Level = 25%
- Color Highlights = Checked
- Glossiness = Medium
- Reflectivity = 0%
- Transparency = 0%

6. And the "pollenbud" surface wasn't much harder.

- Surface Color = 70,55,30
- Luminosity = 0.0%
- Diffuse Level = 70%
- Specular Level = 10%
- Color Highlights = Un-checked
- Glossiness = Medium
- Reflectivity = 0%
- Transparency = 0%

Well, that's about it for the texturing. The last step in the whole process is simply to assemble the lily and set up some lights.

The Assembly

So now we have all of the objects modeled and textured, but we still don't have anything that resembles a lily. No problem, that's about to change. First, parent all of the objects to the main stem ("stembig.lwo"). Create a Null object and name it "Lily Parent Null." Now parent the main stem to the null. What we have just done is given ourselves the ability to adjust the position of the entire lily through one object.

We are now able to arrange the objects that comprise the lily into what we feel best matches our reference image or our imagination. Also, by having modeled the "stemsmall.lwo" object, we can clone this around the plant in various places so that we can attach some more flowers. Have fun! This is where all the work that we have done pays off!

Once you have assembled the lily to your liking, save the scene as something like "lilyloader.lws." Guess what, that's it! Now, anytime you wish to use the lilies in a scene, simply go to the Objects panel, choose Load From Scene, choose "lilyloader.lws, and all the objects will be loaded into your current scene. Their hierarchies will be intact, and their texture maps will be perfectly aligned, just the way you left them. You may even want to set up a few scenes, each with slightly different versions of the plant to avoid obvious repetition.

This is a very useful technique for getting around the lack of UV Mapping support in LightWave as it allows you to align the textures properly while still being able to replicate a group of objects as many times as is necessary. This technique can be applied to any type of object that requires similar control over the texturing and positioning.

The final product that I ended up with after this tutorial is what you see in Figure 2.22.

Of course, yours will probably look substantially different due to the variation in texture maps.

Wrap Up

The technique described in this tutorial can be used as a basis for the creation of an entire scene, as shown by the work-in-progress in Figure 2.23. Once you

Figure 2.22 The final image.

Figure 2.23 Another example of digital botany.

get the hang of it, you'll find that it works wonders for digital botany no matter how daunting the task.

Although greenery does add a lot to an image, be careful not to rely on it to make your image look good. Always keep in mind that proper lighting, modeling, texturing, and composition all come together to form the final image. Hopefully, this tutorial showed you that beautiful and intricate flowers and plants can be created with relative ease. The realism that they add to your images is certainly well worth the effort it takes to create them.

A Bouquet from an Alien Friend (3D Studio MAX)

By Eni Oken

C reating organic live objects using 3D computer graphics has always been a challenge for even the most talented artist. Plants and trees represent a particularly difficult task simply due to the sheer number of leaves and other little living details usually present in plants. Because I have already been face to face with such a challenge before, I know that it can be a tough ride.

So when I decided to create some alien plants, it was mostly because I was interested in taking an alternative route from traditional greenery. Besides, alien plants offer so many opportunities of fun design and concept!

Reference Material: Homework First

The first thing I usually do when approaching a new project, before even touching any modeling, is a lot of research. I do most of my research in the library or in a bookstore. (Owning your own reference books is always fun, although it is not really practical.) For this task, I wondered at first where could I possibly find reference material to serve as inspiration for alien plants. I found three interesting sources. The most obvious was books about exotic plants from the Amazon rain forest. A second source of inspiration was found in books that show microscopic photography, and a third source—usually forgotten by most people—was children's picture books. Microscopic photography usually shows bacteria and microorganisms that have the weirdest shapes, and children's books are full of rich, colorful, wacky, out-of-this-world scenarios.

I usually stack a pile of books, all marked with Post-Its on the pages of the most interesting objects and things. At this stage, I don't really worry about choosing the appropriate ones yet; it's just food for the imagination.

For this project, I used the following books as reference guides:

- *Structure in Nature as a Strategy for Design*. Peter Pearce. MIT Press, 1990.
- *Design Lessons from Nature*. Benjamin Debrie Taylor. Watson Guptill Publications, 1974.
- *Art Forms in Nature*. Ernst Haeckel. Dover Publications, 1974. (No respectable creator of alien landscapes should start without this one—it's amazing.)
- *Art Forms in the Plant World*. Karl Blossfeldt. Dover Publications, 1985. (This book includes perfect examples of microcosm photography, in which minuscule grass looks like giant threatening trees).
- *Chiaroscuro*. Tim White. Paper Tiger, 1994. (Tim is a traditional fantasy artist whom I admire enormously.)
- *The Secret Art of Dr. Seuss*. Random House, Inc., 1995. (Who could ever paint wackier landscapes than Dr. Seuss?)
- *Here Come the Aliens*. Colin McNaughton. Candlewick Press, 1995.

As you can see, you can never do too much research. Well, maybe you could, but it would be difficult. Once your research is complete, you will need to decide which colors you want to use in the image.

Choosing the Color Palette

Another task that I assigned to myself before starting the dirty work on the computer was choosing the palette of colors. A color palette, or even better, a color scheme, is composed of the main hues to be used throughout the project. I make it a point to never go beyond my original palette; in addition to giving an image a more finished look, it also shows control and makes it easier to create textures.

I had been working on a project that would fit perfectly as a scenario for the alien plants; a real-time virtual world. The palette used for the project was orange, purple, yellow, and some red and teal, a blue-green color, as seen in Figure 3.1.

Figure 3.1   The color scheme: orange, purple, yellow, and some red and teal.

I usually don't use so many colors, but in this case I felt it necessary to have a range that would allow me to experiment on different plants.

The next step in planning your project is to consider the actual concept.

The Concept

Although many artists sketch their projects before starting to work, I usually feel more comfortable just letting my imagination run wild while modeling. However, the peculiarities and technical limitations of each project, in this case, a real-time 3D world, to a large extent determine the direction the project will take.

For real-time projects, each engine has its own limitations and allowances. For this virtual Web world, the engine allowed for very few polygons, but at the same time, the texture restraints were generous compared with other real-time projects that I have encountered. I could use almost any number of textures, as long as they were all 128 x 128. They could be tiled or stitched together on panels to use larger images.

This made the modeling decisions pretty obvious. The plants would be created in small clusters, such as flower pots, that would then be used as textures for flat polygonal panels. The panels would act like billboards, holding the detailed pictures of the alien plants, as seen in Figure 3.2.

Analysis of a Plant Arrangement

When the main concept was broken down, I needed to go further and investigate how a single cluster of plants would be structured. While analyzing traditional gardening and flower arrangement books, I noticed that the size and color of plants was usually of great importance for the results (and in the process I acquired a new respect for people with such skills). Figure 3.3 shows a suggested plant arrangement.

The arrangement structure that was most suitable for the purposes and limitations of this project usually had the following elements:

- One or two large or tall plants in the background. The placement could be central or lateral.

Figure 3.2 Billboard holding a panel of plants.

Figure 3.3   Structure of a typical plant arrangement.

- Several medium-sized plants in the middle ground, about one third of the height of the larger plants and surrounding the larger plants.
- Several smaller plants in the foreground, usually new plants, grass, fillers, sometimes draped down. These were usually very small or had tiny leaves and flowers. A base made of rocks, sand, a vase, or container.

Generally speaking, as far as colors are concerned, flowers are usually presented in monochromatic schemes, with subtle variations, or even two colors, sometimes contrasting strongly. Green and brown tones are always present in a neutral way. Shapes and texture usually contrast sharply or are extremely similar in type. Plants always come in a variety of ages, meaning that even full-grown adult plants usually have smaller newer buds nearby.

Because I chose to create weird alien plants, my first decision regarded the neutral colors, which are usually green and brown. I decided to choose something else, a color that would be totally unusual, perhaps purple-blue. This would automatically make the garden look weird and foreign. I also decided to make the texture bulbous and thick, similar to cactus, but not monochromatic with a cellular texture.

Let's get started modeling these alien creations.

Modeling the First Plant

The first plant to be modeled was one of the large plants in the background, mostly because all the other plants would gravitate around it. I will go into quite a lot of detail to show how this plant was modeled and textured, because all the other plants were made using a similar technique. To model organic shapes using 3D Studio Max, there are several alternatives including NURBS and patches, however, I usually use what is called, by some artists, the "box method."

This method consists of starting with a plain box or other simple geometric shape and then extruding faces and manipulating vertices to form other elements and details. After creating a simple structure, the entire object is smoothed out using the MeshSmooth command.

EXERCISE: CREATING THE FIRST PLANT

1. Inside 3D Studio Max, I created a simple long box. Under the Modify tab, I first converted the box into an editable mesh. I then chose the sub-object "Face" and then picked the top face of the box and extruded it. With the Reference Coordinate System set to Local (very important for future steps), I scaled the selected face up a little and then extruded again. This formed the bulge on the top as shown in Figure 3.4.

2. The next step can be done two ways. One option was to select individual faces around the top of the plant and extrude them, scaling and rotating them individually. Another option was to use a MaxScript called FaceScape, which performs the task automatically (although in a random way) to most or all of the selected faces (see Figure 3.5). In case you are trying this without the MaxScript, it will be necessary to select and extrude the individual faces one by one on the first time, or the entire top will be extruded, and that is not the desired effect.

3. After the first extrusion, it was not necessary to extrude each branch individually, all I had to do was select the faces that were at the very end of each branch and extrude them all at once. Also, by keeping the Reference Coordinate System set to Local, I was able to scale down or rotate all the faces at once. I repeated this a couple of times, until the branches started to acquire a pleasing shape, shown in Figure 3.6.

4. When the branches started to become thin, I extruded another couple of times, forming small buds at the very tip of each branch. As the plant

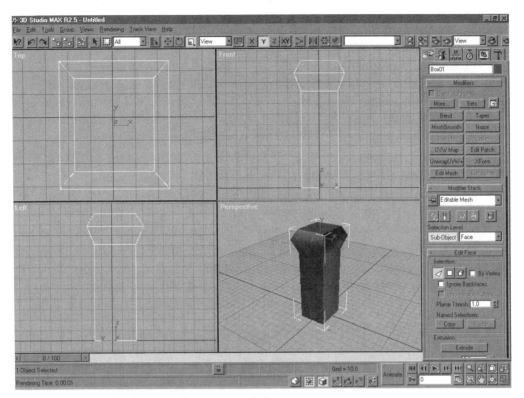

Figure 3.4　A simple box with the top extruded twice.

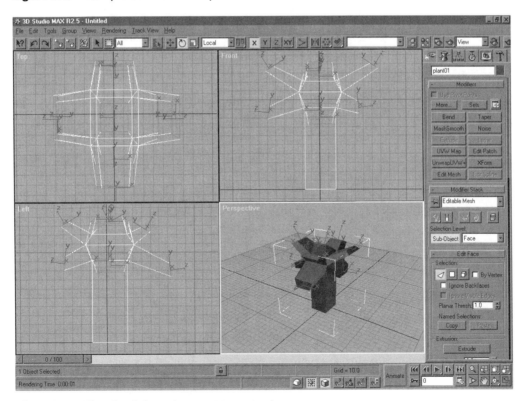

Figure 3.5　The plant's branches start to protrude.

started taking shape, I realized it was necessary to run a small test, which was only temporary, using the MeshSmooth command. With the sub-object unclicked, I applied the modifier MeshSmooth once and viewed the results in the Perspective window with the option to see with Smooth and Highlights. Figure 3.7 shows the results.

5. I deleted the MeshSmooth modifier soon after, for there was still a lot of modeling to do. I continued to manipulate the plant, this time going down, to form a sort of trunk. I continued in this manner, selecting faces, extruding and manipulating them (scale, move, rotate) to extend the main trunk. A smaller patch in the middle section of the plant was left intentionally, as a starting point to extrude some smaller buds, seen in Figure 3.8.

6. The first smaller bud was created the same way as the main plant. A single face was extruded, scaled, and rotated—always using the Local Coordinate System—until the necessary shape was formed (see Figure 3.9).

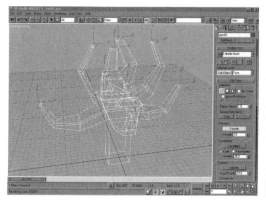

Figure 3.6 The branches start to take their final shape.

Figure 3.7 A test with MeshSmooth shows some temporary results.

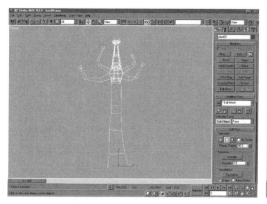

Figure 3.8 Extruding the trunk and preparing for smaller buds.

Figure 3.9 The first bud was created by extruding one of the faces of the trunk.

7. At the very end of the first bud, I selected faces individually and extruded them again, in the same manner as the top of the plant, forming a sort of young flower. I also created a second bud, even smaller than the first one. This concluded the rough modeling of the plant, so I applied a final MeshSmooth to create the final results, which can be seen in Figure 3.10. This command usually works with best results when used with Quad Output and Smooth Results checked.

Applying UVW Mapping

I consider modeling to be only the first part of a successful 3D project. In fact, I tend to focus much more on the texturing work than I do on modeling. Good texture work gives the object a more finished look and makes it look more realistic.

Before creating any materials, it is necessary to apply the UV mapping coordinates, and with such an irregular shape as this plant, one would imagine that it would be quite a task. Well, it was, but it was made much easier by breaking the geometry into main groups. This approach makes it possible to texture any kind of irregular object.

The easiest way to assign mapping coordinates is to select logical groups of faces that fit into a certain type of mapping (spherical, cylindrical, or planar) and to assign them different material IDs. By assigning different material IDs, it also becomes easier to select the same faces later on for manipulation and to update multi/sub-object materials.

I decided to divide the plant into the following groups: Top, Bud1, Bud2, and Trunk (see Figure 3.11).

Figure 3.10 Final plant geometry with MeshSmooth applied.

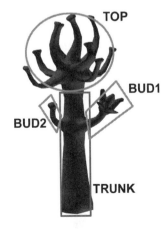

Figure 3.11 The plant divided into logical groups.

The Top would be mapped spherically, while all the other groups would be mapped cylindrically, following the most natural shape line. The next exercise outlines how I selected the objects and assigned different IDs.

EXERCISE: ASSIGNING THE MATERIAL IDS

1. Under the Modify tab, I clicked on the Sub-Object and activated the Face selection mode. I selected the upper part of the plant and immediately assigned the material ID 1 to that group of faces. Then I assigned a spherical UV Mapping, controlling the Gizmo to position it in the center of the selected Faces, as seen in Figure 3.12.

2. I repeated the same procedure with the faces of Bud1, Bud2, and the Trunk (see Figure 3.13).

It is important to remember to assign the UV mapping a little looser than necessary, meaning, make it larger than the faces selected. This way, there is always room in the texture to move around, and there is little risk of creating undesirable seams.

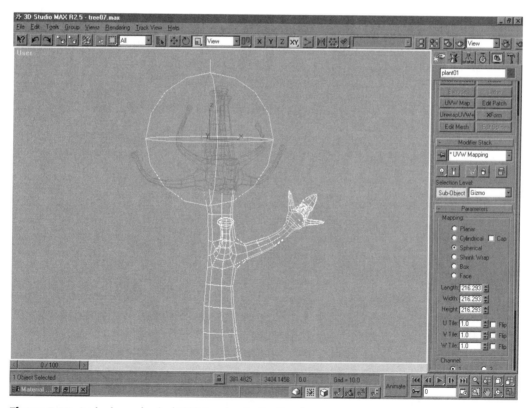

Figure 3.12 Assigning spherical UV Mapping to the Top faces.

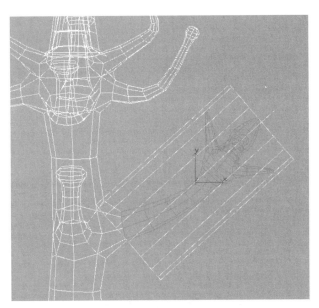

Figure 3.13 Cylindrical UV mapping for the Trunk and Bud1.

Speaking of mapping, let's take a look at creating the painting templates for our image maps.

Creating a Template for Texture Painting

Before creating textures for the plant, it is necessary to create a template, that is, to mark where specific features should be painted. For this example, it had been established that the overall color would be a bluish-purple, but I wanted the tips of the buds to be bright and colorful, resembling fruit or flowers. Therefore, the tips of the buds need to be located on the texture map. I also needed to know where the seams and connections would be placed, so I would not make the mistake of creating something that would show a seam.

A template can be created using several methods. A well-known method is to use a 3D painting program. A few plug-in packages are compatible with 3D Studio Max, and occasionally I use 4D Paint by 4D Vision. This can easily be done by assigning mapping coordinates to the object (which I had done already) and then assigning a temporary material of any kind and painting in 3D a few markings on the features that are worth distinction. After that, it is pretty easy to use this template in any other painting package, as shown in Figure 3.14.

In case you do not have a 3D painting program, you can create a template by using a simple MaxScript that comes with 3D Studio Max 2.5 called UV

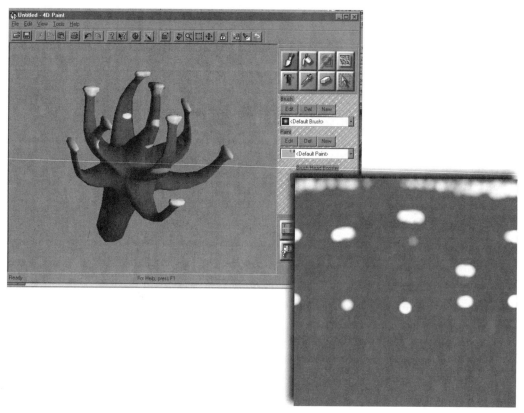

Figure 3.14 Template for materials created using a 3D painting package.

Unwrap (this is not the modifier of the same name that comes with the program). To create a template using the MaxScript, this is how I proceeded:

EXERCISE: CREATING A PAINTING TEMPLATE WITH UV UNWRAP

1. The example used here was the group of faces named Trunk. First, I selected the faces of the Trunk (easily done by using the command Select by ID under Edit Mesh). Using the Shift-Click command, I inserted a clone of those faces into a new object, shown in Figure 3.15. That made it easier to use the MaxScript UV Unwrap.

2. I hid the original plant so I could easily work with the clone. Under the Tools tab, I loaded the UVW Unwrap MaxScript and assigned the clone Trunk to be the selected object. The default size of the map is 256, but I prefer to work with 500 because the markings and wireframe can be seen more clearly. This particular MaxScript then generated an image that showed the markings of the trunk as if they were spread out on a flat panel, literally unwrapping the cylindrical mapping on to a plane (see Figure 3.16).

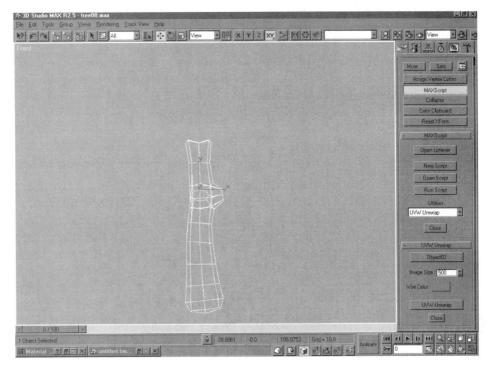

Figure 3.15 MaxScript UVW Unwrap was applied to a clone of the Trunk faces.

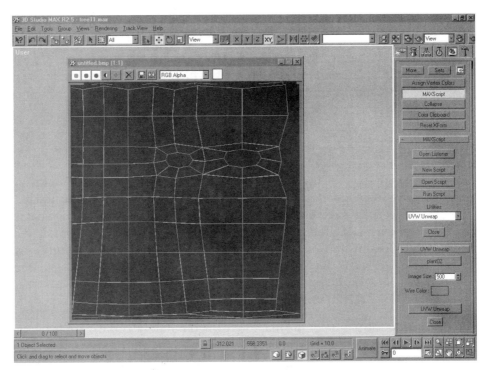

Figure 3.16 The unwrapped UVW mapping coordinates from the Trunk clone.

I then repeated this process with the other groups of faces, creating four templates, one for each group. These helped me tremendously when creating the colored textures for the plant.

Creating the Materials

My texture work usually includes a combination of several textures and materials. It is naïve to think that one can achieve good-quality texture work with a single texture pass. Even in real-time games and interactive projects, good textures are usually made of several layers of "paint" on top of the original, that is, texture over texture, which results in a rich and deep color effect on the final map.

The First Base Material

The first material to be created was a basic material called Cellular, conveniently named since it was created based on the 3D map Cellular. 3D maps are independent of mapping coordinates and spread out through odd-shaped objects in a uniform manner, making them the best choice for the base color of the plant.

The same Cellular material was used as material color and as bump map, and the result was an organic but odd-colored texture, shown in Figure 3.17.

To achieve the bluish-purple tone I was looking for, I combined three colors in the cellular procedural settings: a light blue, medium gray, and purple. I used the same material for the bump map and assigned very little shininess to the material.

The Structure of the Final Material

On top of the base material, I planned to add another coat of "paint"; this time adding some unique features to each one of the face groups created before. The logical choice to do this would be to use Blend materials, which combine two materials mixing them through the use of a black-and-white mask. (Of course, other options do exist, but they do not offer the masking abilities needed for the final effect). Because four distinct groups needed special features (Top, Bud1, Bud2, and Trunk), I would also have to create a Multi/Sub-Object material, where each ID would correspond to the respective groups.

The final structure of the material turned out to be quite complex, but it is easier to understand if we break it into a tree diagram, as shown in Figure 3.18.

The example shown in Figure 3.18 uses the Blend material for the Bud2 group: it was made out of two materials, blended with a black-and-white mask, and

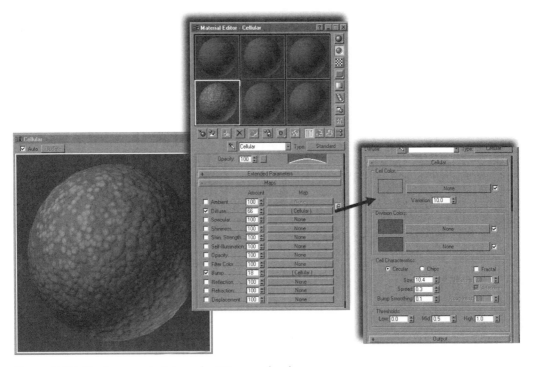

Figure 3.17 The base material used a 3D procedural map.

assigned the material ID 3. For now, I won't enter into the specifics of how to create the Blend and the Multi/Sub-Object material.

Because the structure is so complex, we will take it one step at a time, starting with the special texture and mask created for each part of the plant, and then following with the actual Materials Editor settings for the Blend material.

Creating the Texture and Mask for Bud2

Because the texture for Bud2 is the easiest example to understand and to verify final results, I started with it. These are the steps I took to create the final texture and mask for the Blend:

EXERCISE: CREATING THE TEXTURE AND MASK

1. Using Photoshop, I opened the template created earlier with the UVW Unwrap MaxScript and created some transparent layers. I then painted some colors, following the lines of the wireframe, as shown in Figure 3.19. To make it easier to see the guidelines, some layers were made slightly transparent, but only temporarily.

2. After the first rough texture was created, I duplicated the image to create the black-and-white mask. This was easily done by using the Desaturate

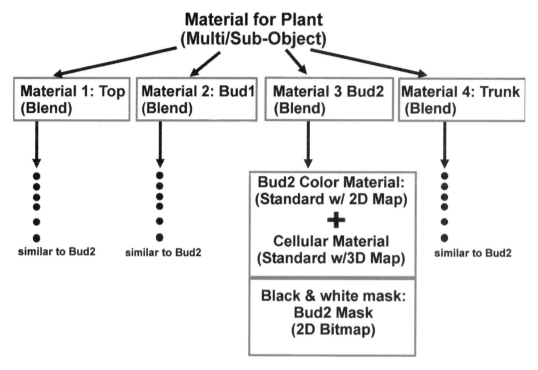

Figure 3.18 The structure of the material created for the plant, using example of Bud2.

command and adjusting the darker areas with Levels. I left the bottom part of the image white (where I wanted the cellular material to show through) and the top part black, or dark gray, where I wanted the painted texture to show (Figure 3.20).

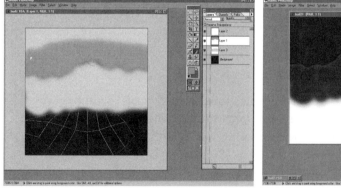

Figure 3.19 The first pass of colors using the template as a guide.

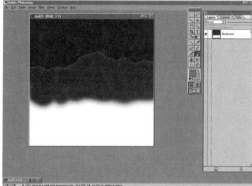

Figure 3.20 The mask was a desaturated duplicate of the colored texture.

3. I then took the colored texture into Fractal Painter 5, where I added some nice little features. I usually go back and forth between Painter and Photoshop, mainly because neither has all the features I really need. This went on for a while, until the final results were achieved, as seen in Figure 3.21. It definitely helps to have a tablet, especially to take advantage of the painterly brushes that Painter offers.

4. In summary; On the first pass, I created the main colors using Photoshop to create new layers (Figure 3.21.1). Then, in Painter, I added some distress and initial blending to each layer. I also created a new transparent floater (equivalent to layers in Photoshop) and added some red pimples (Figure 3.21.2). Still in Painter, I added surface texture to give the texture a rough look. Back into Photoshop, I used Alien Skin's Eye Candy to add some HSB Noise (Figure 3.21.3). I also blurred out some of the more obvious strikes of brush (Figure 3.21.4).

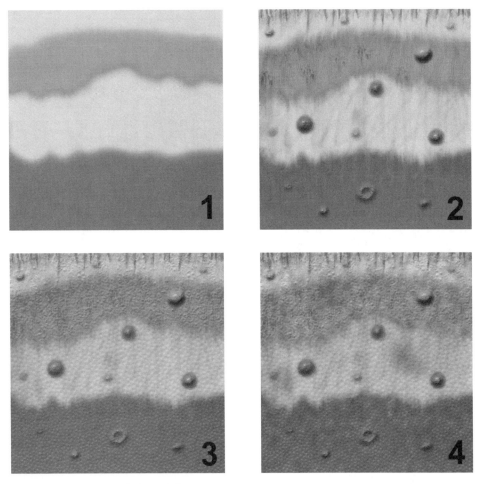

Figure 3.21 The evolution of the texture.

5. After creating the colored texture and mask for the Blend, I had to go into the Material's Editor and create the Blend material. Figure 3.22 shows the settings for the Blend; the top material was made using the painted texture, and the bottom one was simply the base color I had created before.

6. Figure 3.22 also shows a detail of the results on the actual plant: The top of the bud shows the texture where it should be, and the texture blends seamlessly with the trunk.

7. The mask is what makes one material show through, while the other one does not; the white parts of the mask make the bottom material (which is the Cellular) show through. If no mask was used, a mix could also be obtained by using the Mix Amount, but that results in a blurrier effect. The Curve settings can be used to make the transition between the two materials smoother. The straighter and the more vertical the curve, the harsher the transition between each material. The Material/Map Browser shows the structure of each individual material. Notice how the Bump

Figure 3.22 The settings for the Blend material.

map for both materials was the same, which helped to make for a more unified look and smoother transition.

Now we have created one of the materials we need. Next, we'll have to repeat the process for each of the four groups.

Creating the Final Multi/Sub-Object Material

I created a painted texture based on the template extracted from the geometry along with its respective black-and-white mask. After that, I created four Blend materials, one for each group, and after that I assembled a final Multi/Sub-Object material and assigned it to the geometry. Figure 3.23 shows the Multi/Sub-Object in the Material's Editor along with the structure of all the Blend materials in the Material/Map Browser.

Figure 3.24 shows the first plant with all the materials in place. While the resulting object looks a little whimsical, it certainly has all the qualities of a plant and can be recognized as such. That is one of the characteristics of the work I've been doing lately: to make objects that can be recognized but would never belong to our common world.

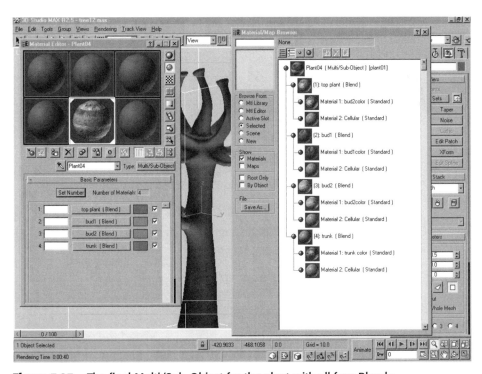

Figure 3.23   The final Multi/Sub-Object for the plant with all four Blends.

Figure 3.24   The first plant, with all materials in place.

Great, we're now finally finished with the first plant. Of course, one plant does not a garden make so let's get cracking.

Secondary Plants

With the first and principal plant in place, I repeated the process to create other plants. I started by duplicating the first plant, making it a little smaller, bent over, and rotated in relation to the first one. This way, the second plant looks like the first one but it is not exactly identical, as shown in Figure 3.25.

Figure 3.25   The second plant is smaller and bent over.

Now that the tall plants are in place, it's time to create the medium-sized plants. I chose to make them like balloons, so they would fill most of the emptiness at the trunk of the larger plants. These plants were created similarly to the first plant, using the "box" method, but instead of starting with a box, I started with a low-poly lathe, shown in Figure 3.26.

Also, instead of applying the MeshSmooth right away, I first applied the UV Mapping coordinates and then duplicated the basic rough shape, creating copies. This allowed me to create different versions of the same plant, some fatter than others, some with longer stems, and others bent over. I kept the original plant model without any MeshSmooth to use as a source for future versions. The final touch for these plants was made by creating an interesting texture, always following the color scheme.

Finally, I needed to create some smaller plants to give the scene a fuller appearance and more richness. I used the same approach as with the other plants, but this time, I created a long six-sided cylinder to use as my basic geometry. The buds were extruded from randomly picked faces, and I proceeded in the exact

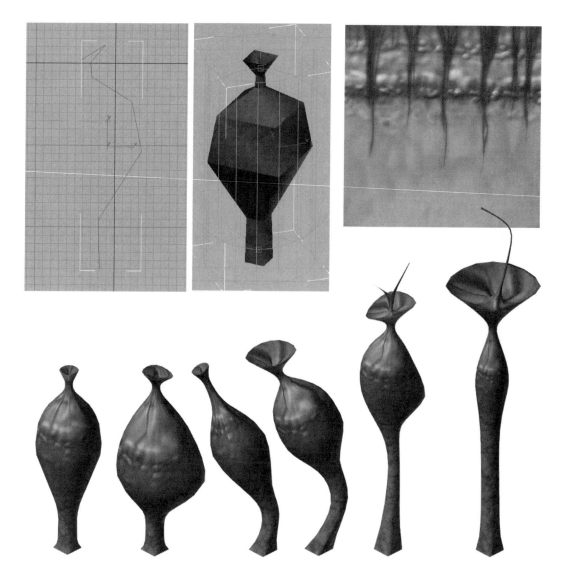

Figure 3.26 The medium plants made out of a simple lathe with variations.

same manner as I did for the other plants: extruding, scaling, and rotating them using Local Coordinate System. Figure 3.27 shows the evolution of the cylinder into the final plant, along with a detail and the texture map used. The last touch was to bend the plant slightly and then to duplicate it a few times to form some interesting variations.

At this point, with all the plants modeled and textured, it is time to start arranging them, just as a florist would position the flowers in a bouquet. I fol-

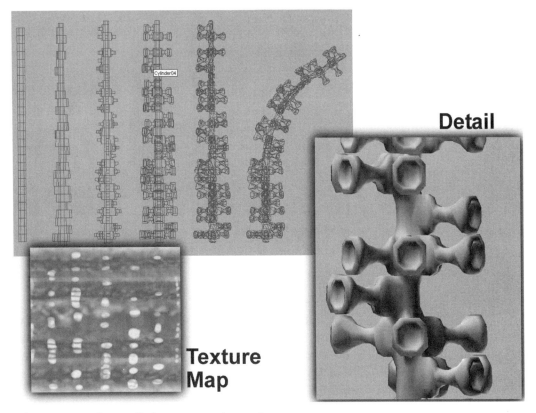

Figure 3.27   The small plant construction and texture.

lowed the formula determined in the structure presented earlier exactly: The larger plants were placed in the back and toward the middle, and the bent plant was positioned slightly toward the side. The medium plants were placed in a "random-looking" way surrounding the larger plants, and the smaller plants were placed in front and toward the side. Some of the smaller plants were heavily bent and rotated to drape in front of the entire arrangement. Figure 3.28 shows the two stages of arranging the plants in place.

The last step in creating our alien botany image is to create the perfect mood lighting to reflect an alien world.

Lighting and Final Touch

No project is ever complete without good lighting. I consider lighting to be one of the most important components of a scene, whatever the theme. Not only

Figure 3.28 Medium plants were arranged first, followed by the smaller filler plants.

does good lighting bring out the colors of textures, but it also plays a game of contrasts with the viewer, hiding or showing parts of the geometry.

Two back lights were installed above the larger plants, with a strong yellow color, to bring out some odd coloration from the plants' surfaces. The main light was positioned slightly to the left and in front, while a filler light, with one third of the value of the main light, was positioned at the right side in front. This is a variation of the classical "three-point light" scheme, which works with most subjects. The only difference here is the addition of an extra back light. Figure 3.29 shows the light positions.

The three-point light usually has three lights arranged in a triangular fashion: two in front and one in the back. One important thing to note is that I always use lights with shadows and set the ambient light to zero. The default environment lighting settings of 3D Studio Max are not zero, and that is an important cause for flatness and lack of realism.

To complete the arrangement, all I needed was a base and some background. The base was created using the box method described earlier. I couldn't resist making it look like a seashell; it just seemed to be the right shape to complete the project. I applied a green metallic material with some noise on it to simulate iridescence. I made the base fairly dark because I did not want to pull the attention away from the main plants. The metallic look gives it just the right amount of attention, with some interest but without detracting from the main subject.

Also, to further enhance the main plants a little, I let my creativity soar by adding two purplish lens flares. I use the plug-in Pro Optic Suite from Cebas, which allows me to create lens flares with a softer look. They almost feel like cotton clouds coming out of the plant's top. The flares have a gradient color that goes from yellow to purple to match the strong yellow back lights. Figure 3.30 shows the final rendered scene.

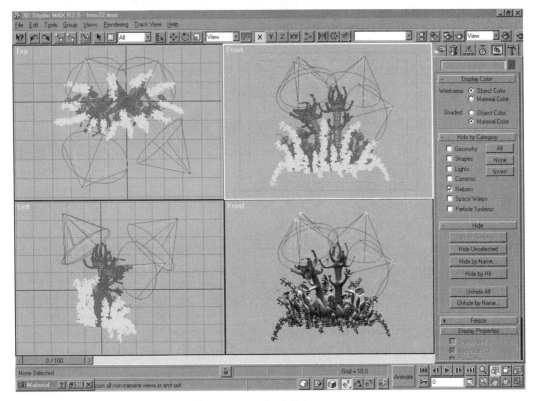

Figure 3.29 Two frontal lights and two strong back lights.

Figure 3.30 The final arrangement complete with base, lens flare, and lighting.

The background was created in Painter 5, and I took care to keep the bottom part of it dark so it would blend in nicely with the base. Because I had no real 3D background set up in this project, this was a particularly important note. Otherwise, the object would appear to be floating in midair.

This completed the final panel. As I mentioned before, plants can be pretty complex to create, but they can also be a source of inspiration for unusual and unexpected projects.

Wrap Up

I thoroughly enjoyed creating this project. I hope you enjoyed it too!

CHAPTER 4

Tackling a Thorny Challenge (trueSpace)

Darris Dobbs

My assignment for this chapter was to devise a tutorial that would demonstrate how to create some type of photorealistic plant life using my chosen software platform. Since I am the trueSpace editor, I wanted to come up with a subject that was appropriate for the program. I decided to create a cactus garden. This may seem a strange choice given the variety of flora I could have chosen, but in many ways the cactus is a fitting symbol for trueSpace. Both tend to be underrated and are often overlooked. Both have a somewhat unusual appearance at first glance. Just as the cactus lacks lush foliage, trueSpace lacks many of the esoteric features of some of the more expensive programs. However, both are efficient and brilliantly engineered for their environment. Both use ingenious and effective unconventional strategies to overcome problems. Finally, both the cactus and trueSpace can only really be appreciated once you come to know them and understand just how well-suited they are for their chosen tasks. Figure 4.1 shows the cactus garden we will be modeling in this tutorial.

As you can see, it's quite a collection. Fortunately, it's not terribly difficult to create all of these plants. It's really a matter of repetition. Let's get started modeling our first cactus, a prickly pear cactus.

Figure 4.1 A digital cactus garden.

A Prickly Problem

We are going to begin this chapter by creating a member of the *opuntias* genus, better known as the prickly pear. Prickly pears are common around the world; often the fruit is eaten in Mexico and other parts of the southwestern United States. The most noticeable feature of these cacti is that their bodies are shaped like flat paddles. These pads are covered with evenly spaced needles. Believe me, you do not want to fall off of your horse and land in a patch of prickly pear. Take my word for it, you will not want to sit back down on the saddle.

There are a variety of ways to approach modeling this particular cactus. In this exercise we are going to concentrate on minimizing the number of polygons. This can be an important consideration when creating digital plants, since creating all of the leaves and branches, or in this case, needles, can require a huge number of polygons. The plants are rarely the focus of the scene, so it makes no sense to waste so many polygons on detail that will never be noticed. You have to decide on a case-by-case basis as to how much detail to put into each plant. If it is not going to be seen up close, use the most efficient method.

EXERCISE: MODELING A PRICKLY PEAR CACTUS

1. To begin crafting our first cactus, switch to top view and use the Draw Spline tool to create the shape shown in Figure 4.2. Think of it as the shape of a beaver's tail.

2. Switch to front view and extrude the shape you just created using the Sweep tool, as shown in Figure 4.3. The idea is to create a somewhat rounded profile.

3. All right, now we need to stand our little cactus upright. Click on the Snap to Grid tool to constrain movement and rotate the object 90° so that it is perpendicular to the ground plane as shown in Figure 4.4.

4. The next step is to create a cube object and scale it to the size seen in Figure 4.5.

   This cube is going to become one of the pads to which the spines of the prickly pear are connected. Although these pads are rounded in reality, we will lower our polygon count significantly by beginning with a cube.

5. Select the front face of the cube using Point Edit/Faces. Next, scale this face so it is smaller. Instead of a cube, the object should now be narrower at the front as shown in Figure 4.6.

6. Move the new object into position on the face of the cactus. Begin copying the object and arranging the copies in a diagonal manner as shown in Figure 4.7. Don't attempt to be precise in their placement. In fact, a little irregularity will add realism. Scale these pad objects larger toward the center of the cactus and smaller toward the edges.

7. Continue placing the pads until the face of the cactus is covered, and then place them around the edges of the cactus. If both sides of the cactus will be seen in your scene, go ahead and add pads to the backside as well. Otherwise, do not waste the polygons.

8. Now that the pads are in place, join them to the cactus using the Object Union Boolean tool. Finally, click on the Smooth Quad Divide tool to round the cactus into a more organic shape. You should notice a real difference. Similar effects can be achieved by using the ThermoClay 2 plug-in or trueSpace4's NURBS tool. Each will give you somewhat different results. Suit the method to the project. See Figure 4.8.

9. Now that we have created the prickly pear itself, it is time to put the prickly in the pear. In other words, it is time to build the spines. Begin by right clicking on the Create Sphere Primitive tool. This will open the Numeric Property panel. Enter 4 for latitude and 4 for longitude. Once again, we are attempting to keep polygons to a minimum. As mentioned

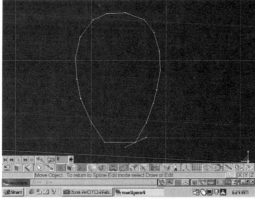

Figure 4.2 Use the Draw Spline tool to create a beaver-tail shape.

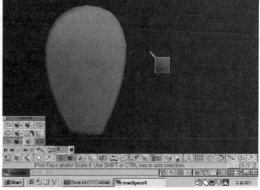

Figure 4.3 Extrude the shape using the Sweep tool.

Figure 4.4 Rotate the cactus into an upright position.

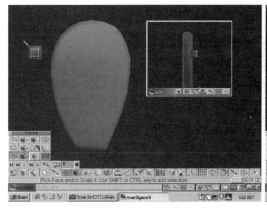

Figure 4.5 Create a small cube.

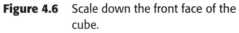

Figure 4.6 Scale down the front face of the cube.

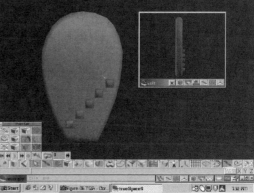

Figure 4.7 Begin arranging the pads.

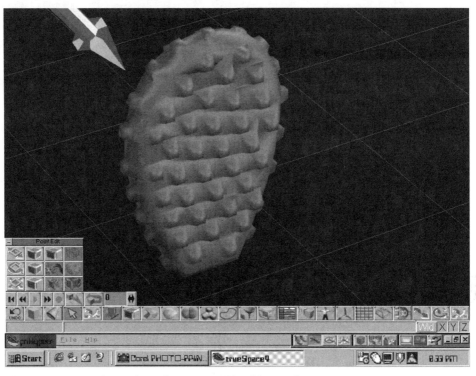

Figure 4.8   Join the pads to the cactus with Object Union.

earlier, this can become a thorny problem. Sorry, no more, I promise. Back to the subject at hand. The spines are going to be so small that once a smoothed texture is applied, the blockiness will be unnoticeable. Click on Create Sphere. The resulting sphere should resemble Figure 4.9.

10. The sphere we just created represents the small fuzzy tuft at the base of a cactus' needles. Apply a pale, yellowish-white color to the object making certain that smooth is selected in the materials panel. Set roughness high and shininess low, and select the Wrapped Rough option for displacement.

11. The next step is to create the actual needles. Before starting, reset the displacement to none. Then switch to Top View and click on the Draw Regular Polygon tool. Set the number of sides to 3. We are still trying to minimize polygons. By creating a three-sided needle instead of a round one, we are saving a lot of polygons when you consider the total number of needles involved. Switch to front view and click on the Tip tool to extrude the triangular polygon into a long needle shape as shown in Figure 4.10.

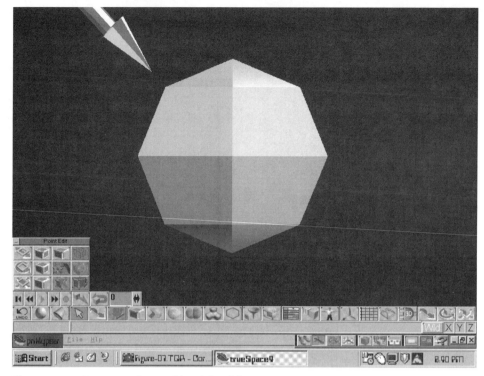

Figure 4.9   Create a sphere with minimal faces.

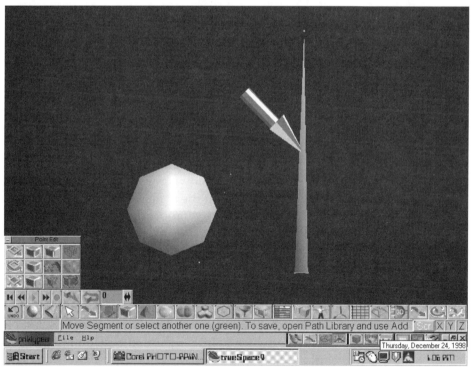

Figure 4.10   Create a needle from a triangular polygon.

12. Position the needle you just created in the center of the white sphere. Next, create six copies of the needle and arrange them in a star pattern as shown in Figure 4.11.

13. The needles around the perimeter should point outwards at an angle of about 45°. It will help if you open a second window in side view while placing the needles. Once the needles are in place, join them to the central sphere using Object Union. Save this new object as spines.cob. To save time, we will be using the same needles on all of the cacti we create. Although the number, color, and arrangement of spines vary from cactus to cactus, these will serve fine for our purposes. When you are actually creating your own plants, however, it will be worth your while to invest a little time researching such details.

14. Take the set of spines that you have created and scale them so that they are in correct proportion to your cactus. Finally, begin positioning a copy of the spines on each pad of the prickly pear. Once you are done, join them to the cactus using Glue as Sibling and save the entire object. Your prickly pear should resemble Figure 4.12.

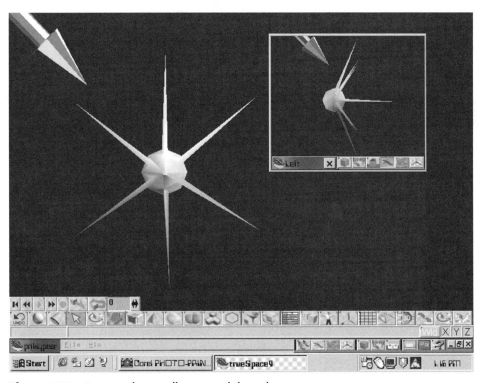

Figure 4.11 Arrange the needles around the sphere.

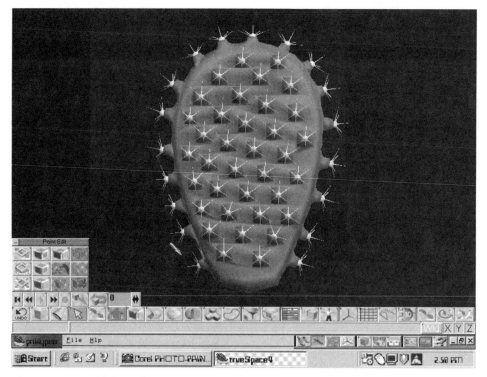

Figure 4.12 Add the spines to your cactus.

15. Prickly pears grow in a strange fashion. New ears branch off of the original cactus. Some miniature indoor varieties are known by such names as Angel Wings and Bunny Ears due to this unusual fact. Therefore, to create a larger and more believable cactus, simply copy the original cactus, scale it smaller, and position the copy on the edge of the original as shown in Figure 4.13.

Prickly Pear cacti tend to grow in clumps. There is a good deal of variation among varieties. Often, the ears are somewhat curled. The prickly pears, which are found in pastures in my native Kansas, have spines that attach directly to the ears without the pads and sport longer needles. I can say this with the confidence born of painful, firsthand experience.

Also, during extreme droughts in Texas, ranchers have been known to take flame-throwers into their pastures and burn the needles off of these cacti to provide sustenance for their starving livestock. Likewise, before eating the meat of this cactus, in Mexico the locals char it to burn off the spines.

Okay, that's one cactus down and four to go! Let's take a stab at the next cactus, the Organ Pipe cactus.

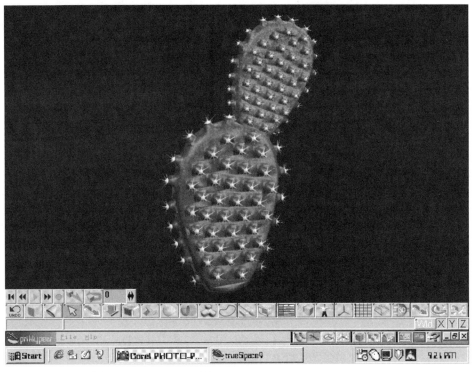

Figure 4.13 Add an ear to your prickly pear.

A Cactus for Music Lovers

The next cactus that we are going to create is part of a genus known as the *Torch cacti*. This same family includes the stately Saguaro, familiar to everyone who loves Western movies. It also includes such oddities as Snake Cacti, a slender variety that grows along the ground and the Old Man, whose long needles resemble rows of bushy whiskers. Our subject, however, is a variety known as Organ Pipe. They are called this because of their unusual shape. They tend to be long and thin, and grow upright in groups so they resemble a pipe organ. Okay, so they are only vaguely reminiscent of an organ—just play along. Whatever they look like, they grow up to 20 feet in height. Let's get started.

EXERCISE: MODELING AN ORGAN PIPE CACTUS

1. The first step in creating the organ pipe cactus is to switch to top view and create a polygon using Draw Spline that resembles the one in Figure 4.14. Don't waste polygons on unnecessary detail, just draw six slightly rounded arms in a vaguely circular arrangement.

2. After you have drawn the polygon, switch to front view. Begin extruding the shape upwards as shown in Figure 4.15, using the Sweep tool. Open a second top view window to make it easier to observe the results. Alternating layers should be scaled larger or smaller in all directions to create the rippled shape shown in Figure 4.15.

3. Rather than create a new set of spines, it is easier to reload the spines.cob object we created while building the prickly pear. Once it is loaded, begin placing copies on each projection of the current cactus. By this I mean the wider areas of the cactus as shown in Figure 4.16.

4. Once again, I remind you not to bother putting the needles on any part of the cactus that will not be viewed by the audience. Placing the spines may prove difficult. Using multiple views can make this task easier. Once the spines are all in position, join them to the cactus with the Glue as Sibling tool. The result is one section of cactus.

5. As you should know by now, good 3D artists are among the laziest people on Earth. Otherwise, we would all go get real jobs. So, if we can save a little time, by all means, let's do it. In other words, let's cheat. Fortunately, cactus are more or less modular in construction, which facilitates shortcuts. Copy the current object and move the copy upward so that the bottom of the copy is embedded just inside the top of the original. Organ pipe cacti grow like this, a section at a time. Repeat this process, but this time, scale the copy so that it is slightly longer. The sections of the cactus grow longer toward the middle and then begin to get smaller as they near the top. Repeat the process until your cactus resembles Figure 4.17.

6. Once your cactus is about seven sections tall, it is time to finish it off. Select the very top face, using Point Edit/Faces in top view. Next you will extrude this upward into a rounded shape, using the sweep tool, as shown in Figure 4.18. You need to make sure that this looks right in both

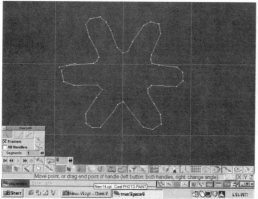 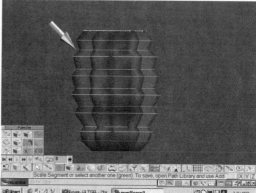

Figure 4.14 Create this shape with the Draw Spline Polygon tool.

Figure 4.15 Extrude the shape upwards using the Sweep tool.

front and side views. Pull the final extrusion down into the cactus slightly to leave a shallow depression. Check the top view to be certain none of the edges protrude through the wall of the cactus.

7. As you have probably guessed, these cacti rarely grow perfectly straight. In fact, they tend to curve upwards and lean slightly outward. The easy way to simulate this is to use the Deform Object tool. Simply create a deformation lattice with four divisions along the z-axis as shown in Figure 4.19.

8. Move and rotate the control planes to create the desired shape. To create an entire stand of these unusual plants, begin with the basic cactus that we have built and vary the size, shape, and number of sections of each copy.

That's two cacti done! Our digital cactus garden is starting to grow. Let's use a little digital fertilizer and see if we can grow a Saguaro cactus.

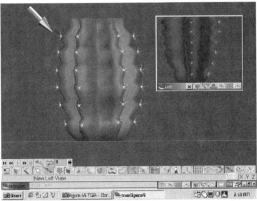

Figure 4.16   Add the spines to the cactus.

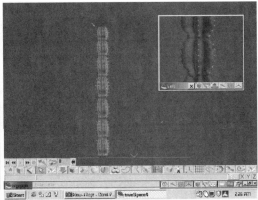

Figure 4.17   Stack the sections, scaling the middle sections longer.

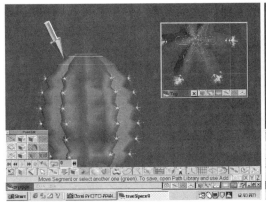

Figure 4.18   Round off the top using Sweep.

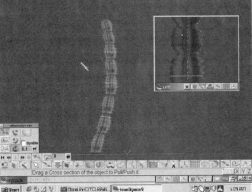

Figure 4.19   Bend the cactus into shape using Deform Object.

Nobody Knows My Saguaro

Our next project is another member of the Torch cacti genus. The stately Saguaro (pronounced *suh-hwa-ro*) is the state flower of Arizona. Most of you will recall seeing this cactus in countless Western movies or on the cover of *Arizona Highways*. Older Saguaros can reach up to 60 feet. Their familiar form often resembles a man with arms raised as if in surrender. Unfortunately, the popularity of these and many other varieties of cacti have made them very popular for landscaping in the Southwest. This has led to a real problem with cactus poachers. Not only has this resulted in making these cacti scarce in many areas, but it also means destruction of habitat and disruption of a fragile ecosystem.

Let's see if we can preserve the environment by creating an immortal Saguaro cactus.

EXERCISE: CREATING A SAGUARO CACTUS

1. Since they are closely related, it should not surprise you that constructing the Saguaro is very similar to building the Organ Pipe cactus. As we did before, start by creating a polygon using the Draw Spline tool. The only difference is that this polygon will have nine lobes rather than six. The new polygon should resemble Figure 4.20.

2. We are going to be building an immature Saguaro such as might be found in an outdoor cactus garden, so we will not have to worry about adding arms or branches. Switch to front view and extrude the polygon you created, using the Sweep tool, as shown in Figure 4.21.

3. At the very top of the cactus, scale the top face smaller and pull it down to create a small depression in the top of the cactus. This is a common fea-

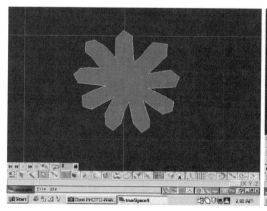
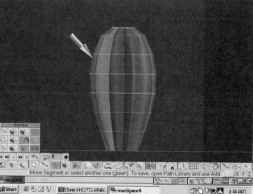

Figure 4.20 Create a new polygon using Draw Spline.

Figure 4.21 Extrude the spline polygon using Sweep.

ture in most cacti as this is where the bud will appear and eventually bloom into a flower. Refer to Figure 4.22.

4. Now that the main body of the cactus is complete, it is time to begin adding the needles again. Load the spines.cob object we saved earlier. Begin positioning copies of this object on the lobes of the cactus. You will notice in Figure 4.23 that the spines are placed in a diagonal or diamond pattern. This pattern is common to most cacti. Nature, with her usual efficiency, has arranged them so that the cactus is completely protected using the smallest number of needles possible.

5. Our last step is to place several copies of the spines.cob object facing straight up in the depression at the top of the cactus. Place them close together so that the spheres are touching. On a real cactus this area is an uneven fuzzy spot with needles pointing outward. Your cactus should now resemble Figure 4.24. Glue all of the pieces together using Glue as Siblings and save the object.

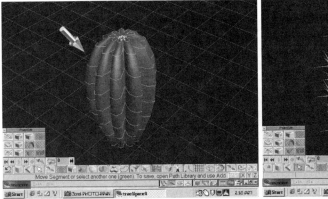

Figure 4.22 Create a depression in the top of the cactus.

Figure 4.23 Place the spines in a diagonal pattern.

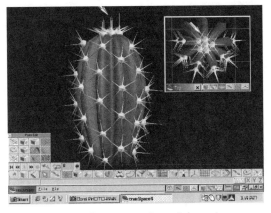

Figure 4.24 Place a number of the spines on top of the cactus.

Another cactus completed. It's a great-looking cactus—very traditional and full of those wonderful trademark spikes. Now we can move on to the mystery of our chapter.

The Mystery Cactus

The next cactus that we are going to attempt to re-create is actually a mystery to me. The model for this cactus resides in a terrarium on my desk. I know that it is a variety of Pincushion cacti, which makes it a member of the genus *Mammilaria*. There is a huge variety of these particular cacti, most of which come from Mexico. Although I don't know exactly which variety my little cactus is, it will nevertheless make an excellent subject. One of the basic characteristics of these cacti is that they are covered with bumps or lobes so that they vaguely resemble a pineapple.

EXERCISE: MODELING THE MYSTERY CACTUS

1. To begin, we will create a sphere primitive in the front view. Boolean Subtract a cube primitive to remove the bottom fifth of the sphere (see Figure

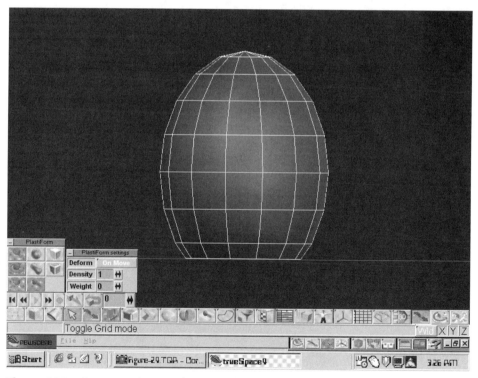

Figure 4.25   Create a sphere and remove the bottom fifth.

4.25). This sphere will serve as the main body of the cactus. We will then cover this sphere with the bumps or lobes.

2. Switch to top view. Using the Draw Spline tool, we will create a polygon like the one shown in Figure 4.26. We are going to extrude this polygon into one of the lobes that cover the exterior of the cactus.

3. Extrude the polygon into a volcano shape using the Sweep tool. The resulting object should resemble Figure 4.27. Be certain to round the object as you near the top. Don't be overly concerned that your effort matches the illustration precisely. These lobes vary a good deal in size, shape, and roundness from variety to variety and plant to plant.

4. Rather than cover the cactus with copies of our lobe object and then repeating the process with our spines, it is much more efficient to simply combine them at the outset. Therefore, rotate the lobe object 90° so that it looks like Figure 4.28. Then load the spines.cob object. Position the spines on the lobe as shown in Figure 4.28, and combine them with Glue as Sibling. Make sure they are a different color.

5. Finally, begin placing copies of the lobe object, with spines attached, so that they cover the entire cactus. Space them as shown in Figure 4.29.

6. This will require quite a bit of effort, and you will need to open multiple windows to be certain the lobes are properly placed. Once this is done, load the spine object again and place a number of the spines pointing directly upward at the very top of the cactus. Join all of the objects using Glue as Sibling and save the resulting object.

We're making progress now. We're done with the cactus portion of this chapter. The last plant we are going to make isn't a cactus, but it does look rather similar.

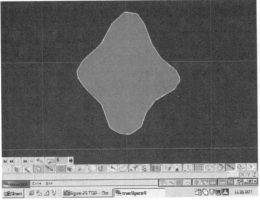

Figure 4.26 Create a polygon with Draw Spline.

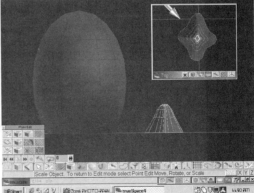

Figure 4.27 Sweep the polygon into a volcano shape.

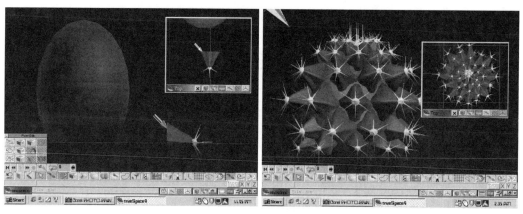

Figure 4.28 Add the spines to the lobe.   **Figure 4.29** Cover the cactus with the lobes.

Now for Something Completely Different

For our final subject I have chosen something completely different. Okay, that's not true. It is not completely different, but it is not a cactus. In fact, it is a succulent (but I should point out that cacti are also succulents). Succulents are plants that have adapted to an arid environment. They have fleshy leaves or stems for storing water and a waxy surface to prevent evaporative water loss. So what is the succulent we are going to create for our finale? I will give you a hint. It belongs to the Lily family. Give up?

Our subject is none other than the aloe. Aloe is not actually native to North America. It was introduced into Mexico and the Southwest by missionaries. They prized this plant for its medicinal value. Aloe is still valued for these properties, and you will find it as an ingredient in everything from hand lotion to shampoo. Speaking of hands, let's get ours busy modeling the aloe plant.

EXERCISE: MODELING AN ALOE PLANT

1. To create our aloe plant we are once more going to turn to the Draw Spline tool. With this tool we are going to create the vaguely triangular shape seen in Figure 4.30. This shape is a cross section of one blade of an aloe plant.

2. Switch to front view and open a second window in side view before continuing. Next, use the sweep tool to extrude the polygon as shown in Figure 4.31. Don't forget to watch the side view and make certain that there is a slight curve to the object on the flat side of the polygon.

3. To create the small teeth along the edges of the blade, create a cone primitive and scale it to size. Apply a different color to this object since it will

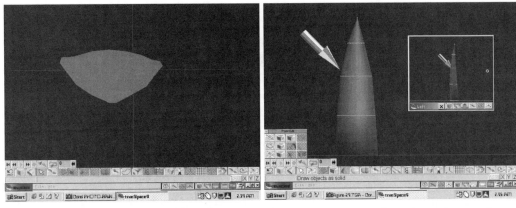

Figure 4.30 Use Draw Spline to create a cross section.

Figure 4.31 Sweep the polygon into an aloe blade.

be lighter than the blade when we texture it. Place this cone at the very tip of the blade. Then begin placing copies at even intervals along the sides of the blade as shown in Figure 4.32. Join the teeth to the blade using Object Union.

4. Rotate the completed blade so that it is at approximately a 40° angle. Next, begin arranging copies of this blade in a rough circle. Don't worry about precision. Just arrange them in a group as shown in Figure 4.33.

5. Finally, begin arranging more copies of the blade in a smaller circle within the first circle. These blades should be rotated into a steeper angle, approximately 70°. Aloe always grows in this sort of star-shaped clump. Refer to Figure 4.34.

6. Glue all of the blades together, and then save the object.

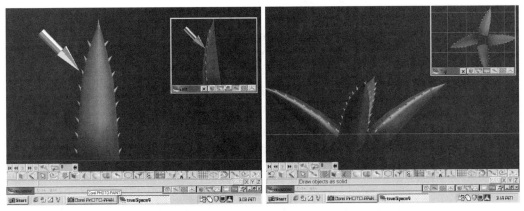

Figure 4.32 Use small cone primitives for the teeth.

Figure 4.33 Arrange copies of the blade in a rough circle.

Figure 4.34 Arrange another circle of blades inside the first.

As you can see, aloe is a relatively simple plant to create. Our digital garden is now complete. Well, nearly complete, all we need to do now is surface the cacti.

Adding the Final Touch

You should now have a pretty thorough grasp on the basics of cactus construction. With only the cacti we have constructed in this tutorial you could create a pretty respectable cactus garden, but unless you add a little color and texture, your garden is going to appear pretty bland.

Texturing these cacti was a piece of cake. I used the same basic approach on all of them, only varying the settings slightly between cacti. I realize some of you will be using trueSpace4, while many others are still using trueSpace3, so I will show you a quick and easy way to add realistic shading to these plants with each program.

If you are using trueSpace3, your best bet is to use the procedural textures. My choice would be to select the granite procedural. I would then set each of the colors to a slightly different shade of green, leaving one color tan or yellow. You can then experiment with the amounts until you get the right mix. I would then apply a bump map such as the orange bump that is included with the program.

Give it a low amplitude and about five repeats. Because cacti tend to be somewhat waxy on the outside, you will want to set the shininess about a third of the way up the slider. The roughness slider needs to be pulled down all the way. The smoothed texture button should be enabled. This basic texture will work for all of the cacti we have created. You will only need to vary the colors and settings to suit your own taste. The color and texture of cacti in the real world is dependent on their location, the soil, the amount of moisture and numerous other variables. Therefore, there are no hard and fast rules.

If you are using trueSpace4, you will want to take advantage of the new Shaders. Left-click on the Color Shader, and select Layered Colors from the Color Property panel. This setting allows you to layer up to eight different colors, textures, or procedural textures and to assign a different level of transparency to each one.

Right-clicking on the Layered Colors sphere will open the Layered Colors panel. Left-click on the top space in this panel, and then select Solid Color from the box that appears. This will set your base color. Right-click on the same space to open a color selector. Choose a medium dark green as your base color.

Left-click on the second space in the Layered Colors panel, and select Solid Clouds from the box that appears. Now right-click on the space and select two different shades of green, and adjust the scaling to suit you. Set the Transparency for this texture to 55%. This means that 55% of the base color will show through this texture.

Right-click on the Displacement sphere and select Wrapped Rough from the box that appears. Play with the scale detail and amplitude until you get the response you are looking for. Although cacti appear smooth at a distance, looking closely reveals a network of bumps similar to the texture of the skin on the back of your hand. Therefore, the key is to keep the amplitude setting low. Make sure that smoothed texture is enabled. Set the ambient light to zero. Set the diffusion to low. Set shininess low and roughness high. This should result in a believable and realistic texture.

Wrap Up

I hope you found this chapter to be entertaining and worthwhile. You never know when you are going to be called on to create a cactus. When and if that time comes, the most important thing to remember in creating a realistic cactus is that these plants lead very difficult lives. They bake in the hot sun in an arid desert, scoured by winds and sand. When it does rain, the usual result is a flash flood. They are also one of the few sources of nutrition and moisture for the animals that dwell in the desert. This means that you must avoid perfection at all costs. The poor suffering cactus is not going to grow straight and tall; it is going to be bent by the wind. The surface of your cactus is going to bear the pits and scars of a difficult life, so add a bump map or textured map to reflect this. Likewise, a cactus in its native environment will not grow uniformly. There will be growth spurts during the infrequent rains and times of almost no growth during the frequent droughts. So avoid uniformity and try to add as much character as you can to these hardy and unique plants.

CHAPTER 5

The Entrance . . .
A Study on Digital Botany
(Strata Studio Pro)

Frank Vitale

This chapter is about digital botany, or creating plants digitally. Plants are great fun to work with because you don't have to be extremely precise. As a matter of fact, it is better not to be precise, or you'll end up with very unnatural-looking vegetation. Inconsistencies, variation in shape, color, and health, and level of growth all contribute to creating something that looks natural. If you plan to create plants, determine the importance of the element in your scene, and if it is a dominant element be sure to research that plant. Go out and find one—find 10. Photograph them and keep those photos handy for reference.

Not only are such photos practical for modeling reference, but they can be invaluable in developing textures that are straight from the source, which is without a doubt the best way to achieve realism. On the other hand, models of plants can quickly get out of hand and slow production to a near halt, so it is important to be careful about how much detail you put into any one element as it is easy to bog down your scene. Having said that, the best way to avoid creating nightmare projects is through the use of *instancing*, not just entire plants but the elements that make them up, such as a blade of grass, a twig, or a leaf. Use texture maps wisely; make sure they are large enough but not too large.

This chapter is set up differently than most. We are going to break down the individual elements of a scene and explore them individually. That way, you can choose the areas that interest you and apply what you discover to your own projects instead of duplicating what somebody else has already done.

When you are through, you will have a work that is truly your own. Conversely, if we were to attempt to go though this particular scene from start to finish, it would consume the whole book and probably a week of your time.

The Tools

I used two applications to create this environment, StudioPro 2.5 and Photoshop 4.0. I used Photoshop exclusively for the development of all the textures and did everything else directly in StudioPro. StudioPro allows the import of several model formats, including outlines from Illustrator, but as a beta tester, I wanted to put StudioPro's pen tool to the test, so I created all the outlines inside of StudioPro. It performed quite well.

StudioPro works with a grid-based environment. The active grid is where the modeling takes place. It can be turned off to allow you to model in full 3D space. Working without the grids, however, can get messy quickly, so I recommend using them. It's very easy to switch between active grids by simply hitting the X, Y, or Z keys on your keyboard. They can also be accessed through the Edit menu. I don't want to bore you too much by going over all the StudioPro features, but I do want to touch on some of the ones we will be using.

First off, I mentioned that with a scene such as this one, with lots of plants, you want to use instancing. Well, you're in luck. StudioPro is based on the idea of instancing, which it calls "shapes," and it is the basis of all modeling in the program. I'll go into more detail in the tutorials, but in a nutshell it works like this. You launch the program, create a new file, and are presented with a window in which you can begin to model. This is your main project window. You can start your modeling process here if you like, or you can create a new shape window and begin modeling within it. When you are through or before you're through you can close the shape window and your "shape" will be saved and can easily be accessed through the Shape tab on the Resource pallet. From the Resource pallet you can insert this saved shape into your environment as many times as you like; it is an *instance*.

Working this way will go a long way toward keeping your project manageable. Any manipulation you do to your shape in its shape window is instantly reflected in all the copies of it within your main project window. If you apply textures to your shape in its shape window all the copies will have that texture. If you don't want them to all have the same texture, you can wait and apply the textures from within the main project window and give each instance its own unique texture. It is a very flexible way of working.

You might ask, why not just copy the object in the main window? Well, if the object you create is 200K in size, then each copy will also be 200K, and before you know it, you'll be slogging through a project that is much larger than it needs to be. Using shapes instead will keep your project substantially smaller as an instance is only a few kilobytes, no matter how large the object.

Some of the other tools or features we will use here include the Skin tool, which allows you to create a Bezier mesh by connecting closed or open Bezier lines. This is a great way to create objects within Studio Pro as it is completely flexible. At any time, you can unskin any portion of your object and not lose the texture-mapping information, unless, of course, you completely unskin the object. You can also reshape the individual ribs or Bezier lines that make up the skin object. Another commonly used tool is the Path Extrude tool, which extrudes an open or closed line along a path. The Path Extrude object can then be converted into any number of object types from Bezier mesh to polygon group including skin object.

Converting to a Skin object allows you to create Path Extrude objects that change shape along their length. The Lathe tool is also quite powerful as it not only allows you to create 3D lathed objects from an open or closed Bezier line, it also allows you to sweep or spiral that shape to create objects like springs or screws. Another useful feature is stencil mapping. Similar to transparency mapping, stencil mapping allows you to use maps to cut out shapes, which is great for grass or leaves. Extreme caution is advised when using stencil mapping or transparency mapping because nothing slows down a render like transparency, except maybe volumetric lighting, which we will also use. Go figure.

The Entrance, What's Up with That?

Before we start the tutorials, I'd like to tell you a bit about the scene pictured in Figure 5.1, titled "The Entrance." First off, the idea is digital botany, but instead of creating a potted plant or a dandelion, I decided to create something that was just a bit darker. Inspired by the Goblin works of Bill Fleming, I decided to play on that theme and create "The Entrance." The entrance to where, you ask. That is part of the allure; only time will tell. This is meant to be a dark environment deep in a wooded area, possibly a jungle that hides a gated entrance to some mysterious place.

I used volumetric light with a gel to simulate a bleak amount of sunlight breaking through the canopy. I then used several other lights to illuminate the scene. The two point lights are fairly obvious as the light from the lanterns on the posts. They are very warm but did not light the scene sufficiently, so I also added two more spotlights to simulate the bounce and fill to give the scene a natural feel. Most of the plants, including the tree and the hillsides, were cre-

Figure 5.1 The Entrance.

ated using Skin objects. The vines, grass, and reeds were done with Path Extrude objects. The steps were also done as Skin objects to simulate the wearing down of the center of the step.

One more useful tool within the program is the Import as 3D Mesh command. This is just like John Knoll's Cybermesh plug-in for Photoshop. It allows you to import grayscale files as meshes and gives you a great deal of control; see the "Water and Algae" section later in this chapter. The grass that caps off the hillsides was created by using a Skin object and mapping with a stencil map, a quick and practical way to achieve the required look. The water is simply a flat plane with the Extend Ripples extension applied. Ripples offers a great deal of control over how many generators are used and how the surface's diffuse attribute is broken, maintaining a natural look.

Tutorial 1: The Tree

The first object I'll cover is the hero of our scene, the tree. The idea here was to create an old tree that could be dead or at least dormant, first to add contrast to the scene and second to keep the database down to a managable size by not creating leaves. One way to create objects such as these is by using the Skin tool. First you create an outline with the Pen tool then duplicate that outline as many times as required adjusting the shapes and then use the Skin tool to test your results.

Moving back and forth between skinning and unskinning and using the Reshape command, you'll be able to create a similar object in a fairly short time. An important consideration before you begin to model a tree or branch is how you plan to texture map it. If it is fairly symmetrical, you could use a cylindrical projection, but that can look a little unnatural because the texture will not follow the natural flow of the shape, and you might end up with some streaking where the normals of the polygons are aligned parallel to the direction of projection. The best way to map such objects is with UV. Using UV mapping your texture map will follow every twist and bend you create, and it will look very natural.

So launch Studio Pro and let's get going.

EXERCISE: CREATING THE TREE

1. First create a new file. Now we will create the first of our ribs, or sections, which will be skinned later. Think about what the cross section of the tree you wish to create will look like; that is what we're creating. We will use the Pen tool, the eighth icon down the tool bar on the right to create that cross section. You should practice with the Pen tool to familiarize yourself with its options. Click once with the Pen tool on the grid. Don't hold the mouse button down; just click once. Move the cursor and you'll notice that a blue line connects it to the vertices you inserted. Now click and hold the mouse button down and drag. You are now adjusting the Bezier curve with one of its handles. Release the mouse and the first curve is created and a straight blue line connects your second vertex to the cursor. The next time you click the mouse a curve will be created that is a mirror of the first curve. If you click once the curve is set, you can click and hold to adjust the curve by dragging the mouse. Don't worry about getting the curve perfect as you lay it down for the first time; reshaping the curve is the way to get it just right. If a closed shape is what you are after, a single click on the first vertex will close the shape. If you wish to keep the curve open, simply move the cursor to the tool bar and single click on the move tool or any other tool to exit the pen.

2. Now that you've created a shape, you can move it around or further manipulate it. Use the move tool, first row second item, and click on the shape you created. Its handles appear allowing you to move it constrained to a direction using the red handles, or you can simply click on it and move it around freely. Next we will reshape the object. With the object selected, click on the Reshape icon at the top of the screen; it is the one with the little curve handles, eighth from the left. You'll now notice that

the tool bar has collapsed to show just the tools for reshaping and all the vertices are visible with curve handles. Using the pointer tool, fourth one down on the left, you can adjust the vertices. Click and drag on a vertex to move it. Shift-click on several vertices to move more than one, or click and drag on a handle to adjust the curve. All of this is taking place on the active y grid. If you need to add a point or break a handle, use the Option key. Be careful, though; if you try to break a handle that lies on the curve, you'll end up adding a vertex instead. If you have a corner vertex, one without handles, and you wish to add handles to create curves, hold down the Command key and click and drag on the vertex. A single handle will emerge from the vertex creating a curve. If you need to have curves from both sides of a vertex repeat this, dragging the other way. This naturally creates a broken set of handles. If you do not want broken handles use the Align Handles tool at the top of the screen; it's the third from the right, the one with the aligned handles. Select the vertex you wish to align, and click on the align handles button. When you are finished adjusting the Bezier curve you'll want to hit the End Reshape button, it's right next to the reshape button, the one that looks like a hemisphere.

3. Now that you've got the Pen tool down, we can make a tree, or at least the trunk of a tree. Start by creating the first cross section, or rib, as we discussed earlier. It often helps to switch views, in the upper left corner of the window, you can switch from an isometric view to a top view to more easily see what you are doing. Since we are going to use UV mapping, do your best to keep the vertices evenly spaced and not too numerous. Our final object is spline-based so it will render smoothly. In this case use about 10 vertices to make up your rib. (I'll use the term *rib* from this point on to describe the cross sections.)

4. After you've completed the first rib, you'll need to duplicate it for the second. Be sure you clicked the End Reshape button. Select the rib with the Object Move tool from the main tool bar and, holding down the Option key, click on the center red dot of the rib and drag a copy vertically. Using the center handle, we are able to move an object perpendicular from the active grid.

5. Now reshape that rib. Generally I'll rotate the rib a few degrees (use the Rotate tool on the main tool bar) just like the move tools, the handles constrain the motion. Use a corner handle to rotate it in y. Next scale it a bit, again, the tool for scaling is on the tool bar directly under rotate. Now reshape it. Be careful how much you reshape because subtle differences are quite noticeable. Repeat this procedure as many times as required to create the shape you're after, each time duplicating the rib you most recently reshaped. For the sake of this lesson, five or six ribs are sufficient. Also, if you like, the ribs can be rotated along any other axis to form

shapes that bend, just keep in mind what it is you wish to create. You might be better off using a path extrude, which we will cover later. Your final set of ribs should look something like Figure 5.2.

6. Next, we'll use the Skin tool to give the object a surface. The Skin tool is a StudioPro extension, and it is accessed through the extension window. If the extension window is not visible, you can bring it up by clicking on the little plug icon in the upper right corner of your monitor. Make sure your modeling window is set to shaded view, in upper right hand corner of the window, either flat or smooth. Select the Skin tool by clicking its icon.

7. Now click and drag from your first rib, and then your second rib. You'll notice that the ribs are highlighted in red as they are skinned. That is important because skinning order is crucial, and it is easy to make mistakes when your ribs are very close together. Also, it is good to know what direction to skin as the UV mapping is affected by direction, and you don't want your texture maps to be upside down.

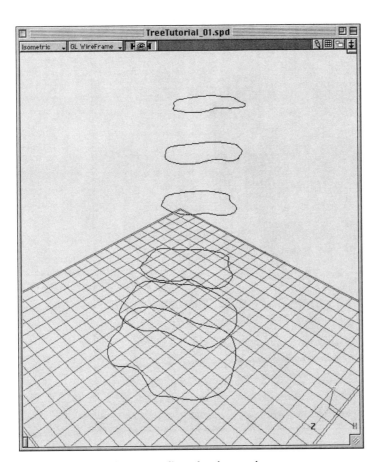

Figure 5.2 The skinning splines for the trunk.

8. Continue skinning your object by clicking and dragging between ribs. Your skinned object should look something like Figure 5.3.

9. If you are happy with your shape great, but if you see that a change is required, don't worry. To unskin the object or just a section of the object use the Unskin tool, located right under the skin tool, and click and drag directly on the object where you wish to unskin it, as shown in Figure 5.4. You can then select that rib or ribs and reshape them as needed. When finished, use the Skin tool again to re-skin by clicking and dragging.

10. Now we will create another branch using instancing and the same technique as before. First we need to set up our new shape window, which is done from the Resource pallet. If the Resource pallet is not up, bring it up by clicking on the little screw icon just above the Extensions icon in the upper right corner of the screen. Click on the Shapes tab, click on New, and name the new shape "Branch." You're now presented with a new

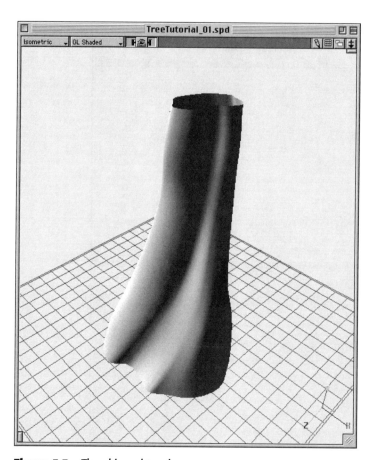

Figure 5.3 The skinned trunk.

modeling window in which to work. Everything you create here will be part of that new shape called Branch. It is a good idea to save very often. If you haven't already saved it, be sure to save your new project; the name is not important—call it whatever you like.

11. We are going to create the new branch in its proper orientation, so hit the X key to make the x grid active. If the grid does not change, hit Y and then hit X. Now just as before, use the Pen tool create a rib to your liking on the x grid. Duplicate straight out along the x axis and then reshape it. Repeat this procedure until you've got about six ribs extending along the x-axis, but this time do not rotate the ribs (see Figure 5.5). Now we need to properly position the ribs relative to each other.

12. Figure 5.6 shows the basic configuration we want for our ribs.

13. Use the Object Move tool to reposition the ribs something like the configuration seen in Figure 5.6.

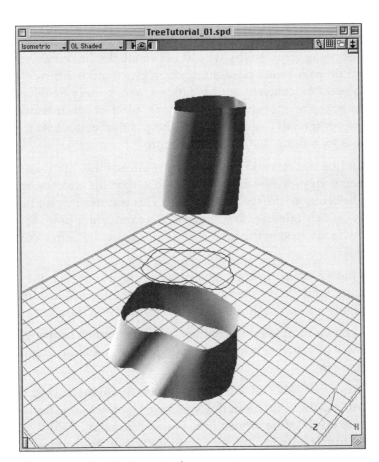

Figure 5.4 Unskinning a trunk segment.

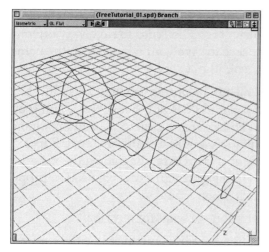

Figure 5.5   The branch ribs.   **Figure 5.6**   The rib positioning.

14. If need be, move your view around to get a better angle for grabbing the control handles on the ribs. Next we'll rotate the ribs to get them aligned better for skinning. This is why we did not rotate the ribs as we made them, it would have made positioning them much more difficult. I use the View Rotate tool extensively for this process, and it really helps me get a better view of the relationships. Also, you should feel free to move the ribs—whatever it takes to get them into the position you want. You should have something that looks like Figure 5.7.

15. Now if you like you can add that twist by rotating the individual ribs around their own y-axis by using the rotate tool on the corners. You might find that the center of the ribs is off center. This is caused by all the reshaping. Go to Modeling/Re-Center to reset the center point to fix this. We are now ready to skin the branch. As before, use the Skin tool to skin the branch.

16. Once you have a skinned shape, you may need to go thorough several skin/unskin rounds to get the ribs in just the right place at just the right scale. In Figure 5.8 I went through several revisions on the ribs.

17. Now that you've completed the branch, close the branch shape window; the shape will be saved. Click on the main project modeling window with your tree base in it.

18. From the Resource pallet click on the Insert button to insert the branch you created into the main modeling window. Use the Move, Rotate, and Scale tools to position the branch how you like. Remember to switch views from front to top to isometric, getting the best angle on your scene. You might decide that you need to further adjust your tree base as I did to make it work better with the branch. Also, you can insert as many

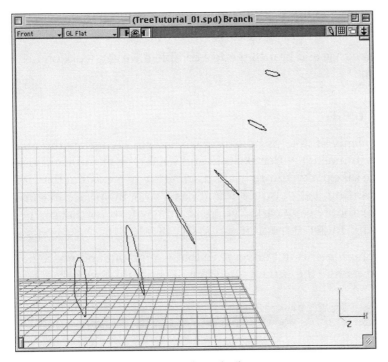

Figure 5.7   Final position of the branch ribs.

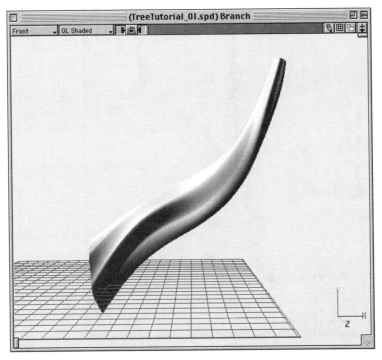

Figure 5.8   Shaping the branch.

branches as you like into the scene as they are instances. I added four branches to the tree, as you can see in Figure 5.9.

With the tree base and branch models complete we can work on texture mapping the tree.

Texturing the Tree

There are plenty of options here, and we have to give some thought to what type of environment the tree exists in and what type of surface you see it having. For the sake of this tutorial, let's assume the tree exists at the water line of a pond or stream. Let's also assume it has a smooth surface like an aspen or other tree without heavy bark. I've created many textures that can be found in the Chapter05 folder of the companion CD-ROM.

Keep in mind that it is not imperative that you go out and photograph a specific tree to capture the surface you want. It certainly does help when creating

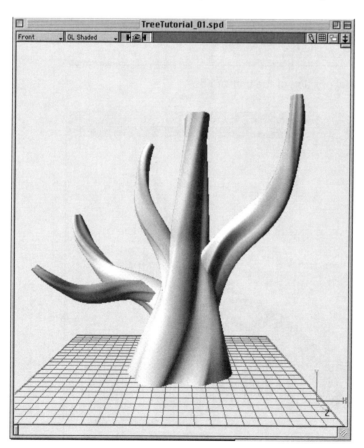

Figure 5.9   Adding the branches to our tree.

photorealism, but is not required for every creation. Here, I instead used a photo of fence slats for the tree texture. You can see the original photo in the Chapter05/images folder of the CD-ROM. It's called "fenceslats1.jpg"

In Photoshop I cleaned up the spaces between the slats, removed some knots, made the texture wrap, and changed the color. I liked the break-up of this photo with the dark areas in contrast to the light and thought it would work well for a tree in a wet environment. I've already developed all the materials you will need for these tutorials, and they can be found in the "Chapter05/materials" folder. Let's get started surfacing the tree.

EXERCISE: SURFACING THE TREE

1. Using File/Import import the material "TreeWrap" into your project. The material will appear on the Texture tab of the Resource pallet. Double-click on the texture on the tab and the Surface Texture Edit window will come up. It is within this window that all the image maps and attributes are applied to a given material or surface texture. Click on the Map button or in the minitexture window directly above it to load a texture. We already have the texture map "TreeWrap_RGB" loaded here.

2. You will also notice that there is a texture loaded in the bump channel. This texture is named "TreeWrap_BMP," and it is a grayscale file. It is a good idea to use grayscale maps for all channels other than Diffuse Color (same as map) and Specular Color. All the other channels use 8 bit and less. If you do put a color map into one of these other channels, it will simply be converted into a gray scale image. Let's apply "TreeWrap" to the tree.

3. Close the Texture Editor window by clicking Cancel, and go to the project window.

4. Now expand the group "Tree" by clicking on the blue arrow to its left. Expand further the Base Proprieties section revealing all the elements of the tree. We want to apply the texture to each part separately for the most control. Apply a texture by selecting the shape you wish the texture to be applied to and clicking on Apply from the Resource pallet. Also, you can drag the material directly onto the shape in its modeling window. When you do this you'll notice the shaded shape has changed color to reflect the new texture.

5. With OpenGL shading you can have StudioPro display more than just a shaded view of your object. Go to Edit/Preferences and click on the Windows tab; then click on Show Textures and close the window. Now your shaded view will actually show your textures in real time. The texture placement will update in real time as you adjust the mapping coordinates, which we will now do.

6. Bring up the Object Properties pallet and click on the Texture tab with your object selected. The little sphere tells us that mapping is set to UV, which is what we want. Click on it to see the other mapping options. The tiling and mixing is set correctly as well. Mixing is used when more than one texture is applied to an object. Click on it to see the options available to you.

7. We now want to adjust the amount of coverage used. The default is 100% in X and 100% in Y. X would be around the circumference of the tree or U and Y would be the length of the tree or V. Make sure the radio button for coverage is clicked and set them both to 50%. Feel free to experiment with these settings to your liking.

8. Now with the render camera at the bottom of the tool bar, select RT Best from the pop-up window and drag a marquee around a portion of your tree to render it, as seen in Figure 5.10.

9. Using the same method, apply the texture to all the other branches, experimenting with different coverage settings so that not all the branches look alike. As you drag the tree texture to the various branches, you might find that the mapping defaults to "planar." If it does, simply use the pop-up menu next to the sphere on the object properties pallet to set it UV. On the smaller branches you might want to set the X coverage value higher than 100 because that is a lot of texture map to squeeze onto a thin branch. I've found that 150 and even 300 work well for smaller branches. Your render should look something like Figure 5.11.

Figure 5.10 Testing the texture.

Figure 5.11 The surfaced tree.

10. We will now add the water line to the tree so that when we add the water it looks more natural. The idea here is that at the water line the tree would get wet, making it more specular and darker; also algae might grow on the surface of the tree in these wet regions. We will use stencil mapping to add this algae. Again, go to Import and bring in the material WaterLine.

11. Double-click it on the Resource pallet and have a look at the various texture maps associated with it. For the stencil map the white areas will show the texture and the black areas will be fully transparent. Close the window and drag the waterline material to the main tree shape, remember that your "tree" group needs to be expanded in the project window to have the material applied to just that one shape. The material should default again to UV. This time, we will change it to planar and set tiling to none. When you set tiling to none, you'll notice the tree appears to be shaded white under the waterline material. Don't worry about this. The render will still show the tree texture beneath.

12. We now need to place the texture properly. On the Object pallet click on the Position button. If it is not available, your modeling window might not be active. If this is the case click on the title bar of the modeling window to make it active. Clicking on the position button will reduce the tool bar to the necessary tools for positioning the projector or mapping coordinates. Using the projector tools, the three bottom ones, position the Planar Projector as shown in Figure 5.12.

13. When you've finished aligning the projector, click on the End Reshape button, the little hemisphere at the top of the screen. This technique of stencil mapping is very useful for layering of textures and can be used to hide those unsightly intersection points. Figure 5.13 shows a render of the waterline.

Great, the tree is now complete. Our next step is to add the grass around the tree.

Tutorial 2: Grasses

The next object, or set of objects, we will cover are the grasses. In this scene we basically have two different types of grasses (not counting the grass atop the mounds or hills that we will cover in the tutorial for the hills). For now we will focus on the reeds and the green grass you see growing up around the tree base and near the dock and stairs. Grass has always plagued designers as being a very difficult thing to create and have look natural. In large, grassy areas, the general idea was to use texture maps on flat planes or on undulating terrain meshes. This worked okay for viewing from a distance, but once you were up close on such an object the suspension of disbelief was quickly lost;

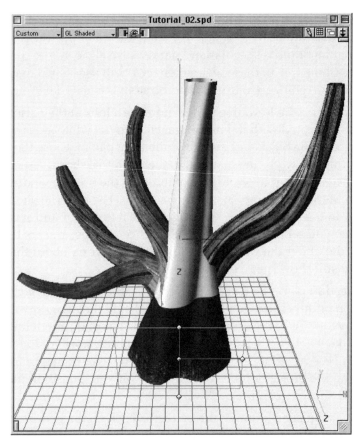

Figure 5.12   Positioning the planar projector.

Figure 5.13   The waterline.

the shadow and shape just was not there. What is needed is a combination of flat texture mapping for distant objects and actual 3D grass for anything up close or even in the middle ground. With the use of instancing you can create large areas of grass that are fully modeled without taxing your memory.

Open your Tree project if it is not already open. If you did not do the tree project, don't worry; just create a new project in which to work. It is a good idea, though, to at least read through the tree tutorial as many tips and techniques on operating in StudioPro were presented. By the time we reach the end of the tutorials a complete scene will have been created.

The way in which we will model the grasses are similar to the way we modeled the tree in that it will be a Skin object. The difference is that it will start out as a Path Extrude object and then be converted into a Skin object. Working as a Path Extrude object allows us to create a fairly complex path that would take too long to create as a Skin object. Before we start creating the grass, let's organize our project a bit by naming the tree parts and grouping them under one name. If you are not working in the tree project, you can skip this step.

If it is not already up, bring up the Project window by clicking on the little film strip icon in the upper right of your screen. This is the window where you can access all your objects and key frame animations. Select one of your objects, say, the tree base, and expand it within the project window by clicking on the blue arrow. The first input field is Name. Go ahead and type in a name like "Tree Main" and hit Enter. If the name doesn't take, add a space after the name and then hit Enter. Click on the arrow again to collapse the attribute list for Tree Main. One at a time select and name the other branches within your project in the same way. After all the objects have been named, Shift-Click to select them all within the project window and go to Modeling/Group to group them all together. Now name this group "Tree." There you have it, all nice and organized. You can still access all the shapes by clicking on the arrow next to Base Properties.

Now on to the grass.

EXERCISE: MODELING THE GRASS

1. If it is not already up, bring up the Resource pallet and click on the Shapes tab. Hit the New Shape button, and name it "Blade of Grass." You now have a new empty shape window. Hit the Z key to activate the Z grid, which is where we will create the path for our blade of grass. Don't be too concerned with scale at this point; we will scale the grass down later.

2. Using the Pen tool, lay down a path similar to the one you see in Figure 5.14.

3. Use Reshape and switching of views to adjust the path to your liking. Remember, to end an open Bezier line and leave the pen tool, all you do is click on another tool such as the Object Move tool.

4. Next, we will create the profile of the path extrude object. Hit the Y key to make that grid active, and using the pen tool in association with the Reshape command, create an open Bezier line something like Figure 5.15.

5. To create this shape you will need to break the middle vertex so you can have the curves at steep angles. Option-drag on handles to break. Now that you have the path and the profile, use the Path Extrude tool to create the extrude shape. If the extensions pallet is not up, bring it up by clicking on the little plug icon, upper right of the screen. Select the Path Extrude tool and as with the Skin tool, click on the profile, hold the mouse down, and drag to the path and release; the profile will be extruded along the path you created. It should look like Figure 5.16.

6. Great, now we need to convert it into a Skin object so we can create the taper and make it look like an actual blade of grass. Select the object if it is not already and go to Modeling/Convert... and select Skin. You can also use the Convert button at the top of the screen; it looks like a sphere with a box around it.

7. Now that you've got a Skin object, next step is to unskin it. Using the Unskin tool from the Extensions pallet, click and drag on your object to unskin it and reveal the ribs. Depending on the complexity of the path you created, you will either have a few ribs or way more than necessary. In this example, I deleted every other rib to simplify my object, as seen in Figure 5.17.

8. Now we need to scale the ribs so that the tip tapers. I like to see to it that by the time I get to the end the last rib is scaled down to about 10%. The

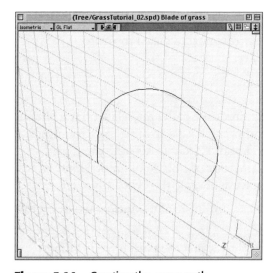

Figure 5.14   Creating the grass path.

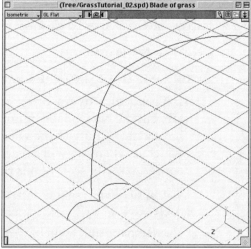

Figure 5.15   The grass extrusion object.

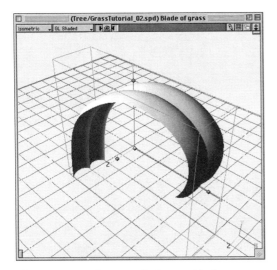

Figure 5.16 The extruded grass blade.

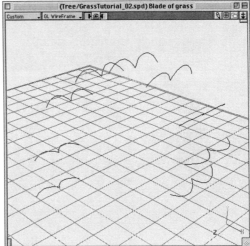

Figure 5.17 The grass ribs.

amount you scale them depends on the look you're after. In your shape modeling window, click on the second rib from the base. Now from the Windows menu bring up the Object Pallet if it is not already up. Click on the Transform tab, and click the blue expansion arrow in the lower left of the window.

9. Now click on the radio button next to the scale icon and click on the little padlock to lock all three axis together. Select the Percentage radio button and double-click in the field next to X to highlight it. Type in 90 to scale that rib down in X, Y, and Z 10%.

10. Now select the next rib and type in, say, 80 to scale it down 20%. Work your way down the length of your object scaling each rib down more and more until you reach the end and around 10% for the final rib.

11. Now that you have scaled down all the ribs, use the Skin tool to patch the ribs back together again, clicking and dragging from rib to rib starting from the base and working your way to the end. Your final skinned object should look something like Figure 5.18.

12. There you have it, a curving blade of grass. Now we need to create a couple of other blades of different shapes and sizes that we will insert into a new shape window called "Patch of grass." Close this shape window, and click on the New Shape button on the Resource pallet, calling it "Blade of Grass 2." Within that window, create another blade with different proportions. Do this one more time, and call it "Blade of Grass 3." What you want to end up with is something like Figure 5.19.

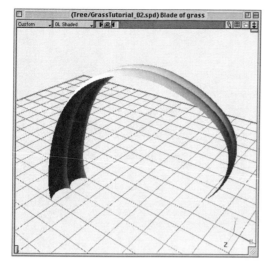

Figure 5.18   The completed grass blade.

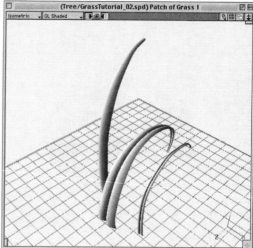

Figure 5.19   The completed grass blades.

13. What I've done here is create my 3 different blades of grass and insert them into a new shape called "Patch of Grass 1." If at this point you decide that you would like to make changes to any particular blade of grass, do so on its shape level, within its own window. You can bring up a shapes window simply by double-clicking on that shape wherever it is.

14. Now insert 10 to 15 of each blade of grass into your new shape, Patch of Grass 1. Using the Move, Rotate, and Scale tools, position each blade in a natural manner. It is a good idea to try to group blades together similar to the way grass grows naturally. It can be a bit tedious to place 30 to 50 blades of grass, but if you stick with it, the results will be worth the effort. "Patch of Grass 1" should look something like Figure 5.20.

15. Now we need to texture map the blades of grass. Go to File/Import and from the saved materials directory load "Grass 1" and "Grass 2." Drag these textures onto the primary shape level of your three different blades of grass. Alternatively, if you decided that you needed to have more than two different texture maps, you could assign the materials on the "Patch of Grass 1" level. You could have a slew of different texture maps on similar objects. Since we have sufficient variety in the models and in the placement, there is really no need for more than two materials. The materials will default to UV, which is the proper mapping method for these objects. That is about it. Your rendered patch of grass should look something like Figure 5.21.

Your patch of grass is ready to insert into your scene. Its placement is up to you, but you might want to wait until you complete the next tutorial, "The Hillside."

Figure 5.20   The completed grass patch.

Figure 5.21   The rendered grass.

Now is a good time to add a flat plane to the scene, which will eventually be water. This water plane will be completely opaque so it will not need to be very high on the tree to be effective. If we were going to make transparent water, we would have to create not only more trees, preferably with roots and all, but the bottom of the pond as well. For this lesson we'll just go with opaque water, and make it really scummy, like pea soup. With your tree project open, go to an isometric view in the main modeling window and drag out a flat plane on the Y grid. The Flat Plane tool is ninth down on the left side of the tool bar. The three 2D tools all have two sides, one is a simple outline and one solid, so be sure to use the solid side. Don't worry about getting the shape perfect with the tool, it's much easier to use the Move and Scale tools to size and position the flat plane exactly where you want it. Your flat plane should look something like Figure 5.22.

The reeds are created the exact same way as the grass. The only exception is a circle used as the object to be swept along the path, not an open Bezier line. When grouping the various reed stalks into a reed patch, it's a good idea to have straight stalks in the center and curving stalks toward the outside, as seen in Figure 5.23.

To texture map the reeds, load the saved materials Reed 1 and Reed 2 from the Chapter05/materials folder on the CD-ROM and apply them to the reed stalks as you did with the grass.

After you've inserted all the grass and reeds to your liking, you should group them together to keep your project window from getting too crowded and to make it easier to turn them on and off as you progress. To group the objects, select them within the project window by shift clicking on their names and then

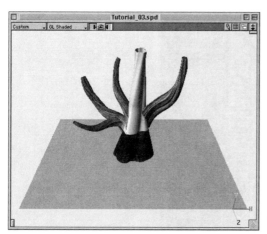

Figure 5.22   The water plane.

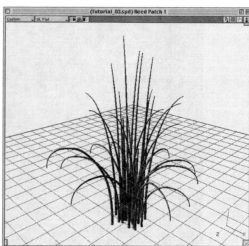

Figure 5.23   The reeds.

make the modeling window active by clicking on its title bar. Click the group icon at the top of the screen or go to the Modeling/Group menu. In the project window, expand the group you just created by clicking on the small arrow to the left and name the group. Do this for the grass and the reeds separately.

Great, now let's move on to creating our hillside behind the pond.

Tutorial 3: The Hillside

Another major element in the scene is the grass-topped hills. They surround the tree and add a mood to the scene. They are also a place to add small details like the roots of other unseen plants. They are quite simple to create using the Skin tool. They could also be created using the Path Extrude tool or by simply converting a flat plane to a Bezier mesh and adjusting. I like the Skin tool approach because it is a clear modeling technique and easily adjusted. In this tutorial we'll use the Skin and the Path Extrude tools.

EXERCISE: CREATING THE HILLSIDE

1. As before we will create the hillside as a shape, so if you wish to have more than one in your scene you can do so with minimal memory usage. From your tree project or from a new project, create a new shape and name it "Small Hill."

2. The first thing to do is to create the cross section, or rib, using the Pen tool. The shape is up to you. What I've created is a shape that will curve off nicely both left and right, and has a bit of a depression or indent for the tree. Remember that when you are using the Pen tool, its handles can be broken by using the Option key on your keyboard. Conversely, if you've already broken handles, they can be realigned by clicking on the Align Handle tool (it's the third icon from the right at the top of the screen). If you're unclear about the use of the Pen tool, please refer to the tree tutorial. Your first rib should look something like Figure 5.24.

3. The number of ribs you duplicate along the Y axis for skinning depends on the amount of variation you'd like in the vertical. Keep in mind that you will want to have fairly even distribution of ribs to keep the texture map from distorting with UV mapping. Duplicate the rib you created by holding down the Option key and dragging the center or Y handle. I created six duplicates to ensure the hillside had detail. What I've done in this example is to make the second rib overlap the first rib to create a bit of an overhang of the bank over the water. I continued to duplicate ribs along the y-axis each time using scale and reshape to get to the shape desired. Switching views goes a long way toward making this process easier. If

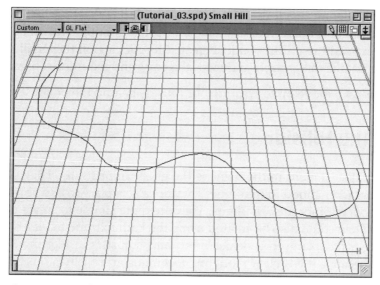

Figure 5.24   The first rib.

you look at Figure 5.25, the top view, you'll notice that it resembles a topographical map.

If you think along these lines, creating land masses with Skin objects will make a lot of sense. Looking at Figure 5.26, you'll notice I've also adjusted the ribs in the vertical to add a bit of rolling to the hill.

You can work from a front view or isometric or whatever works for you as long as the proper grid is active, either Z or X.

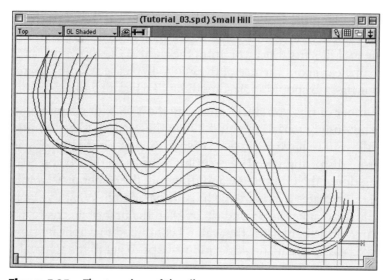

Figure 5.25   The top view of the ribs.

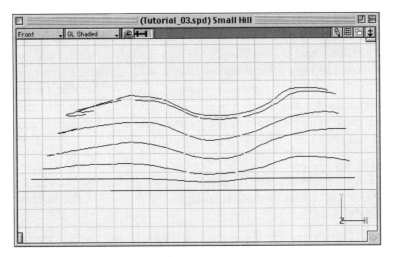

Figure 5.26   Tweaking the ribs.

4. Figure 5.27 shows the hill shape in a shaded view after it has been skinned.

5. Use the Skin tool as you did in previous tutorials, clicking on a rib and dragging to the next. Shapes like this one at times are more difficult to skin properly, so be sure to watch which rib highlights in red as you proceed through skinning. If you find that the Skin tool keeps wanting to use rib 1 when you are skinning ribs 3 and 4, try changing your view a bit and skinning from the back or inside of the object.

6. Now that you have the main portion of the hill, it's time to create the grassy top. We will use a Path Extrude object for this shape, and we'll

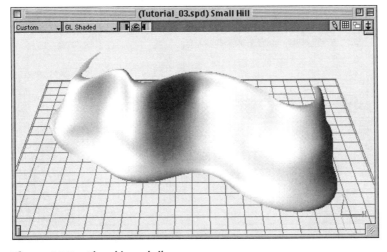

Figure 5.27   The skinned ribs.

map it with a stencil map. Don't confuse stencil map with opacity map. With an opacity map, it is not possible to achieve 100% transparency. Opacity maps affect the way light passes through an object and need to be used in conjunction with diffuse, ambient, and specular maps to work properly. Whereas stencil maps simply cut away at the object without the need for any other supporting maps. The first thing to do is to create the path for the extrusion. From an isometric view use the Unskin tool to unskin just the very top section of the hill.

7. Select the top rib and with Option-drag, copy the rib moving it vertically along the y-axis, and then reskin the top rib. You now have a path for the extrusion that perfectly matches the top rib of the hill, as seen in Figure 5.28.

8. Next, we'll create the profile of the extrusion. Using the Pen tool create a Bezier line something like the one seen in Figure 5.29.

   I've shown this line in reshape mode so that you can see the starting point is at the bottom of the line. This is very important as where you start will affect the way the Path Extrude object is created. Also, notice that I am at the right side of the path. That is important, and it will affect the final shape.

9. After you complete the profile, go ahead and use the Path Extrude tool from the Extensions pallet and create the Path Extrude object by clicking on first the profile and dragging to the path. Your object should look something like Figure 5.30. I've scaled and lowered the object a bit to keep from having too much intersection with my hill object.

10. Now that our shapes are complete, we can add the texture maps. Go to File/Import and bring in Grass Cap and Dirt Bank. Drag Grass Cap onto

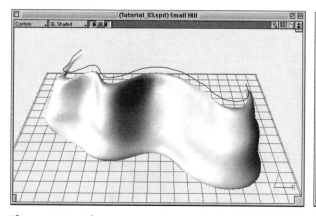

Figure 5.28 The grass extrusion path.

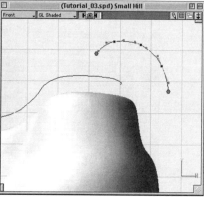

Figure 5.29 The extrusion Bezier line.

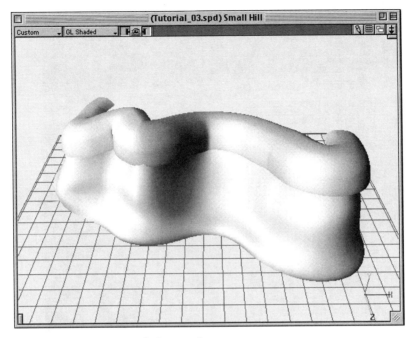

Figure 5.30   The extruded grass shape.

the shape you created for the grass. On the Object Properties pallet go to the Texture tab and set the Y to 10%. This texture wraps and will repeat 10 times along the length of the extruded shape. I had to adjust the orientation of the maps using Compose Maps under the texture editor as the texture was created as a horizontal texture not vertical. A quick snapshot and your objects should look something like Figure 5.31.

11. Now repeat the process with "Dirt Bank". This time set X to about 20%. Because we are working with a skin object, the orientation of the maps are correct: X is along the horizontal, and Y is along the vertical. However, you might find that the map is upside down, depending on how you created the Skin object, so now is a good time to work with Compose Maps. Figure 5.35 shows the surfaced hillside, if your map is indeed upside down double click on the material Dirt Bank and then click on the Compose Maps button. Here you can use the circle that is half gray and half white to rotate the individual channels of your material. Just click on the horizon line within the circle and drag it around. Be sure and do that for each channel; you can select them at the top of the window.

We're getting closer to completing our scene. The next object we'll need to make is the goo on top of the water to make our pond appear old and murky.

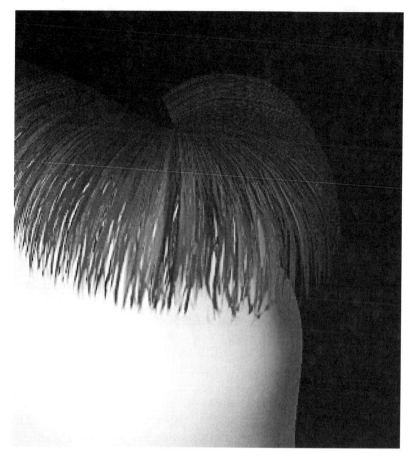

Figure 5.31 The surfaced grass object.

Tutorial 4: Water and Algae

All of the detail in the water comes from the surfacing and the addition of the algae; the water itself is simply a flat plane.

EXERCISE: CREATING THE WATER AND ALGAE

1. Use the Scale and Move tools to position the water plane as shown in Figure 5.32.

2. The next step is to build the shader or material for the water. From the Resource pallet, click on the Texture tab to bring it to the front if it is not already. Click on New, and select Surface Texture. In the Surface Texture window that comes up, click on the Color button and choose a color,

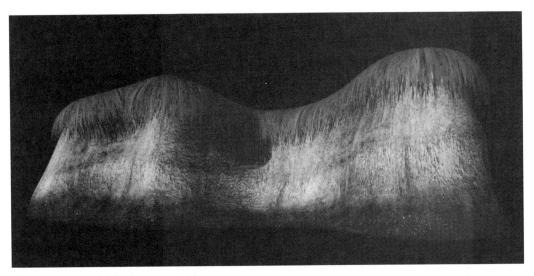

Figure 5.32   Editing the water plane.

preferably something muted and dark. I used a dark blue green, but you can use any color you like—we'll probably change it later, anyway.

3. Where it says "reflect" set the first % field to about 20 and the second to about 50, and then set specularity to 100%. Name the material "water," and close the window. You'll notice we did not make it transparent. That is because as I mentioned earlier we will not be modeling below the surface of the water.

4. Click on the New button again, and select Extend Ripples. The panel in Figure 5.33 appears, which is a plug-in for StudioPro that allows the creation and animation of ripples.

5. Using this plug-in, you can create shaders that will add the illusion of ripples to your objects either as a still or animated effect. You can add more than one ripple effect if you like. For example, you could have a random ripple effect, atop a linear effect, possibly caused by a boat rocking and then a circular effect from perhaps a leaf that dropped into the water. In addition, this plug-in will break up the way the surface reacts to diffuse light, which is great for making water look scummy or cloudy, and great for simulating depth.

6. Have a look at Figures 5.34 and 5.35 for the settings used for this ripple shader. The best way to arrive at appropriate settings is through experimentation. The values here require very subtle changes to alter the appearance of the image. Both of these materials have already been created for you, and they can be imported from the saved materials directory (see Figure 5.36).

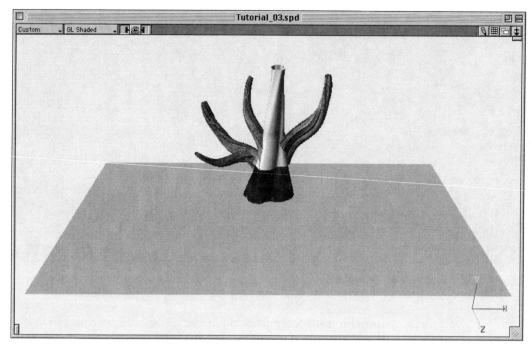

Figure 5.33 The Extended Ripples plug-in.

7. Now for the Algae. A quick and easy way to create such an object is through the use of a feature in StudioPro similar to John Knoll's Cybermesh called Import as 3D Mesh. From the Import command under File, you can import grayscale files as 3D geometry. Figure 5.37 shows the Import as 3D Mesh pallet.

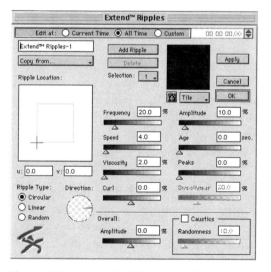

Figure 5.34 Extended Ripples settings.

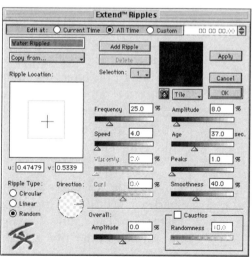

Figure 5.35 The surfaced hillside.

Figure 5.36   Extended Ripples effect.

8. Information about the pict file is seen at the top of the window. Below that are all the settings for converting that grayscale file into geometry. These are the settings used for the algae shape. Clicking on the camera icon renders the shape with the current settings and clicking and dragging on the shape itself allows you to rotate it for better views. The important thing to keep in mind for shapes like this one is to keep the smoothing set quite high, otherwise you will end up with faceting on the shape where steep angles occur.

9. To create the algae shape import the file "AlgeCyber.pict" from the textures directory and input these settings: Grid Divisions 250 _ 167, don't adjust the size, and set the Height to .2, keep it set to Trimesh and Point

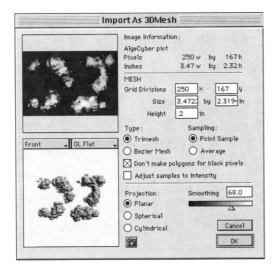

Figure 5.37 The Import as 3D mesh pallet.

Sample. Click the Don't make polygons for black pixels box and set the Smoothing around 70-smoothing can actually be cranked to 100 because the whole object is to be smooth. Click the camera and your results should resemble these.

10. After you've imported the algae, you need to position and scale it to your liking. Using the Rotate, Move, and Scale tools, position the algae so that the base of it is just barely below the water's surface with most of the shape visible above.

11. Now you can see the line that is the water and the flat bottom of the algae shape. Drag it down in Y using the red handle so that the base is just below the surface. Using the Magnifying tool to zoom in on the center of the shape makes selecting it much easier. Remember that "command =" will fit view to all objects and "command -" will fit to selected—two very useful key commands to remember. Note that if in shaded view, it appears that your algae is below the surface of the water plane it is most likely not. When it comes to subtle differences in distance between two shapes sometimes the OpenGL shading can't distinguish between the shapes and it gives an inaccurate representation. The best way to be sure is to drag with the render camera, a quick snapshot of the area in question.

12. Next we'll apply an algae texture to the shape. Go to File/Import and import the saved material "Algae Wrap," and then drag this material from the resource pallet to the algae shape. Bring up the Object Properties pallet and bring forward the texture tab. Now click on Position and scale down the projector to cover about one third of the shape. Finally, hit the End Reshape button at the top of the screen and that's it, you're set. Take a snapshot of your scene and it should look something like Figure 5.38.

Figure 5.38 The rendered water.

Well, all of our scene elements are now complete. Our next step is to bring them all together and position them to create a natural and interesting scene.

Tutorial 5: Building the Scene and Inserting a Camera

Now that we have a surface from which to work, we can proceed with inserting the hill shape and inserting some patches of grass. The placement of these objects is up to you. You can scale, move, and rotate them to your liking. One of the good things about shape objects is that with an object like the grass you can insert, say, five iterations of the shape into your scene and then scale them to different values in Y to give the appearance of multiple different objects.

EXERCISE: ARRANGING THE SCENE

1. Insert the other objects into your scene by bringing forward the Shapes tab on the Resource pallet, selecting the shape you wish to insert, and clicking on the Insert button. As your scene gets larger the screen redraws are going to get slower. What I generally do is set my view to point cloud or wireframe, make my changes, and then switch back to shaded view.

2. This is also a good time to insert a camera into the scene. Up to now we've been working with the standard modeling window, which is quite flexible and is sufficient for most views of any given scene. For final renders, though, it is best to use the Camera window. StudioPro allows you to insert as many cameras as you like. The cameras are fully editable, and most of all their parameters can be animated. Have a look at Figures 5.39 and 5.40, which should give you an idea of how to place your grass and reeds into the scene. Remember you can always move elements around to suit your needs. Feel free to change the water level, the placement of the hillside, or the tree and algae.

3. Next, the camera. The camera is inserted into the scene using the camera tool, it is the third from the bottom on the left side of the tool bar. Simply clicking once with the camera tool in your scene will insert a camera. You can also click and drag if you like. The first click sets the camera's reference point and then dragging positions the camera body. Once the camera is in your scene, you can make all the fine adjustments to its position. For now, from the front view of your scene, set to point cloud to speed things up, click once with the Camera tool to insert a camera. The camera appears outlined in red with a black body. The default is the camera pointing left, so switch to the top view and by clicking on the body, position the camera so it's pointing forward and by clicking on the reference point, position the camera so that it is oriented something like Figure 5.41.

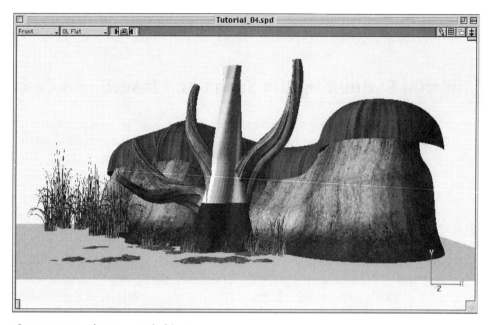

Figure 5.39   Placement of objects.

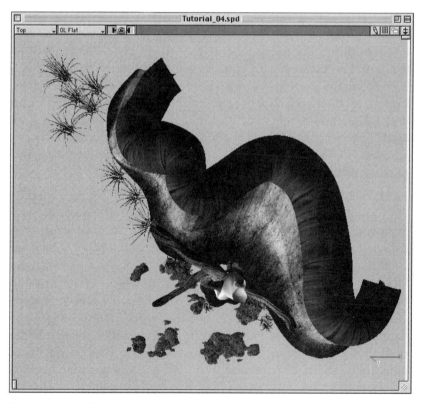

Figure 5.40   Placement of objects.

4. The fine adjustments we will do in the camera window itself, for now have a look at the Object Properties pallet with the camera selected. You can select the camera either in the main modeling window or the Camera's Object Properties, seen in Figure 5.42.

5. This is where you can set the depth of field, view angle, motion blur, targeting and tracking info, and more. Now in your modeling window, with the Object Move tool, double-click on the camera body. This brings up the camera view window, seen in Figure 5.43. It's here that you can make all the fine adjustments to the camera position.

6. The arrow icons at the top of the camera window allow you to move the camera around its reference point. If you wish to move the camera and the reference point, use the set of arrows in the upper right of the camera window. Again, it is best to keep the view set to point cloud to speed redraws when adjusting the camera. The slider at the top of the window affects the view angle of the camera, and if you like, you can choose from a list of presets directly to the left. If you decide you would like to play with field of view, the way it works is the number you input in the range field on the

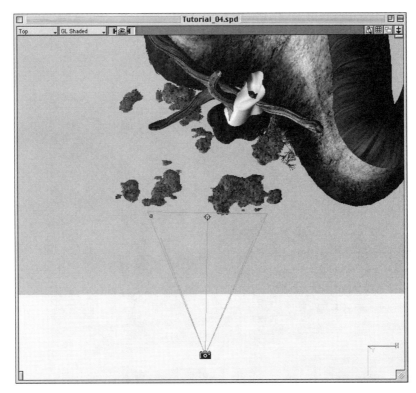

Figure 5.41 Positioning the camera.

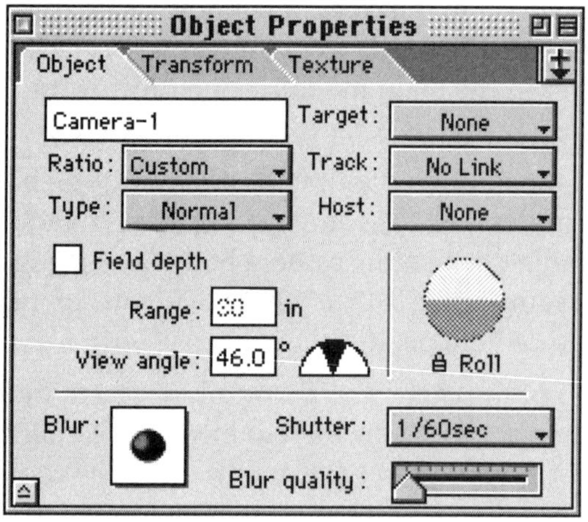

Object Properties

Object / Transform / Texture

Camera-1   Target: None

Ratio: Custom   Track: No Link

Type: Normal   Host: None

☐ Field depth

Range: 30 in

View angle: 46.0°   🔒 Roll

Blur: ●   Shutter: 1/60sec

Blur quality:

Figure 5.42   The Camera Object Properties window.

Camera Object Properties pallet will remain in focus both in front of and behind the camera's reference point. You also need to be sure Field Depth is checked. Depth of field (DOF) is best saved for situations when the camera is very close to an object or the scene is a very small one such as a fish tank. In Figure 5.44 I have activated the DOF, which makes the scene look like it is a miniature environment.

Figure 5.43   The camera view.

Figure 5.44   Depth of Field applied.

7. Since our camera position is very close to the object we won't want to use a DOF effect. Everything should be in clear view. The only time a natural DOF effect would apply is if the elements in the background of the scene were rather far away.

Well, now that we've arranged our scene and positioned our camera we can tackle the last step in the construction of this pond scene, the lighting.

Tutorial 6: Lighting

The next issue to take into consideration is lighting. All too often overlooked lighting is a very important aspect of any scene and can make or break all your hard work. It would be quite easy to write page after page on this issue alone as there are so many variables to consider. I will stick with the basics for this tutorial.

EXERCISE: LIGHTING THE SCENE

1. Up to now, we've been working with the default lighting model. It consists of a setting for ambient light and a single parallel light. Both of these

lighting types are accessed through the Environment pallet. If this pallet is not up, bring it up by clicking on the yellow circle or sun icon in the upper right of your screen (Figure 5.45).

2. The gray circle on this window represents the scene and the line with the circle on the end represents the direction the parallel light comes from. Think of parallel light as sunlight or a light source at an infinite distance, which covers the entire scene. You can select this light by clicking on it and dragging it around. As you change views in your modeling window those changes are reflected here. You can change its intensity, add color, and specify if it casts shadows. You can also delete the light or add as many as you wish. I use this light type when modeling but rarely for final renders unless the scene is quite large, such as expansive outdoor scenes. You can also adjust the ambient light from this pallet. Clicking on the Ambient button will bring up a color requester, where you can change its settings. One of the big mistakes made very often is setting the ambient light too high. Think of the ambient light as how bright it is in the deepest shadows, which in the real world is very dark. For this scene set your ambient to about 6%. You can also set a color for this light type handy for simulating night scenes with a bit of blue. Go easy on color though as a little goes a long way.

3. For this scene we will not use a parallel light, but we will use three spot-lights. One will act as our main or fill light, one will act as our bounce light simulating light bouncing off the water, and the other will act as a special effect, volumetric light streaming through the unseen canopy of trees above. Select the parallel light or lights on the environment pallet and hit delete to remove them from the scene.

4. First a bit about spotlights. They are added to the scene with the spotlight tool, which is the fourth from the bottom on right side of the tool bar. They

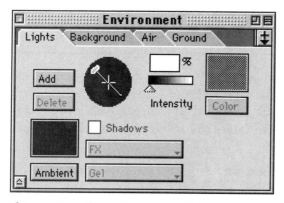

Figure 5.45   The Environment pallet.

act just like the camera in the way they are positioned and the way they attach themselves to objects you drag over, see tip above. Additional controls are the two red circles that control the areas of intensity and the two red nodes that control the fall off from the source, see Figures 5.46 and 5.47.

5. Here you see a top view and a front view of the fill light. You don't need to match this placement exactly, but something like this is recommended. What we have here is a very soft spotlight, the idea is it's filtered from the trees above. The fall off nodes are below the surface of the water as we want full intensity of the light across our scene. Double-clicking on a spotlight will bring up a spotlight view window very similar to the camera view window. This window can also be used to position the spotlight. With the spotlight selected bring up the Object Properties pallet for complete control of the light, seen in Figure 5.48.

6. Here you can name the light, add gels and effects, and set all its parameters. If you click where it says Light source radius, you'll see the Full intensity distance and Total falloff distance reflect the positions of the two red nodes you dragged out. The angle and edge softness reflect the size of the two red circles. You can also control the way the light falls off, either exponential or linear. For now, exponential is fine. Make sure the shadows box is checked, and click the color button to set the color to a pale yellow; very little saturation. Another mistake often made is not giving just a bit of color to natural lights. There is really no such thing as a white light. They're either cool or warm. A bit of color will add a great deal of life to your scenes. That about does it for the fill light.

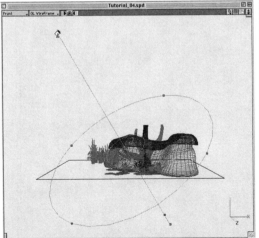

Figure 5.46 Spotlight control circles.

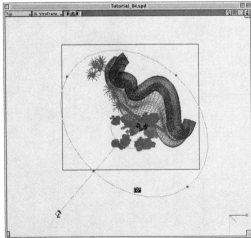

Figure 5.47 Spotlight control circles.

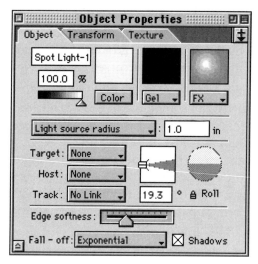

Figure 5.48 The Light Object Properties pallet.

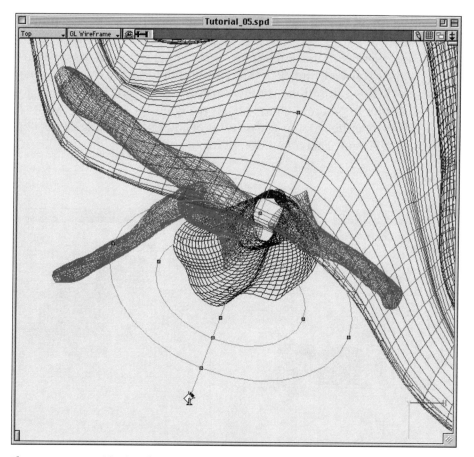

Figure 5.49 Positioning the new spotlight.

7. Now we'll add the bounce light. Bounce light is very area-specific. If we wanted to add bounce to the entire scene, we would have to insert a great many lights to cover the entire length of the bank, so for now we will just focus on the area around the tree. For bounce we need to pay close attention to the falloff of the light as we don't want the bounced light to reach very high, that would look unnatural. For this process I've turned off all my grass and reeds by clicking on the eyes next to their groups in the project window.

8. Now insert another spotlight and position it as seen in Figures 5.49 and 5.50.

9. I've also switched my view to orthographic to get a better view. The idea here is the light is just below the surface of the water and just in front of the tree. The light points at the tree and the fall off begins at the water's surface and ends about half way up. The light is set to a dark green color and the intensity is set to about 90%. Also, it's important to turn off shadows for this

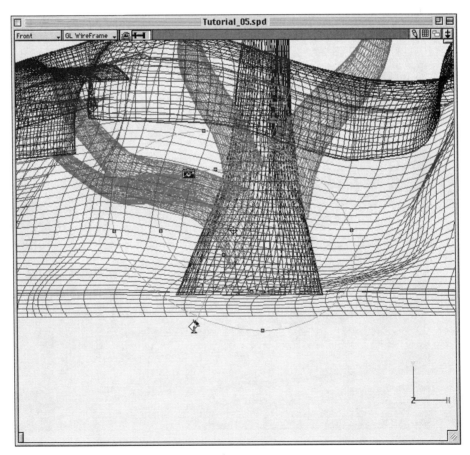

Figure 5.50 Positioning the new spotlight.

light, or else the water plane will cast a shadow and you'll see nothing. This is all very flexible depending on the scene you develop. This type of light placement requires a lot of test renders, and the snapshot feature of Studio-Pro makes this quite easy. Just drag out the area you wish to render with the render camera, the last item on tool bar. I generally do test renders with the camera set to RT Good or Best and cancel or close the render window before it's complete. This is the best way to get a good feel for what the light is doing. Your test render should look something like Figure 5.51.

Feel free to add more lights. In a scene like this, you should add several around the tree to illuminate the bank and all sides of the tree. Just watch the intensity because it can get out of control quickly.

10. The third and final light we'll add is the volumetric light. It starts out as a copy of the fill light as it needs to be in the same general area. Click once on the fill light to select it and then hold down the Option key and drag a copy. Position the light and adjust the falloff and edge softness approximately as shown in Figures 5.52 and 5.53.

Figure 5.51   The test render.

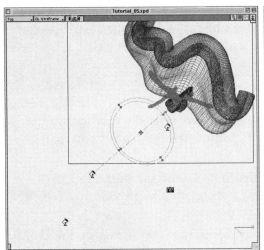
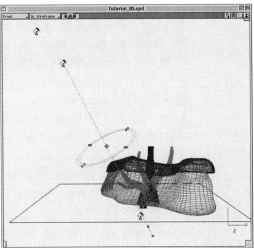

Figure 5.52 Positioning the volumetric light.   **Figure 5.53** Positioning the volumetric light.

11. Set the spotlight's intensity to 100% and reduce the amount of color saturation. Also, make sure shadows is not checked, we don't want double shadows.

12. With the light positioned and set up properly, the next step is to make the gel. From the Resource pallet click on the Gel tab to bring it forward. Click on the New button and make a new image gel. Click on the map button and load from the textures folder, gel 6. Leave the tiling set to its default and that's it, you just created a custom image gel.

13. Now, to assign that gel to the spotlight, select the light and from the Object Properties pallet click where it says Gel and select Image Gel 1, this is the gel you just created. When a gel is selected, a black dot will appear to its left. If you like, more than one image gel can be applied to any given light. When you first assign the gel to the light, the gel moves up in the list to between the two lines, which means it is loaded. If you choose not to use the gel, simply select it again, and the black dot next to it will disappear, which means it is not being used.

    That gel is now set, and if you like you can do some test renders to see how the light falls on your scene. It should render quickly because we've not yet added the volumetric. If you are pleased with the placement, move on to the next step, adding the volumetrics.

14. First, you will need to create either a fog or a mist shader, which you'll apply to the light; either will work fine. With mist, you'll get a breakup to the visible light, just like real mist. You have complete control over the scale and detail of this breakup, and it is fully animatable. With fog your

options are a bit more limited because the visible light is a constant tone throughout, although it does render a bit faster. From the Texture tab on the Resource pallet, click on New and select Fog. The Fog dialog box, seen in Figure 5.54, now appears.

15. Click on Color and set it to a pale yellow, and then click on Link colors. The Enable shadows box does not need to be checked because this spot-light does not cast shadows. Enable shadows is used when you want objects to cast shadows through the volumetric light, a very dramatic effect.

16. Set the density to about 35, max depth to 30, and the start depth to .1. Leave the falloff set to linear. These settings should provide an effective volumetric light.

17. Next we need to assign the fog shader to the light. Bring up the Lights Properties pallet to assign the fog just as you did for the image gel. Fog and mist are set under the F/X list as are other special effects like lens flare, pixie dust, fire, and smoke, but that's another tutorial. With the fog and image gel set to your spotlight, you're ready to render. One last important thing to note when using volumetric lighting: The render samples the light a set number of times between the source and the reference point. The default is 32, and this is often not sufficient. I've noticed, at times, that I've needed to take that number as high as 200. The higher you set this number, the longer the render will take, but the smoother the visible light will appear. This amount is changed under the Render window. To access it, hold the Shift key down while dragging or clicking a render, the Render window will appear, as seen in Figure 5.55.

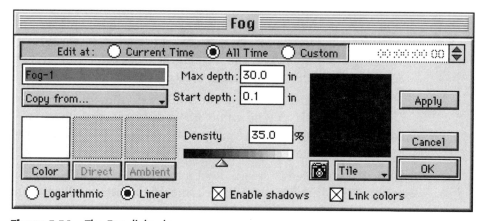

Figure 5.54   The Fog dialog box.

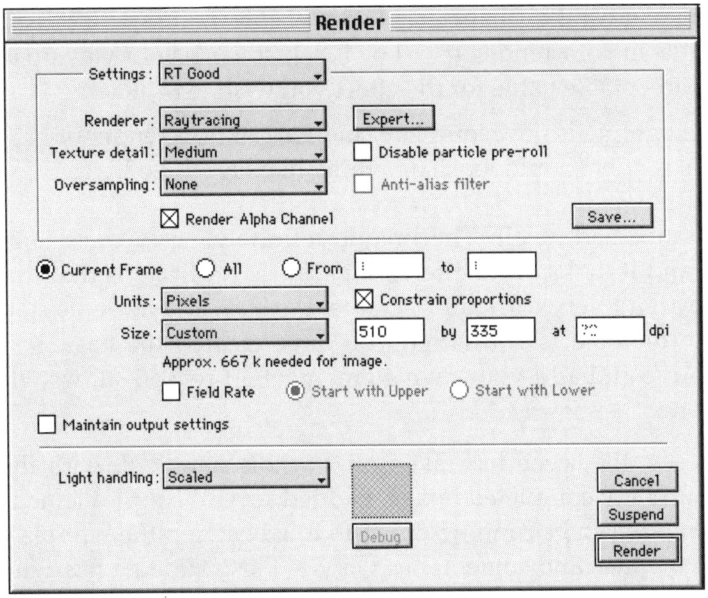

Figure 5.55 The Render window.

This window controls all aspects of how the image is rendered. It is also where you tell the renderer that you are rendering an animation and what frames to render.

18. Next, make sure the Renderer is set to Raytracing, and click on the Expert button. The Raytracing Esoterica window opens, as seen in Figure 5.56.

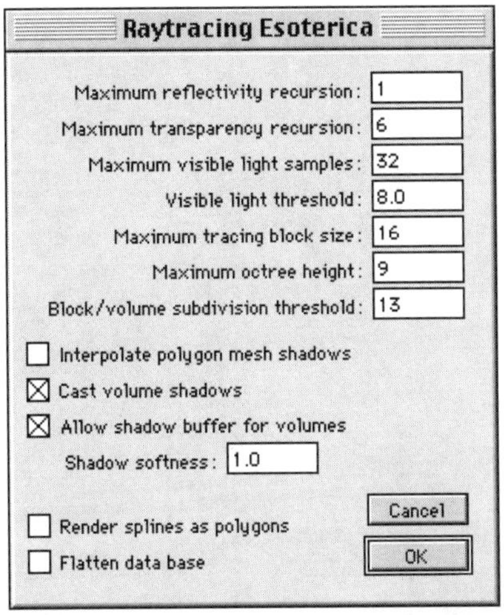

Figure 5.56 The Raytracing Esoterica window.

19. The value you want to change is Maxim visible light samples. If 32 yields poor results in your render, try 64 or 128. Just work your way up until you reach an acceptable value for the effect you wish to achieve.

20. Okay, the lighting is now complete, and we can do a render of the scene. Your final render should look something like Figure 5.57.

We'll, that's not bad at all. The image definitely has a dark and murky mood to it, and it looks quite interesting. The great thing is that the objects in the scene aren't very difficult to create. We basically added detailed surfacing to simple objects. Now that you have created the basic scene, you can get creative and add your own elements. Figure 5.58 shows what I did with the scene.

As you can see, the scene has taken on a whole new look with the added details. To build my completed image, I added several simple elements, like a dock with wooden steps running down to it, a boat, a rather simple yet very cool door in the tree, and some lights. Oh yes, I also added a few vines hanging from the tree. In reality, all of these objects were rather easy to create, but they transformed a somewhat barren scene into a living reality. The key to developing visually stunning scenes is detail. The more you add, the more interesting and believable the scene becomes.

Figure 5.57 The final render.

Figure 5.58   The Entrance.

Wrap Up

We covered a great deal of information in this chapter, but we have actually just scratched the surface. Two very important aspects of creating digital plants are surfacing and modeling. If you have models that possess too few polygons and show faceting around the edges, realism is gone. Also, in regard to surfacing, try to stay away from flat colors. All plants have variations in their color and tone, and if you want realism, you have to mimic that. Do your research and whenever possible use scans from the real thing. Even if you don't have access to a scanner, go out and take photos for reference material. You'll be glad you did, and before you know it you'll have volumes of invaluable photos.

As for StudioPro, I've just barely touched on all the tools it has to offer. Personally, I use the application because I feel it has one of the best renderers you can buy, and the surfacing control is hard to beat. Also, I've found that it is one of the most comfortable applications in which to work, and that means a great deal when you are staring into your monitor for 10 hours straight. From this digital artist, it comes highly recommended.

CHAPTER 6

Surfacing: Half the Battle (Photoshop)

Frank Vitale

COLOR FIGURES ON THE CD-ROM

All the figures in this book are in color on the CD-ROM. This chapter deals heavily with color, so you should refer to the color figures in the Chapter08/Figures folder on the companion CD-ROM before continuing with this chapter.

There is so much to cover when it comes to creating realism no matter what the topic. This is especially true when creating plant life. That is why it is necessary to narrow the focus a bit and talk about surfacing specifically. Surfacing is such an important aspect of any 3D illustration or animation. It really deserves a great deal more attention than most people are willing to give. For me it's 25% modeling, 25% lighting, and 50% surfacing. Nothing captivates the viewer more than an image that has them wondering whether it's real or manufactured. Quality surfacing is one of those areas where you really can create absolute realism. It's more than just creating the perfect texture map. It's creating the perfect combination of texture maps and knowing how to adjust the material attributes.

This chapter is going to focus on using Adobe Photoshop 4.0 to develop texture maps for the leaves of the flower seen in Figure 6.1.

We will also touch on how to set the material attributes. My 3D application of choice is Strata StudioPro, but these principles carry over to any and all applications. Specularity is specularity whether you use Ray Dream or Houdini.

Figure 6.1 A 3D flower painted with Photoshop.

I hope the flower I've created here will have florists around the world scratching their heads. It's based loosely on a Gloriosa Lily, but I've taken several artistic liberties to create a more thorough surfacing lesson. Basically, we are going to develop textures for four parts: the stem, leaves, petals, and the pod, which includes the pistels. We will start with the leaves. A few things need to be taken into consideration while developing the textures for the leaves.

Whenever possible I use a scan of the real thing. I firmly believe that the best way to achieve realism is to start with realism. The leaf is a perfect example of this. Easily acquired fairly flat, just slap it down on the flatbed and scan away. But not everybody has access to a scanner, and you might have a very specific look in mind that either does not exist or can't be found. So for the sake of this tutorial we will paint the leaf textures. Another important thing to think about is the edge of the leaf. You might have created the perfect model and the perfect textures, but your render still looks unreal. That's because leaves do not have perfectly smooth edges, whereas, unfortunately, most models do have perfect edges that are nice and smooth, with no flaws. The way around this is to use a stencil or clipping map, which is basically a texture map that cuts away at your shape, allowing you to use any edge treatment you like.

Having said all that we can get started.

EXERCISE: PAINTING A LEAF TEXTURE

1. If you haven't already, launch Photoshop and make a new file 700 pixels high by 400 pixels wide and save it as "Leaf1.psd." Within this document we will create all the different texture maps necessary for the leaf shader. I'll be using rather straightforward colors here, mostly green and a bit of yellow, but feel free to experiment with color or value. Subtle adjustments to value and hue can make a great difference in the final render.

2. Pick foreground and background colors by clicking on the color squares at the bottom of the tool bar. For foreground, choose something like RGB 91, 150, 31, and for the background 54, 78, 32. These will give you a nice light and dark green.

3. Now go up to Filter/Render/Clouds, which will give you a natural-looking break-up to the base color for the leaf. I use the Clouds filter a great deal in all sorts of situations. It is much better than using a solid color.

4. Next we'll darken the center of the texture to further break up the color. Keep in mind that there is practically an infinite variety of leaf types, so there are no wrong decisions, within reason. Make a rectangular selection that runs the length of the texture vertically and occupies the center third of the horizontal. Go to Select/Feather... and type 50.

5. Now bring up the Levels control, Image/Adjust/Levels, and move the Output level's black arrow to about 144, about in the middle, and then move the Input level's black arrow to about 10. Your textures should now look something like Figure 6.2.

6. Next we'll add some yellow to the edges of the leaf. For this and the rest of the lesson we will use Photoshop's layers. Bring up the Layers window now, and you'll see you've been working on the background layer up to this point. Click on the Background layer within the Layers window, and drag it to the little page icon at the bottom of the window to duplicate that layer. Now double-click on the layer you just created (background copy) and name it "Yellow."

7. Double-click on the Background layer as well, and name it "Green." It's easy to blow off naming your layers and channels, but I highly recommend doing so because it will make your development process much

Figure 6.2 The underling color layer.

smoother. Next, select the yellow layer and go to Image/Adjust/Hue Saturation. Set the value to -25, +53, and +35, respectively to turn your layer from green to yellow. If you decide later to change this color, it is very easy to do-that's the beauty of working with layers.

8. Now is a good time to save your file again. Actually, anytime is a good time to save your file; do it often.

9. Now we need to remove or, in this case, mask off most of the yellow on this layer so that it appears only on the edges and in a natural way. Use the rectangular marquee tool to select about one quarter of an inch on each side of the texture, running the full length in the vertical. First select the left side of the file, and then use the Shift key to add to your selection and select a similar region on the right side.

Figure 6.3 The saved channel.

10. Now with that selection active make sure your Channels window is open and at the bottom of that window, click on the Save selection icon; it's the second one, the gray square with the white circle in the center. This saves our selection as Channel #4, and it should look something like Figure 6.3.

11. Clicking on Channel #4 on the Channels window will bring it up. Clicking back on RGB at the top of the Channels window will bring you back to your color layer.

12. Now to break up the image. There are several ways to do this, but two of my favorites are to use Spatter or EyeCandy 3.0 Jiggle. Both are found under the Filter menu. I'll use Spatter here as it ships with Photoshop. With Spatter you'll need to break the surface up a bit manually first using the paintbrush. Select the paint brush and using two different sized brushes,

one 20 pixels and one around 40, and alternating between black and white, paint away at Channel #4 until it looks something like Figure 6.4.

13. Next go to Filter/Gausian Blur and blur the channel by about 5. Now go to Image/Adjust/Brightness Contrast and set it to 49, 93. This tightens up the blurred image-it's an effect I use a great deal. It takes our hard-edged painted image and makes it look much more natural. At this point your image should look like Figure 6.5.

14. To break the image up further we'll now use Spatter. First, blur the image a bit as we did before, again using 5. Then go to Filter/BrushStrokes/Spatter... and set it to a spray radius of 20 and a smoothness of 7. Move the cursor into the black preview window and drag the hand around until you can see your image; it defaults to center. Your image should now look like this, see Figure 6.6. Again, you can run Brightness Contrast on it to tighten it up a bit.

15. The next step is to add a layer mask to the Yellow layer. If you are not familiar with layer masks, it's a good idea to read up on them in the Pho-

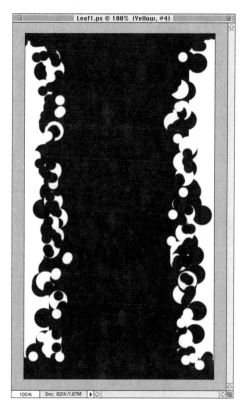

Figure 6.4 The channel broken up by painting.

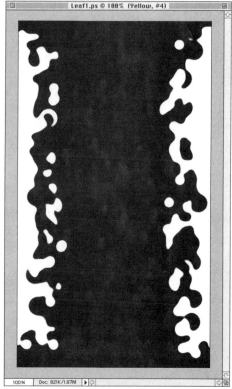

Figure 6.5 The channel blurred and then tightened up.

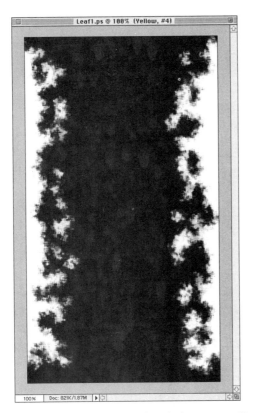

Figure 6.6 The channel with the Spatter filter effect.

toshop manual or in *The Photoshop 4 Wow!* book, a highly recommended book published by Peachpit Press. Be sure to check out page 190, Windows version. The first thing to do is to load the selection from the channel #4. Do this by selecting channel #4 so that you can see it and then clicking on the load selection icon at the bottom of the channels window. It's the first icon in the row, a simple circle on white. If you hold your cursor over the icon, its function will appear in a small window above. Click this icon to load the selection.

16. Click on the RGB channel within the channels window, click the Yellow layer within the layers window to make it active, and then click the first icon at the bottom of the layers window, the add layer mask icon. Your yellow layer now has a layer mask associated with it. The black regions of the mask allow the layer below it (the green layer) to show through. This is the most flexible way to work with multiple layers. You can add or subtract from the layer mask at any time, see Figure 6.7.

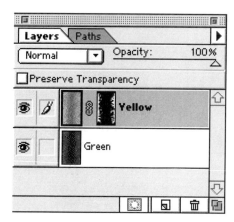

Figure 6.7   The Layers window.

17. Next to the layer swatch for the yellow layer you'll see a paintbrush, which tells us that we are on the RGB value for that layer. The swatch also has a black outline around it. If we click on the layer mask swatch directly to the right, that icon changes to a square with a circle in the center, the layer mask icon. This tells us that we are on the layer mask portion of this layer. Fully understanding channels, layers, and layer masks will go a long way toward helping you create textures in Photoshop.

18. Now we'll further affect the values of the colors within both layers using the Burn and Dodgetools. Burn/Dodge/Sponge are all accessed through the sixth icon down on the right side of the tool bar. Using a large soft brush, around 75 pixels, use these three tools on both layers to make your image look something like Figure 6.8.

19. I like to use a light exposure setting, around 10% or 15% set at the Options window where you can also switch tools and set the effect. Dodge will lighten and remove color from the image. Burn will darken and add color to the image, and Saturate will either increase or decrease the saturation of the image. The default is Saturate, so be careful.

20. I further blurred and ran Brightness Contrast on the layer mask to smooth out the edges a bit. I also used the airbrush tool to paint black over some of the white areas within the mask using a low opacity setting to allow the green to show through a bit more.

21. Now we will make the veins that run through the leaf. The trick to making these look real I believe is keeping them very thin. To create them we will use the Pen tool to draw the path. It will show up in the Paths window, so make sure that window is open. Generally, if it is open, it will be under the Layers window. Layers, Channels, and Paths windows can be

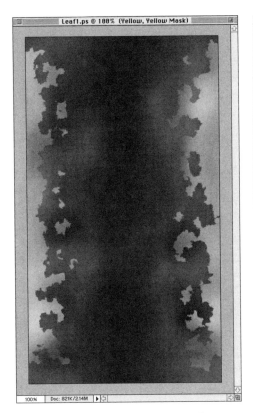

Figure 6.8 The yellow and green layers.

Figure 6.9 Green, yellow, and veins layers.

combined by dragging their tabs to the same window. If you like, you can drag the Paths tab out of the Layers window to create its own window. The Paths or Pen tool is the seventh down on the left of the tool bar and expands to reveal several options. The first option is the Pen tool itself, which is what you'll use to lay down the paths. The second option, the white arrow, is the Adjust tool, which you'll use to deselect a finished path and adjust the vertices position and curve. These are the only two options you need to worry about at this time. As you can see in Figure 6.9, each line is a separate path.

22. The idea is to lay down a path (a single line) using the Pen tool, and then using the Adjust tool click off the path to deselect. Then, again using the Pen tool, lay down a second path and so on. It's tedious, but it works well. Another option would be to go into Illustrator to do this or simply to use the paintbrush with a very small brush. The brush technique will work well if you have a tablet; but if you are using a mouse, you might find it difficult. For the sake of this lesson I'll use the Pen tool. After you've created all the veins for one side of the leaf, go back to your layers window

and create a new layer (using the page icon at the bottom of the window) and name it veins. Make sure it is active as it is in this layer, which we will use to stroke our paths.

23. Using the Adjustment tool found in the Pen tool pop out, drag a selection marquee around all the paths. With all the paths selected, go to the Paths window and click on the Stroke paths icon at the bottom of the window, second from the left. You've just stroked the paths with your foreground color in the layer you created, veins.

24. Now to save that layer as a channel or selection. If you're on a Mac, Command-click directly on the layer in the layers window. The icon should change to a hand with a small outlined box on top. If you're on a PC, it's Ctrl-click. This action will load a layers contents as a selection-a very handy feature. Now on the bottom of the Channels window, click the save selection icon, second from left. You now have a saved selection of the vein pattern we will use.

25. Now we need to duplicate it to fill both sides and adjust its thickness as it is way too thick at this point. To duplicate it use the rectangular marquee tool to select just the right side of the channel; then using the layer move tool drag a copy horizontally. With the copies marquee still active, go to Layer/Transform/Flip horizontal. Your image should now look like Figure 6.10.

26. Next, we need to thin up the lines a bit. We do this by blurring them with Gausian Blur and then using Brightness Contrast or Levels to tighten them back up. This needs to be done slowly about three times blurring only about 1 to 1.5 pixels each time. If you don't do it that way, some of the lines will break up. After you've thinned up the lines, the ones that end abruptly need to be faded out. Use an airbrush about 20 pixels in diameter set to about 50% and paint black over these sections to soften the ends of the veins. Your finished image should look something like Figure 6.11.

27. Now that you've got your Channel set, go back to the Layers window and to your veins layer. Select all and hit Delete to delete the original veins we created with the Pen tool. Now load the selection from the channel you just created, (Command-click directly on the channel in the Channels window to quickly load any selection). Pick two shades of green using the Eye Dropper tool (Option-click to select background colors) and run the Clouds filter. This will fill your selection with the clouds texture. Veins in leaves come in all colors and values, sometimes darker and sometimes lighter than the leaf. In this case, I'll use both. I've used the Dodge, Burn, and Sponge tools to darken the veins where intersections occur and lighten them toward the ends-how you do this is really up to you. Also, I duplicated the veins layer (drag it down to the page icon at the bottom of

Leaf1.ps @ 100% (Veins, #5)

100% | Doc: 821K/3.09M

Figure 6.10 The veins saved channel.

Leaf1.ps @ 100% (Veins, #6)

100% | Doc: 821K/3.09M

Figure 6.11 The thinned up and faded veins.

the window) and applied a blur of about 3 to it. This gives the effect of more depth and is optional. After all those adjustments, your image should look like Figure 6.12.

28. That about wraps it up for the RGB value of the leaf texture. Your Photoshop file should have four layers and two extra channels that look like Figure 6.13.

29. Now Save a Copy as "LeafColor.jpg."

30. The next step is to create Specularity and Bump maps, which we will do using channels. First we'll work on the bump map. The idea here is to create a sort of pillowy effect around the veins as well as have a smaller bumpy effect across the entire surface. Make a new channel by clicking on the new channel icon at the bottom of the channels window and name it Bump.

31. In this new window add noise at the amount of 175, Filters/Noise/Add Noise. Next apply a Gausian blur to the noise of 8 pixels. Now bring up levels, Image/Adjust/Levels and set the input values to 52, 1, and 82 and blur again with a value of 2. Next go to Filter/Other/Offset and offset the

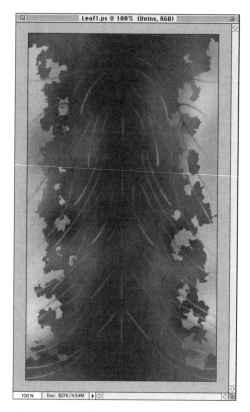

Figure 6.12   The three color layers.

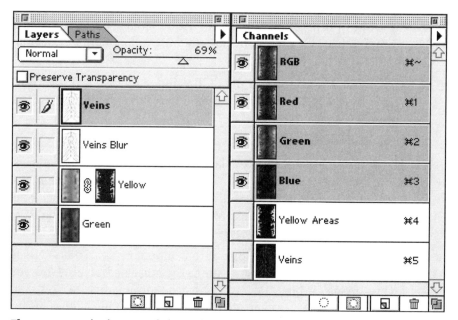

Figure 6.13   The layers and channels windows.

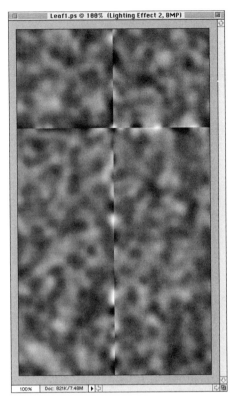

Leaf1.ps @ 100% (Lighting Effect 2, BMP)

100%   Doc: 821K/7.48M

Figure 6.14   The blurred noise showing harsh seams.

image 200 _ 200 making sure it is set to Wrap Around, your image should look like Figure 6.14.

32. This is the beginning of the process of making a texture wrap with no seams. Now use the Rubber Stamp tool (fifth down on left side of tool bar) to eliminate the seams. Option-click sets the tools reference spot and then painting with the tool will clone that spot's pixels to the area you are painting. Use a large soft brush of about 50 to 70 pixels.

33. After you've finished, Offset the texture again. You should see a faint seam caused when you painted on the edges. Remove that as well. You might need to repeat this a couple of times to totally remove the seam. Now you'll need to run Curves on the image, so the bump created is nice and rounded, Image/Adjust/Curves (see Figure 6.15).

34. Run Levels once again, setting the input values to 66, 1, and 231. This gives us a good range of values to work with for the bump map. This next process is what will give us a good pillowy effect, which is also great for making bumpy animal skins. In the Bump channel, select all and copy to the Clipboard. Then offset the channel and paste the Clipboard contents back down on top.

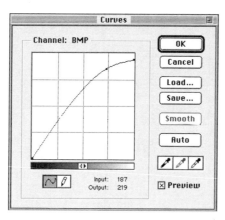

Figure 6.15 The Curves window.

35. While the selection is still active, go to the Layers window; set the blending to lighten only. Continue to do this pasting of the Clipboard contents, setting to lighten and offsetting four or five times, and then run Levels on

Figure 6.16 The pillowy effect.

it again for a good range of values. Your images should look something like Figure 6.16.

36. That last process built the small raised surfaces you often find on leaves. The next process will build the pillowing that occurs between the veins of the leaf. It requires the use of KPT Gradient Designer, so if you do not have that plug-in, you can skip this step.

37. Make a new channel and load the veins selection. Select the inverse, so that everything but the veins are selected and run Gradient Designer on the selection. Your blend should be white to black and you should choose Circular shape burst for the mode. Your results should look something like Figure 6.17.

38. Now give it a Gausian Blur of 5, and run Curves on it to round out the blend. Go back to the Bump channel and run Levels on it setting the output levels to 0 and 45. It should look quite dark. Now load the channel you created using the KPT Gradient Designer and lighten; see Figure 6.18 for reference.

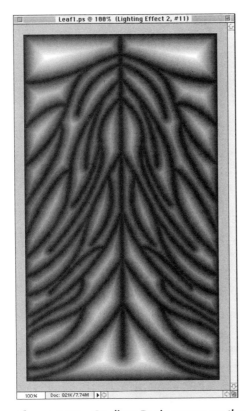

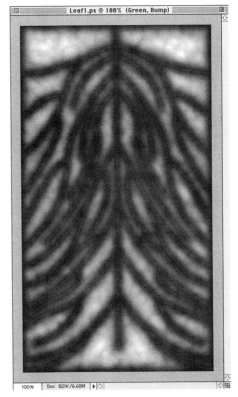

Figure 6.17 Gradient Designer run on the inverse of the veins selection.

Figure 6.18 The completed bump map.

39. Now duplicate the veins channel and blur it by 1 pixel. Next, load that channel into the Bump channel and lighten (see Figure 6.18). There you have it. Your bump map is complete. Save a copy as "LeafBump.jpg." See Figure 6.19 for a layer with lighting effects run to test the map.

40. Now for the specularity map. Don't worry, this is a quick one. The leaf itself will be quite shiny, but the veins will have little specularity. All you need to do is make a new channel, name it SPC, load the veins selection, fill it with black, or delete to black (Option-Delete deletes to foreground color). Then you blur it by about 3 or 4, load the veins again, fill with black again and blur just a bit, something like .5. Now lighten the whole channel a little using Levels and you're done (see Figure 6.20).

41. Now save a copy as "LeafSpec.jpg."

42. The final map to create is the stencil or clipping map. It takes about two seconds to make, but it would be worth it if it took two hours. Make a new channel and name it Stencil or Clipping—whatever your software calls it. Using the Lasso tool, create a selection that runs the length of the map in the vertical with rough edges and fill with white (see Figure 6.21).

Figure 6.19 Testing the bump map with lighting effects.

Figure 6.20 The specularity map.

Figure 6.21 The clipping map.

That does it! Figures 6.22 and 6.23 show a render of my final leaf.

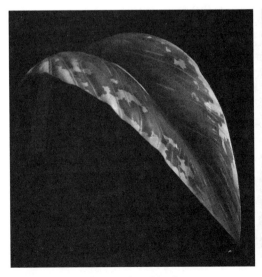

Figure 6.22 The rendered leaf.

Figure 6.23 The rendered leaf.

I created it as a shape object in StudioPro, so that I can insert as many instances as I like into my scene. With more time I would create several leaves for more realism. The image maps were applied as Planar maps. Figure 6.24 shows the completed scene.

There is enough going on in this scene that the use of a single leaf is not that detrimental, but I certainly recommend doing more than just one. Finally, Figures 6.25–6.27 show the image maps used for the flower petals.

Figure 6.24 The completed flower scene.

Figure 6.25 The petal color map.

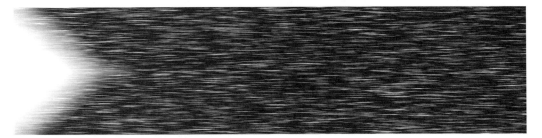

Figure 6.26 The petal specularity map.

Figure 6.27 The petal bump map.

43. Notice the specularity map for the petals. The streaking creates an effect similar to the way light reflects off of a petal. This map will be loaded into the stencil channel in StudioPro or the Clipping channel for 3DStudio Max, LightWave, and most other 3D programs. It will cut away at the shape, giving it a rough asymmetrical edge, which is much more natural than a perfect clean mesh. Now save a copy as "LeafClip.jpg."

Notice the specularity map for the petals. The streaking creates an effect similar to the way light reflects off real flower petals. If I were to use these flowers in an animation I might even use a reflectivity map that creates a similar effect. That is an effective way of adding a colorful sheen to the surface, similar to the feather of a hummingbird. Have fun and experiment, all those channels are there for a reason, so use them.

Wrap Up

Unfortunately, we don't have the time or the space to cover each texture map in this chapter. The same basic techniques are used for all of these textures. The most important thing to remember when developing texture maps is to keep your PhotoShop file layered. I am constantly making changes to the layer masks to get to the desired effect. After you apply your maps to objects in your scene, you'll likely find that they don't quite fit the way you want them to, and you will need to come back to PhotoShop to make changes. If you've not saved layered files, this will be very difficult.

PART TWO

Creepy Insects

What's cooler than an insect? Well, it really depends on your view. They can be quite the irritant in your kitchen or a park bench during a picnic, but when you consider the benefits of a 3D insect, well, they are just plain cool. Nothing has more detail or more visual appeal than an insect. Yes, they are annoying little critters, and giant insects don't usually dominate our entertainment, but when you think about it, most Hollywood creatures are based on insects. Just take a look at *Aliens*, and you'll see plenty of insect attributes in those creatures. How about the B- movie *Pumpkinhead*? That creature had attributes that were definitely based on an insect. And let's not forget the alien in *Predator*. That face was clearly insectoid.

There's something about the freaky mechanical detail of an insect exoskeleton that makes them rather frightening. Of course, they always have the freakiest faces imaginable. It's these attributes that make them perfect source material for any horror creature and definitely some of the best creatures for 3D since they are full of fascinating details. If it's details that make a 3D object appear realistic, then insects have the best opportunity to be the most photorealistic of any creature we could approach. They are also the easiest to make photorealistic, since they are inherently full of detail.

In this part we'll be exploring how to create 3D creepy insects with LightWave, 3D Studio Max, trueSpace, and Strata Studio Pro. Although we didn't have enough space to cover every 3D program in this book, you will find equally detailed digital botany tutorials for Electric Image, Animation:Master, Ray Dream Studio, Bryce, Soft F/X Pro, Cinema 4D, and Rhinoceros 3D on the companion CD-ROM. See the "What's on the CD-ROM" section of the book for a detailed listing of the CD contents.

CHAPTER 7

What's Under the Fridge?
Part 1: The Model (LightWave)

Bill Fleming

What's cooler than a creepy insect? Not much. Insects are the most extraordinary of creatures. They are extremely common and populate the planet more than any other form of life, but they look so darn freaky. Almost everyone is afraid of at least one type of insect, particularly spiders. These creatures are typically less than 1 inch in size and yet they intimidate even the most macho of people. Insects are the closest things we have to aliens on earth-well, that we know of anyway.

In fact, insects are the foundation of most very cool alien creatures in films, such as the creatures from the movie *Aliens* or the *ID4* aliens. You'll find the *Predator* creature is based on insects; just take a look at those gruesome mandibles on his face. Of course, there were the giant insects in *Starship Troopers*, but they were alien insects, like the creature in *The Fly*.

Insects are an amazing resource for creating very cool 3D creatures. They are also far easier to animate than organic creatures because they are literally, jointed. You don't have to worry about bone deformations. Sure, the IK can be a bit tricky, but it's a welcome tangent from the horrors of bones animation. When you are contemplating your next 3D creature, you might want to take a walk outside and lift up a few rocks or rotting logs. You'll find plenty of source material scampering around. If you want something that doesn't run all over the place, you can always buy dead insects from collectors' resources. These are awesome resources since they don't move. Here is a list of on-line resources for purchasing insects:

- www.bio-arts.com/
- www.L5.net/bughouse/
- www.worldbutterfly.com/
- www.insectworld.com/

Of course, a living insect has its advantages because you can see how it moves for animation purposes. I remember sitting here in the studio watching a wolf spider run around my desk to see how it moved. I also remember chasing it all over the studio since it didn't want to simply walk around in circles. I also let an African Giant Millipede (*Scaphiostreptus parilis acuticonus*) run around on my desk, but they actually do run in circles, which is convenient. They also make a great pet. They are more than 10 inches long and eat an amazing volume of vegetables. One will eat an entire large cucumber in a week! They really are quite cool. Another insect that makes a great pet is a cockroach. Yes, it sounds disgusting, but they really do make a great pet.

There are nearly 4,000 species of cockroaches (*Dictyoptera*, *Blattodea*) in the world, of which only 25 to 30 have pest status, the rest are innocent members of the earth's fauna. Of course, the pet roaches are the clean, gentle, and peaceful ones, making them great pets. The largest known cockroaches in the world are (largest wingspan up to 18 cm) *Megaloblatta longipennis*, and the *Macropanesthia rhinocerus* from Australia, which has the largest mass weighing in at up to 50 grams.

The smallest known roach is the *Attaphilla fungicola*, which lives in the nests of Leaf Cutter ants in North America. They feed on the fungus they farm. This little critter is a mere 4 mm long. Cockroaches have been on the Earth for at least 250 million years, and it is possible that in the late Carboniferous period, cockroaches outnumbered (in terms of number of individuals) all other flying insects. Most cockroaches are tropical in habitat and are typically diurnal, although several are exclusively nocturnal. Many are forest floor species, a few are cave dwellers, and some are even semi-aquatic.

The most popular cockroach-as-pet is the Giant Madagascar Hissing Cockroach (*Gromphadorhina portentosa*), which is the focus of this tutorial. The Giant Madagascar Hissing Cockroaches, shown in Figure 7.1, are found on the island nation of Madagascar, which is off the east coast of Africa. As decomposers, they perform an important role in nature.

They eat leaf litter and other decaying plant and animal tissue, and then break these materials down for nature to reuse. They are quite large. The adults can measure up to 10 cm in length and weigh up to 24 grams.

Figure 7.1 Giant Madagascar Hissing roaches.

Madagascar Hissing Cockroaches get their name from a defensive warning sound they produce through small openings on their sides, which are used for breathing. When air is pumped out of these small openings, it produces a hiss, which can be heard from 12 feet away! Madagascan Hissing Cockroaches have been found to be almost identical to fossilized roaches that lived more than 300 million years ago—long before the dinosaur era. Being around for millions of years has made these living fossils quite popular. They can be seen in many movies and broadcast productions. They are truly the most attractive and well-armored of the roach family and the star of our tutorial.

This is a two-part tutorial. In the first part we will explore the modeling of our Madagascar Hissing roach. In the second part we will cover the techniques for surfacing it. The modeling is covered in this chapter, and surfacing is covered in Chapter 8. It's a big tutorial, so be ready to chain yourself to your computer for several hours.

Okay, enough chatter, let's get cracking with our creepy critter.

Creating the Roach

A Madagascar Hissing Cockroach is a combination of a grasshopper and a beetle, with a little alien-like armor to top it off, as you can see by the model in Figure 7.2.

Since it's an insect we can build the body in several segments. There are many places we can begin the body, but the armored tail is the best since it defines the general shape of the body mass and it doesn't require a lot of polygons. It's important to start the model in a place where the polygon density is low. It's easy to add polygons for detail but rather complicated to reduce the polygon count. We always want to aim for the lowest polygon count required to achieve the desired effect, so the animation will be expedited.

Let's begin modeling.

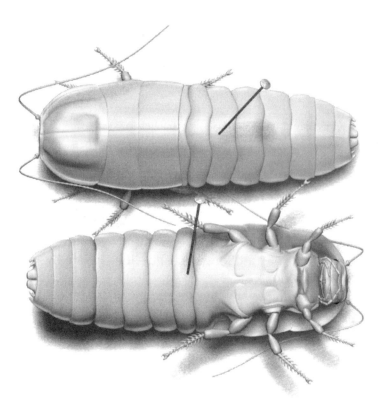

Figure 7.2 The Madagascar Hissing roach model.

EXERCISE: MODELING THE TAIL

1. To begin the tail, we'll start with a cross section that represents half the tail width since we'll be mirroring it to create the other half. The cross section is started with a simple plane. Create a plane with six segments along the x-axis, as shown in Figure 7.3.

2. Now we need to move the polygons, so we have a concentration on the left side, where we want the body segment to be rounded, as seen in Figure 7.4.

3. Now we add some shape to the cross section by dragging the points, as shown in Figure 7.5.

4. When you get to the last points on the left, merge them to create a single-point termination. Now we are ready to add depth to the segment by extruding it with four segments, as shown in Figure 7.6.

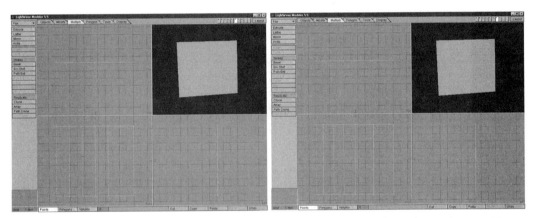

Figure 7.3   Creating the cross-sectional plane.   **Figure 7.4**   Moving the polygons into position.

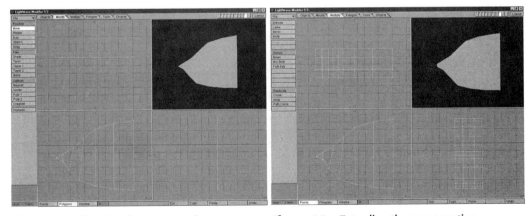

Figure 7.5   Shaping the cross section.   **Figure 7.6**   Extruding the cross section.

5. Great, now we're starting to see the segment shape come together. Next we want to add the organic curve to the outer edge of the segment. Select the Bend tool and then press N to pull up the Bend panel. Now set the Sense to "-" and then press Keep. Now, from the X Axis Viewport place the cursor on the middle of the mesh and drag it to the left to bend the segment so it resembles Figure 7.7.

6. Now we are ready to create the inset on the end of the segment, so we can create the next segment of the tail. The inset will create the socket for the next segment. Smooth Shift the polygons on the end with an Offset of "0," then Scale them down slightly and position them as shown in Figure 7.8.

7. Now repeat the Smooth Shift and Scale, but this time move the polygons inward to the position shown in Figure 7.9.

8. Next, Smooth Shift the polygons again, Scale them up, and position them at the opening of the inset, as shown in Figure 7.10.

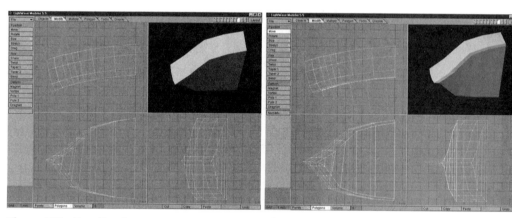

Figure 7.7 Bending the segment.   **Figure 7.8** Positioning the new segment.

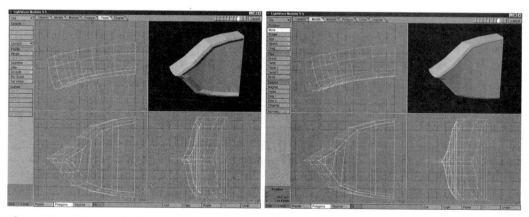

Figure 7.9 Creating the inset polygons.   **Figure 7.10** The complete first segment.

9. Now the first segment is complete. To complete the tail we will create several more segments in the same fashion. In fact, why don't you repeat the preceding steps to create another segment like the one shown in Figure 7.11.

10. Notice how I added a rounded shape to the new segment. This will make the tail more organic when we apply the Metaform upon completion. Of course, now we need to make the first segment more organic, so grab your Magnet tool and compress the top and bottom of the first segment where it meets the second by pulling them down in the x-axis Viewport as seen in Figure 7.12.

11. You should now round the back of the first segment using the same technique. The last step is to delete the unwanted polygons that lay along the x-axis. Select these now, and delete them so you have something similar to Figure 7.13.

12. Okay, now we can complete the tail mass by adding five more segments in the same manner. The tail should now look something like Figure 7.14.

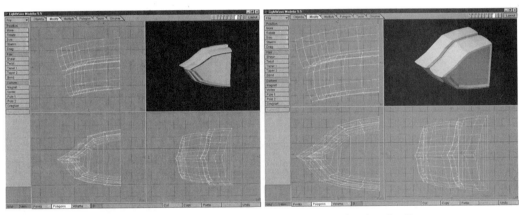

Figure 7.11 Creating the second segment.   **Figure 7.12** Shaping the first segment.

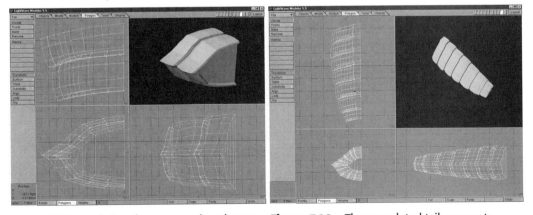

Figure 7.13 Deleting the center axis polygons. **Figure 7.14** The completed tail segments.

13. We definitely have something rather crustacean going here. We're almost done with the tail; the last step is to complete the hook segment at the base. We'll start the segment with the same technique we used with the others. Smooth Shift the polygons and move them outward to be parallel with the inset opening, then Smooth Shift two more segments, scaling them as shown in Figure 7.15.

14. Now deselect the last two polygons on the left, near the edge, and Smooth Shift them. Then Scale down the polygons a bit, making sure they are aligned with the parent polygons, as seen in Figure 7.16.

15. This will create a rim on the end of the tail. Deselecting the last two polygons gives us the foundation for the outside tail Hook, which we will create in a minute. Right, now let's complete the inset for the inner tail hooks. Smooth Shift the polygons, Scale them slightly, and move them back into the tail as shown in Figure 7.17.

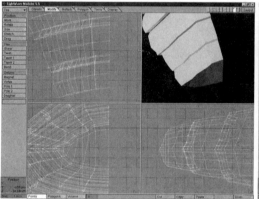

Figure 7.15 Starting the last segment.

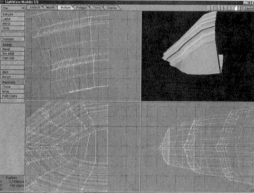

Figure 7.16 Creating the rim.

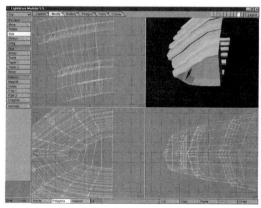

Figure 7.17 Creating the tail hook inset.

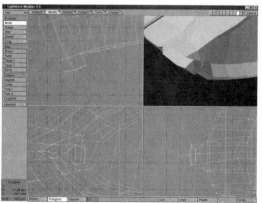

Figure 7.18 Starting the tail hook.

16. Now we're ready for the first tail hook. We'll start with the outside hook. On the end of the tail, select the two outer polygons we deselected earlier. Then Smooth Shift them once, Scaling them slightly and dragging the points to create a round shape as seen in Figure 7.18.

17. Now Smooth Shift the polygons two more times, Scaling them and Rotating them slightly to create the hook shown in Figure 7.19.

18. The last step on this hook is to Drag the points on the base at the inside so the hook will blend into the inside hooks smoothly, as shown in Figure 7.20.

19. Now let's attack the inside hooks. The first step is to Smooth Shift the inset polygons and place them evenly with the opening, as shown in Figure 7.21.

20. Now deselect all but the last two polygons on the left. Then Smooth Shift these polygons three times, Scaling and Rotating them to create the inner hook, as seen in Figure 7.22.

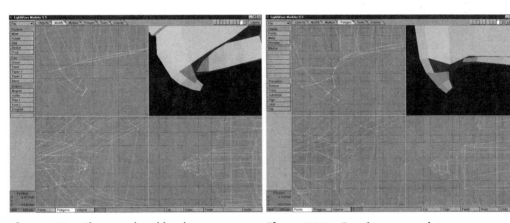

Figure 7.19 The completed hook.   **Figure 7.20** Creating a smooth taper.

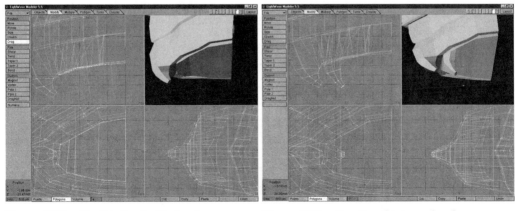

Figure 7.21 Starting the inside hooks.   **Figure 7.22** Creating the inner hook.

21. The last step is to create the inside protrusion. First, select the two remaining polygons on the inside and Smooth Shift them once. Then Scale them slightly, keeping the inside edge just left of the center axis, as shown in Figure 7.23.

22. Now Smooth Shift the polygons again and Scale them down slightly, keeping the inside edge parallel to the center axis, as shown in Figure 7.24.

23. To complete the protrusion Smooth Shift the polygons again and Scale them down slightly, as seen in Figure 7.25.

24. Great, the protrusion is complete, as is the tail. All we need to do now is test our work. Mirror the tail along the x-axis and Merge the points along the centerline. Now Subdivide/Metaform the object with a Max Smoothing Angle of 179 to create the smooth tail shown in Figure 7.26.

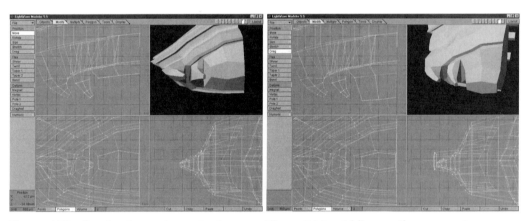

Figure 7.23 Starting the center protrusion.   **Figure 7.24** Adding another segment.

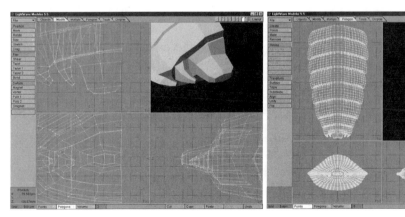

Figure 7.25 Adding the final segment.   **Figure 7.26** The smoothed tail.

That looks great! We now have a completed tail with plenty of detail. Of course, now we need to Undo the Metaform so we can continue to model the body. As you can see it wasn't terribly difficult to create the tail. It's really nothing more than repetition. That's one of the good things about insects: They are really just a lot of repetition.

Well, now we're ready to work on the body, which is more complicated in detail but really just plenty of Smooth Shifting and tweaking. Let's get started on the body.

Modeling the Body

The body has a great deal of detail. We need to create the multiple body plates, sockets for the legs, and a head with high detail. We'll be working on these elements one at a time since they are actually separate objects on the roach. We'll start with the main bulk of the body, which contains the leg sockets.

EXERCISE: MODELING THE BODY

1. Before we start adding the body detail, we need to do a little "body work" on the tail. The outside edges of the tail need to be drawn forward to make the tail more organic and to create a more logical flow for the plates. Using your Magnet tool pull the outside edges of the tail forward, as shown in Figure 7.27. Be sure to make the start of the tail relatively flat, which makes it easier to build the body.

2. Select the polygons on the beginning of the tail and Smooth Shift seven segments, as shown in Figure 7.28.

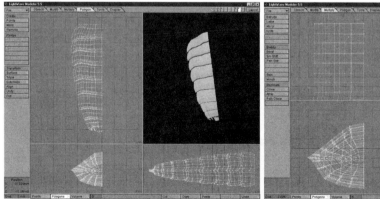
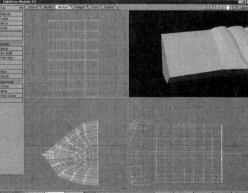

Figure 7.27 Pulling the outside of the tail forward.

Figure 7.28 Starting the body.

3. Select the tail polygons and hide them so we can see what we are doing with the body. Now drag the point on the body polygons in the Z Axis Viewport to make them rounded, as seen in Figure 7.29.

4. The next step is to shape the body. While we don't have all the body polygons yet (only the back half featuring the two hind legs), we need to shape the portion we have to form the protrusions where the legs are placed. Using the Morph tool, from the Y Axis Viewport, pull the side of the body inward, as seen in Figure 7.30.

5. Now we're ready to start building the hind segment of the body. The first step is to create a physical segment, which is really quite simple. Before we add any depth, we'll need to modify the alignment of the points to create a smooth shape, so using the Magnet tool, drag the points to create flowing lines, as shown in Figure 7.31.

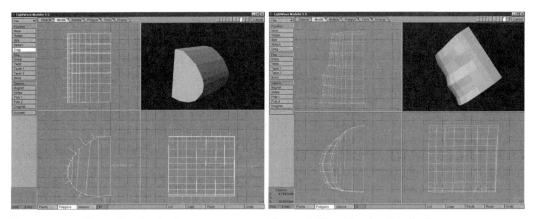

Figure 7.29   Rounding the body.   **Figure 7.30**   Shaping the body.

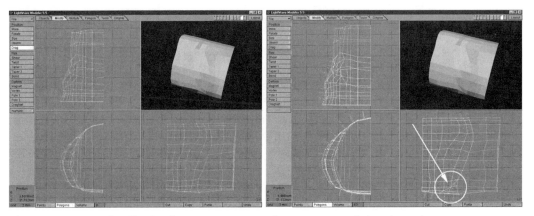

Figure 7.31   Creating flowing lines.   **Figure 7.32**   Splitting the polygons.

6. Although this creates a great base for a clean line, we have a bit of a sharp angle at the base of the body where the curved lines terminate. We don't want to drag the points back to make it smooth because it will cause undesirable pinching when we Metaform. Instead, we'll split the last few polygons to make a clean line. Figure 7.32 shows the polygons to be split.

7. Next we select the back half of the body, as seen in Figure 7.33.

8. Then we Smooth Shift the polygons. Once this is done, deselect the row of polygons on the leading edge of the model, which are marked in Figure 7.33. We don't want these polygons to be modified because it will create an undesired bulge where the body meets the tail. We want this area to be a smooth blend. Now we Scale the polygons slightly larger and position the front edge to be parallel to the underlying points, as shown in Figure 7.33. We want them to be parallel so they smooth properly when we Metaform. If we allowed them to overlap, the smoothing would leave a sharp edge, which wouldn't be realistic.

9. The last step is to Merge points, which will merge the points on the leading edge of the body where we created the new polygons with the Smooth Shift but didn't move them. The Merge will create several undesirable two-

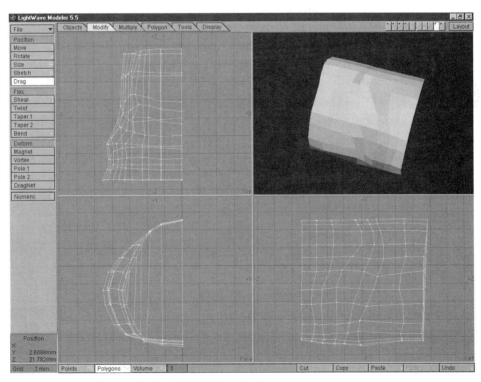

Figure 7.33   Selecting the back half of the body.

point polygons, which we need to delete so press the W key in Polygon selection mode and press the +key next to the 2 Vertices line item, and then press Delete. Great, now we're ready to build the hind leg protrusion.

Building the Leg Protrusion

10. We'll need to create a rounded group of polygons on the lower side of the back segment for the start of the protrusion. This is accomplished by selecting the polygons in this region and dragging points until we have a fairly round trailing edge, as seen in Figure 7.34.

11. Of course, we have a bit of a problem in the upper right corner of the circle. It's not quite possible to make it round without really stretching a polygon, so we split the polygon, as shown in Figure 7.34.

12. Now for the fun part. We want the protrusion to come out at an angle backwards so the leg can rotate backward to the extreme. To do this, we Smooth Shift the polygons once, and then deselect the leading polygons. Finally, we rotate the selected polygons outward, to the left, as seen in Figure 7.35.

13. Now we drag the points of the selected polygons to create a relatively round shape, then we Smooth Shift them once, Scaling them slightly, and keeping them lined up with the parent polygons. This created the ridge of the leg socket. Then we Smooth Shift the polygons two more times, Scaling them down and moving them inward to create the leg socket, shown in Figure 7.36.

14. Phew, that was fun. Of course, we aren't finished yet. Insects have a great variety of subtle details so we need to bear down and add the nitty-gritty

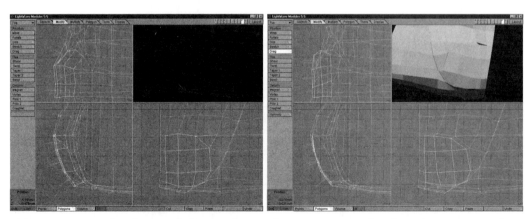

Figure 7.34 Creating the rounded protrusion polygons.

Figure 7.35 Rotating the polygons outward.

details before we move on to the next segment of the body. We'll start by creating a nice soft ridge that flows around the top of the leg protrusion. Select the polygons shown in Figure 7.37.

15. Now Smooth Shift them once, then hide all unselected polygons and select the lower points as seen in Figure 7.38.

16. Now move these points outward a bit to add a little depth around the edge of the leg socket. Then unhide the polygons, but be sure to hide the tail again. Then select Merge Points and delete the two-point polygons that are created. You should now have something similar to Figure 7.39.

17. Great, now we have one last major detail to add to this segment. We're going to create a nice groove running diagonally down the segment and into the leg socket. This is a bit tricky, but the effect is worth it. Start by selecting the polygons that run diagonally up the segment as shown in Figure 7.40.

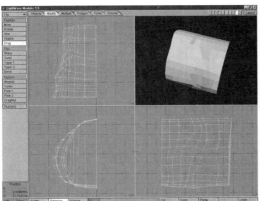

Figure 7.36 The completed leg socket.

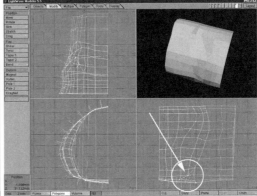

Figure 7.37 The ridge polygons.

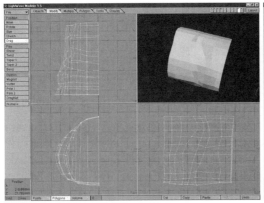

Figure 7.38 The points to be selected.

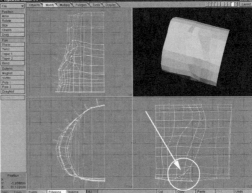

Figure 7.39 The soft protrusion ridge.

18. Now drag the points on the left inward so they divide the polygon evenly as shown in the figure. Now select the points running up the middle and pull them inward slightly, as seen in Figure 7.41.

19. We now have the start of our groove. The next step is to create a small crease in the groove by splitting the polygons using the Knife tool, as seen in Figure 7.42.

20. Then drag the points inward a bit and line them up so they are almost directly behind the front points, as shown in Figure 7.43.

21. Okay, the crease is now complete. If we do a Metaform test we will see a great crease running diagonally down the segment and a nice ridge around the leg protrusion, as shown in Figure 7.44.

22. Well, that's not too bad. We're starting to see some nice progress here. You might have noticed that modeling insects in detail can be quite exhausting. Although they are much easier to animate than an organic creature,

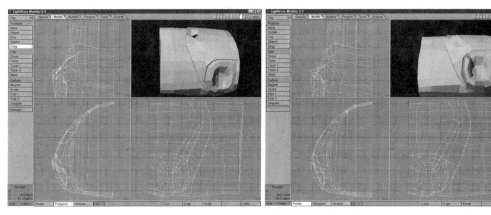

Figure 7.40 Creating the groove.   **Figure 7.41** Pulling the points inward.

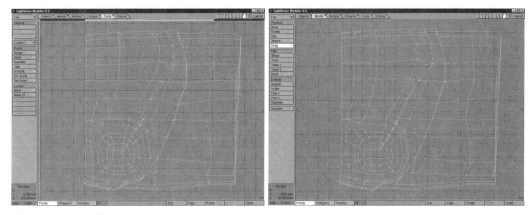

Figure 7.42 Splitting the polygons.   **Figure 7.43** Moving the points.

they do have far more detail, making them very complicated to model. It will take real commitment and patience to create a photorealistic insect.

Let's continue with our modeling.

Creating the Second Body Segment

23. The second segment of the body is created in similar fashion to the first. To create the segment ridge we start by selecting the first segment polygons and Smooth Shifting them. Then we deselect the polygon on the right edge and scale the selected polygons, positioning them so they are lined up with the leading edge, as seen in Figure 7.45.

24. Now we Merge Points and delete the two-point polygons. The next step is to create the leg socket protrusion, as we did with the first segment. Of course, the detail of this protrusion is slightly different. It has a circular ridge ring running around the base of the protrusion, unlike the first. The first step is to select the protrusion polygons and drag the points to make a rough circle, as shown in Figure 7.46.

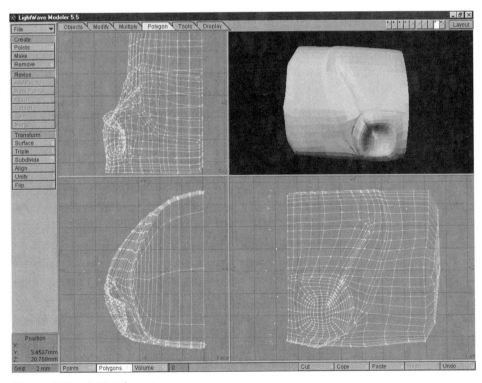

Figure 7.44 A Metaform test.

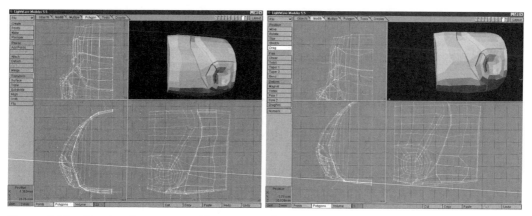

Figure 7.45 Creating the segment ridge.

Figure 7.46 Making the circular protrusion polygons.

25. Now Smooth Shift these polygons and Scale them slightly, keeping them parallel to the original polygons, as seen in Figure 7.47.

26. This creates the polygons for the ring around the protrusion. Now Smooth Shift the polygons again, Scaling them down slightly and moving them inward, as you see in Figure 7.48.

27. Next, Smooth Shift the polygons inward a bit, then once again outward, as shown in Figure 7.49.

28. Now Smooth Shift the polygons again, Scale them down, drag the points until you have a round shape, and move them to the front edge of the protrusion. Then rotate them outward as seen in Figure 7.50.

29. Okay, now we can create the socket by performing several Smooth Shift operations as we have done previously. Smooth Shift the polygons once,

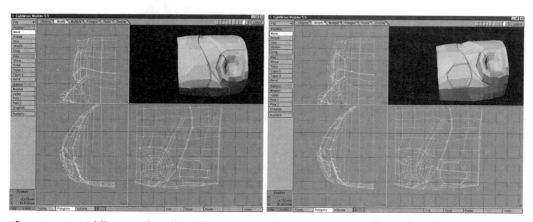

Figure 7.47 Adding Depth to the ridge.

Figure 7.48 Completing the ridge.

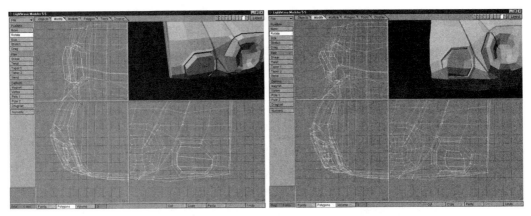

Figure 7.49   Starting the protrusion.   **Figure 7.50**   Starting the socket.

Scale them down slightly, and keep them parallel to the original. Then Smooth Shift them again, Scaling them down and moving them inward, as shown in Figure 7.51.

Now the leg socket is complete and so is this segment of the body. We're very close to completing the body so let's move on to the third and final segment.

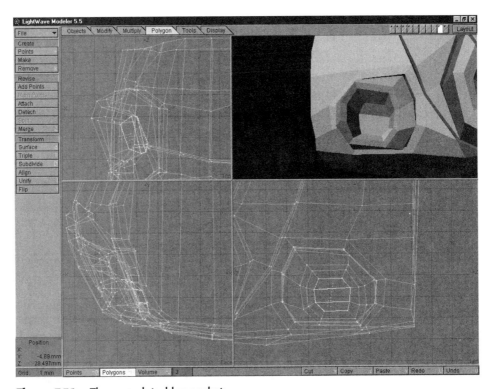

Figure 7.51   The completed leg socket.

Modeling the Third Body Segment

The third segment of the body is unique because it has a nice armor plating on the top to protect the upper torso. We'll be tackling this plating soon, but first we need to add polygons for the third segment.

EXERCISE: MODELING THE THIRD BODY SEGMENT

1. Select the polygons on the end of the object and Smooth Shift them forward four times, as shown in Figure 7.52.

2. Now it's time for a little body work. With your Magnet tool in hand, drag the new polygons until they look something like Figure 7.53.

3. Now we're ready to add some armor to this critter. This, of course, requires liberal use of the Split polygon tool since we need to create a smooth flowing plate on the back of the roach. Figure 7.54 shows the alignment and splitting of the polygons to create the armor. Go ahead and manipulate the points and polygons on your model to match.

4. Now Smooth Shift these polygons and Stretch them so they are slightly larger than the original polygons, but don't move them upward. Leaving the polygons flush with the original will create a very nice seam and overlap for the armor. Figure 7.55 shows position of the new polygons.

5. We are using Stretch instead of Scale because Stretching allows us to keep the polygons from Scaling down to an odd size. We want the same border width on all sides, and Scaling won't do this. Using Stretch allows us precise control. You simply Stretch the polygons from different viewports until you have the desired size.

6. Now Smooth Shift the polygons again and raise them upward, and then Stretch them outward a bit so they create a nice thick edge for the armor, as seen in Figure 7.56.

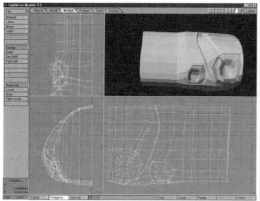 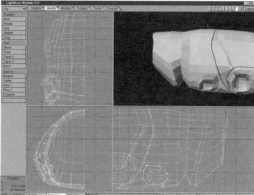

Figure 7.52 Adding the third segment polygons.

Figure 7.53 Shaping the third segment.

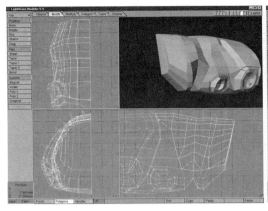 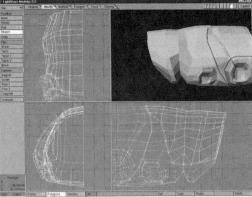

Figure 7.54 Creating the Armor polygons.   **Figure 7.55** The new polygon position.

7. Next, Smooth Shift the polygons again, Stretch them to be slightly smaller than the originals, and then move them up and out a bit, as shown in Figure 7.57.

8. This will reinforce the top edge of the armor so it creates a rounded edge when Metaformed, rather than a sharp edge.

9. Okay, we now want to create a nice ridge around the edge of the armor so we need to Smooth Shift the polygons again and Stretch them a bit smaller, then move them inward a little, as shown in Figure 7.58.

10. The next step is to add a rounded lift on the inside of the ridge, so we Smooth Shift the polygons again, Stretch them to be smaller, and move them upward, as seen in Figure 7.59.

11. Well, the basic shape of our armor is now complete. The final step is to add segmented ridges to the armor. Basically, we select rows of polygons,

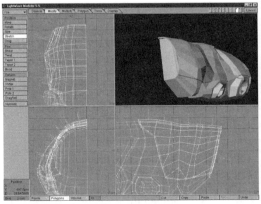 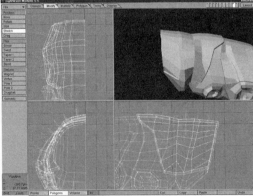

Figure 7.56 The armor thickness.   **Figure 7.57** Another Smooth Shift.

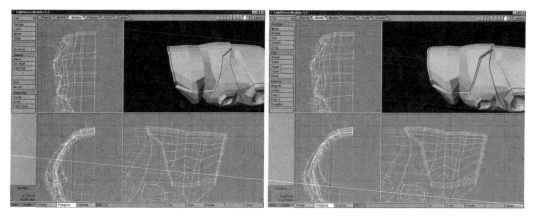

Figure 7.58 Creating the ridge.

Figure 7.59 Creating the inside lift.

Smooth Shift them and Stretch them to be smaller, then move them upward, as shown in Figure 7.60.

12. Now we repeat the process to create two additional ridges, as seen in Figure 7.61.

13. Great, the armor is now complete and the body is nearly finished. All we have left is a little detail to make the object more realistic. Insects are heavily segmented with many lifts and cavities, so we should add a few to our roach to make it more realistic. We'll start by adding a lift on the side. Select the polygons shown in Figure 7.62, Smooth Shift them, Scale them down, and move them outward, as shown in the figure.

14. Oops, I almost forgot the socket for our front legs. I guess we'd better get that completed before we add the rest of our body details.

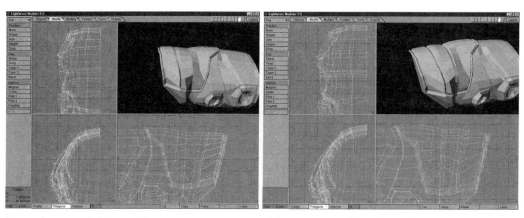

Figure 7.60 Creating a ridge.

Figure 7.61 Adding the additional ridges.

15. The front leg socket is very similar to the others. First, we select some polygons on the outside of the front segment and drag the points to make a round shape, like the one seen in Figure 7.63.

16. Now we Smooth Shift this once, Scaling it but not moving it, to create a ridge for the socket. Then we Smooth Shift once more and Scale it inward to create the socket depression seen in Figure 7.64.

17. Well, that wasn't too bad. Now let's add those final details. To finish off the body, we should add some plates to the underside, which is really quite simple. We select rows of polygons, Smooth Shift them, Scale them down, and then move them down to create lifted plates, as shown in Figure 7.65.

18. Phew, that was a lot of work, but we really made some progress. In fact, the body is now complete with the exception of one detail, the shoulder segment for the front legs. We need to create a little segment for the front

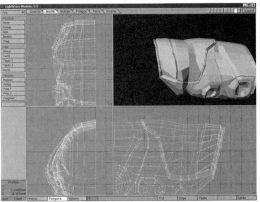

Figure 7.62 Adding a lift.

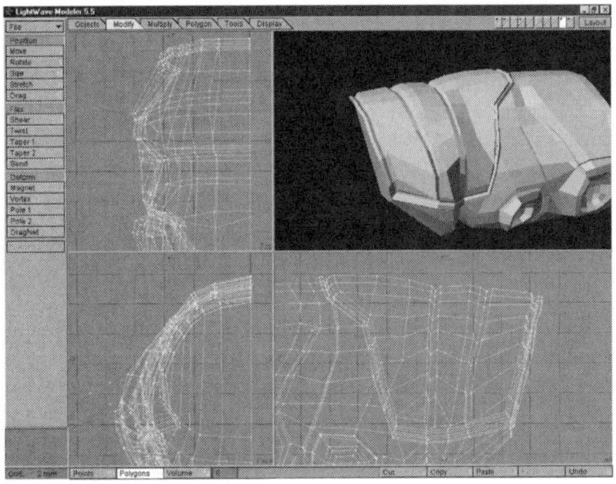

Figure 7.63 Creating the front leg socket shape.

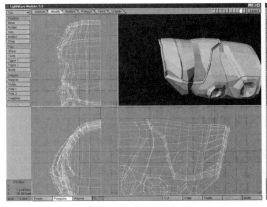

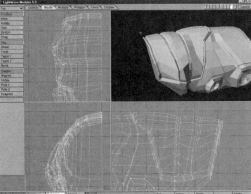

Figure 7.64 The completed front leg socket.

Figure 7.65 The completed belly plates.

legs to attach to the body. The back legs don't need to rotate over nearly as wide a range, so they have rather fixed shoulders, while the front legs need a full 180° of rotation, so we must build a shoulder segment. Of course, this is a welcome change from the complex body we just finished.

Creating the Shoulder Segment

19. We'll start the shoulder segment with a plane that has nine polygons, as seen in Figure 7.66.

20. Then, with the body in the background layer, we drag the points on the outside of the plane to make a rounded shape that matches the depression of the front leg socket, as shown in Figure 7.67.

21. Now we extrude the plane with two segments, as seen in Figure 7.68.

22. Next we add a slight rim to the end of the segment by performing two Smooth Shift operations. The first is Scaled down and moved out while the second is Scaled down and moved in, as seen in Figure 7.69.

23. Now, with the body on an active layer, select the entire shoulder segment and then use your Magnet tool to bend it upward and manipulate it to fit into the front leg socket on the body, as shown in Figure 7.70.

24. Okay, now cut and paste the shoulder segment into the body layer and Metaform the object to see what it looks like. It should resemble Figure 7.71.

Now that looks awesome. It definitely looks like an insect body. Notice how the plating on the torso really helps to make the object appear more realistic, even if it's not completely accurate. We certainly have come a long way, but unfortunately we have much more to do! We need to create a head for this creepy crawler, but first we should Undo the Metaform.

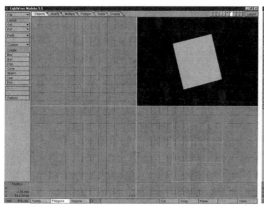

Figure 7.66 Starting the shoulder segment.

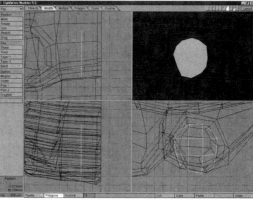

Figure 7.67 Shaping the plane.

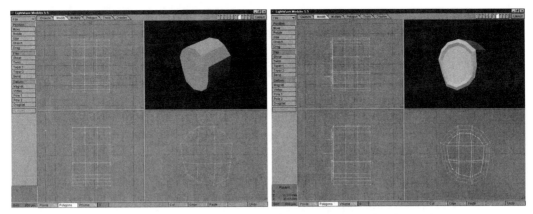

Figure 7.68 Extruding the plane.   **Figure 7.69** Creating the socket.

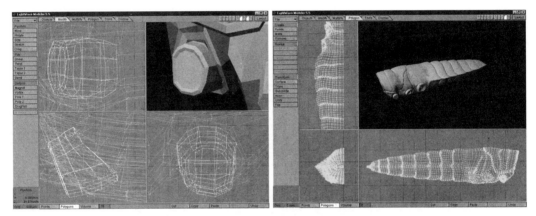

Figure 7.70 Shaping the shoulder segment.   **Figure 7.71** The completed body.

Let's take a stab at the head now.

Creating the Head

The head is a rather complicated object because the mouth is quite detailed. Fortunately, it's really just a matter of redundancy to create the head. We'll be using the flat mesh modeling technique for creating the head since it's the fastest method, and we've already been at this critter for too long.

EXERCISE: MODELING THE HEAD

1. The head is started with a simple flat plane, which has 10 horizontal segments and 11 vertical ones, as seen in Figure 7.72.

2. Now we define the cross-sectional shape of the head by splitting polygons and dragging points to create the outline of the head profile, as shown in Figure 7.73.

3. Next we delete the unwanted polygons to reveal the head profile displayed in Figure 7.74.

4. Now we extrude the mesh slightly, as seen in Figure 7.75.

5. The next step is to add some depth and shape to the head, which is accomplished by first Smooth Shifting the outer polygons, and then Scaling them down and moving them outward a bit, as seen in Figure 7.76.

6. The head is taking shape, but it's not terribly organic. This is where we have a little fun with the Magnet tool, manipulating the head, pulling out the center of the outer polygons, and softening the edges, as shown in Figure 7.77.

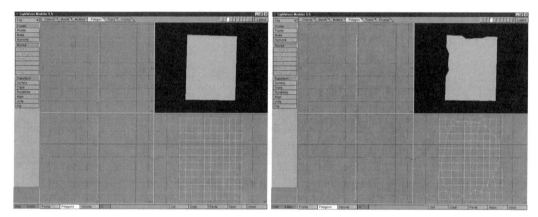

Figure 7.72 Starting the head.

Figure 7.73 Defining the head shape.

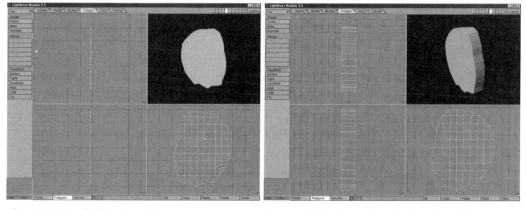

Figure 7.74 The head profile.

Figure 7.75 Extruding the head profile.

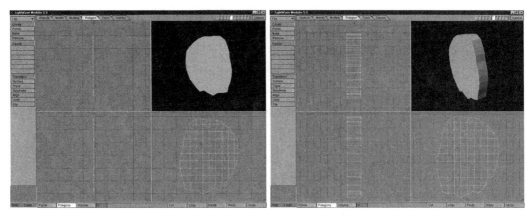

Figure 7.76 Adding depth to the head.   **Figure 7.77** Shaping the head.

The head is starting to look recognizable, and it is ready for the eye. Let's take a stab at modeling the eye.

Creating the Eye

7. The first step in creating the eye is to shape the eye socket, which is accomplished by dragging points and splitting polygons, as you can see in Figure 7.78.

8. This is the general shape of the eye. Now to add the socket, we Smooth Shift the polygons, Scale them, and push them into the head a bit, as seen in Figure 7.79.

9. To add the eye, first Smooth Shift the polygons into the head a bit. Then give them a new surface named "eye." Now Smooth Shift the polygons outward to the point where they are flush with the socket opening. Then Smooth Shift them again, Scaling them down and moving them outward to complete the eye, as shown in Figure 7.80.

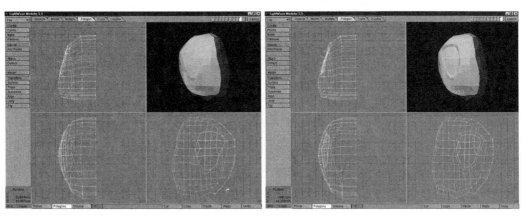

Figure 7.78 Defining the eye socket shape.   **Figure 7.79** Creating the eye socket.

10. Okay, that was easy. Now for some additional armor-plating fun, we'll be adding a heavy plate to the front of the head. First, we select the polygons to be manipulated, as shown in Figure 7.81.

11. These polygons define the plate shape, but we had to split one on the lower end so we could have a nice rounded shape. You'll also notice there is a lone polygon on the lower portion of the selection, which will create a cool tab on the plate. We'll be making this plate like the body armor we did earlier. First, we Smooth Shift the polygons. Then we deselect the upper row of polygons, so we have a smooth blend. Now we Stretch the selected polygons so they extend slightly beyond the parent polygons, as seen in Figure 7.82.

12. Next we add the upper row of polygons to our selection, Smooth Shift them again, deselect the upper row and rotate the selected polygons outward at the base, as shown in Figure 7.83.

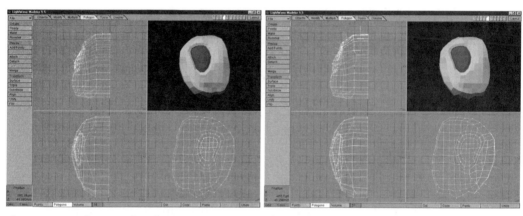

Figure 7.80　The completed eye.

Figure 7.81　The forehead armor plates.

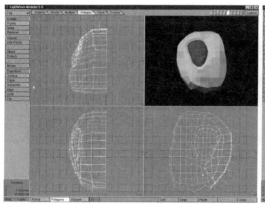
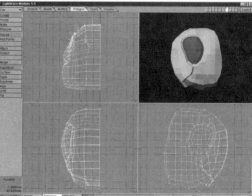

Figure 7.82　Starting the armor.

Figure 7.83　Adding depth to the forehead armor.

13. Great, the forehead armor is now complete. Our next step is to create the mouth plates. There are several of them, but they are all created using the same technique as the forehead armor. We'll walk through the first one, and then you can create the others. First, select the polygons highlighted in Figure 7.84.

14. Be sure to drag them to form the shape seen in Figure 7.84. Then Smooth Shift them and Stretch the new polygons so they are slightly larger than the parent polygons, as seen in Figure 7.85.

15. Now Smooth Shift them again and move them out to be the same distance as the forehead plate, as shown in Figure 7.86.

16. Okay, now complete the other two plates, as shown in Figure 7.87.

17. Next, select the polygons surrounding the mouth plates and create another plate, like the one shown in Figure 7.88.

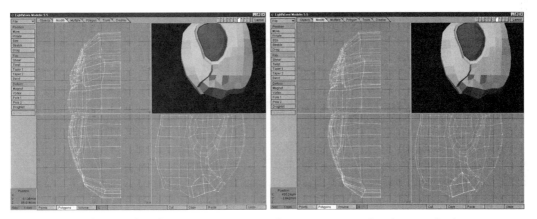

Figure 7.84 The mouth polygons.   **Figure 7.85** Starting the mouth plate.

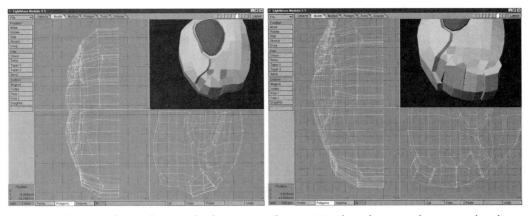

Figure 7.86 Completing the mouth plate.   **Figure 7.87** The other two plates completed.

18. Now select the two polygons on the back of the new plate and Smooth Shift them outward beyond the other plates, as seen in Figure 7.89.

19. Very nice, we now have a rather detailed mouth. It doesn't look like much now, but it will look awesome when we Metaform the model in a few minutes.

20. Okay, let's wrap up the head by adding the small details. First, we'll add a token bump to the front of the head. It never hurts to add the occasional bump detail to an insect model. It makes them more eerie, particularly when they are added to the face.

21. Select a polygon on the lower outside portion of the forehead plate and Smooth Shift to about half the size of the original keeping it parallel, as seen in Figure 7.90.

22. Now Smooth Shift it outward a bit like Figure 7.91.

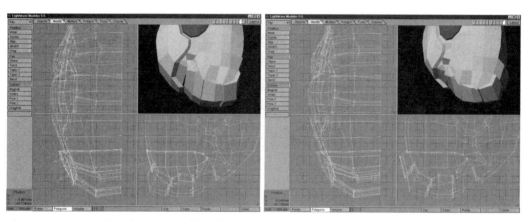

Figure 7.88 Creating the surrounding plate.   **Figure 7.89** Completing the surrounding plate.

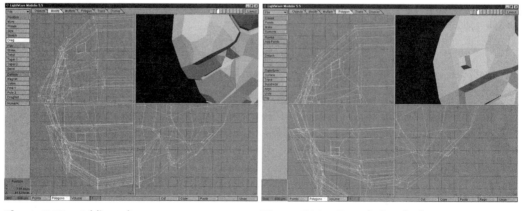

Figure 7.90 Adding a bump.   **Figure 7.91** Completing the bump.

23. Great, now we have a cool bump. The last element we need is a socket for the antenna. First, we define the shape of the protrusion. Select the four polygons in front of the eye and drag the points until they make a circle, as seen in Figure 7.92.

24. Now, using Smooth Shift, create a socket for the antenna base, as shown in Figure 7.93.

25. Now Smooth Shift out the beginning of the antenna base, as shown in Figure 7.94.

26. Then, using the Smooth Shifting techniques we've used throughout the tutorial, complete the antenna base socket shown in Figure 7.95.

27. Excellent, now let's test our head by Metaforming it, as shown in Figure 7.96.

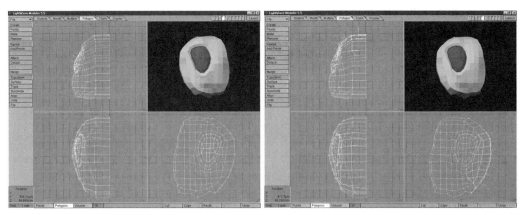

Figure 7.92 Defining the antenna socket shape. **Figure 7.93** Creating the antenna socket.

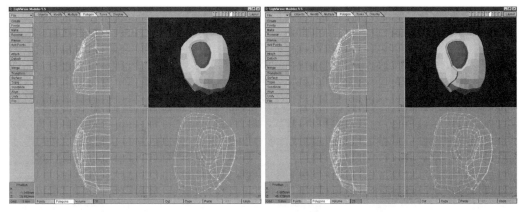

Figure 7.94 Starting the antenna base. **Figure 7.95** The completed antenna base socket.

28. Very nice, it definitely looks like an insect head. In fact, you could even use this head for a grasshopper, since they are nearly identical. Now, Undo the Metaform before we forget, and paste the head on the body layer to complete the body mass shown in Figure 7.97.

Well, that's definitely a very cool insect. Even in the simple model form, without surfacing, it's already incredibly realistic. We've covered a lot of ground, and it's really starting to show. Since we're on a roll, we might as well complete the top layer of armor that protects the torso. Let's get cracking.

Modeling the Body Armor

A Madagascar Hissing roach has many layers of armor, making it one of the toughest insects on the planet. It can take quite a major blow without injury. It's one tough bug. The torso armor is really quite simple, so let's get started.

EXERCISE: MODELING THE BODY ARMOR

1. First, hide the tail on the roach, as seen in Figure 7.98.

2. Now create a plane just above the body with 13 segments, as seen in Figure 7.99.

3. Using your Drag tool, shape the polygons to conform to the body, as shown in Figure 7.100.

4. Be sure to create a dip along the centerline so there will be a crease down the middle of the armor when we Metaform it.

5. Now Extrude the plane with five segments and shape the object using your Magnet tool to resemble Figure 7.101.

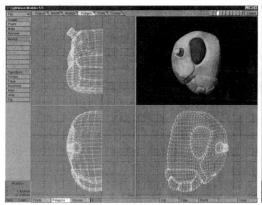

Figure 7.96 The Metaformed head.

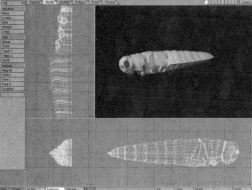

Figure 7.97 The complete body.

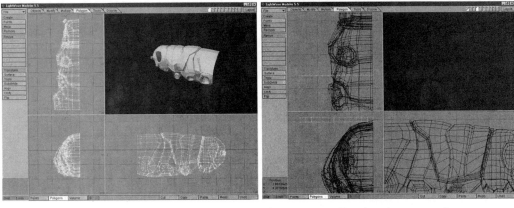

Figure 7.98 Hiding the tail.

Figure 7.99 Creating the armor plane.

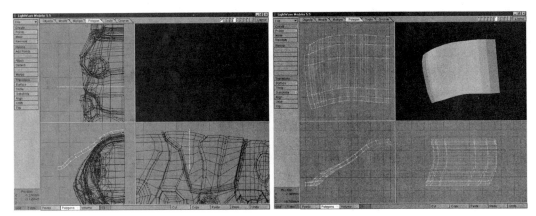

Figure 7.100 Shaping the armor.

Figure 7.101 Shaping the plate.

6. Now select the points on the right end, and move them down so this plate will slide under the next one we create. Then select the last two rows of points on the left side and move them up a bit, as seen in Figure 7.102.

7. Next, copy the plate to a new layer and move it to the position in Figure 7.103.

8. Using your Magnet tool, pull the end of the new plate upward where it overlaps the first plate so they don't penetrate, as seen in Figure 7.104.

Okay, now we move on to the final plate that lies over the head.

Creating the Head Armor

This armor plate is a bit different to the others because it needs to be rounded on the leading edge, and it must have a nice rim around the entire shape. This

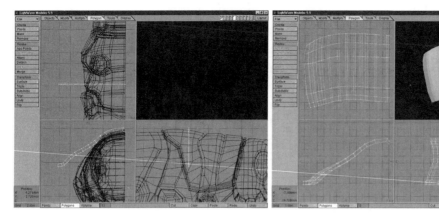

Figure 7.102 Tweaking the ends.   **Figure 7.103** Adding a new plate.

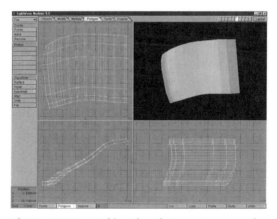

Figure 7.104 Making the plates seam properly.

means we need to model the plate from scratch using the flat modeling technique but with a twist. This time we will manually construct the polygons so we have the perfect shape.

EXERCISE: MODELING THE HEAD ARMOR

1. To begin, we need to be in the Y Axis Viewport, looking down on the head of the roach in the background layer. Then we lay down a series of points with the Point tool to outline the general shape of our armor plate. Use the right mouse key to create the points, and try to make sure the points along the top and bottom align so we can make clean polygons. Once completed, we copy those points and Scale them down to create a dual line of points, as shown in Figure 7.105.

2. Now we make polygons by selecting four points in series and pressing the P key to make the polygons. Complete the entire ring of polygons, as shown in Figure 7.106.

3. Now use the same process to create inner polygons, as shown in Figure 7.107.

4. We need to divide the inner polygons so we can shape the armor later, so select the Knife tool and split the polygons horizontally, as seen in Figure 7.108.

5. Now Extrude the mesh slightly to add depth, as shown in Figure 7.109.

6. Now for the fun part! Grab that Magnet tool and use it to pull the inner portion of the mesh upward to create a rounded shape, and then, using the same tool make sure the portion that overlaps the other armor plates lines overlap properly. You should end up with something similar to Figure 7.110.

7. Great, now select the top polygons around the rim of the shell, as shown in Figure 7.111.

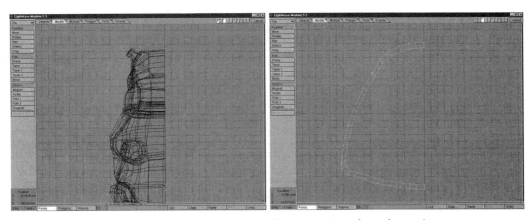

Figure 7.105   Placing the points.

Figure 7.106   The polygon rim.

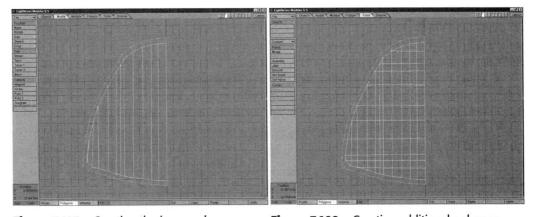

Figure 7.107   Creating the inner polygons.

Figure 7.108   Creating additional polygons.

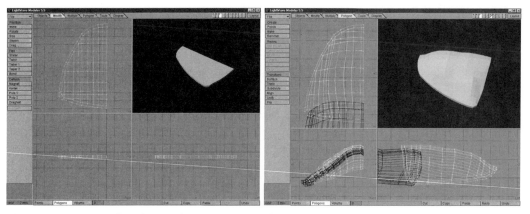

Figure 7.109   Extruding the mesh.   **Figure 7.110**   Shaping the head armor.

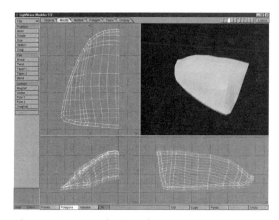

Figure 7.111   Selecting the rim polygons.

8. Now Smooth Shift them upward a bit to create the rim shown in Figure 7.112.

9. Well, we've finished the torso armor, so combine all the armor layers and paste them in the body layer to complete the roach body mass shown in Figure 7.113.

10. Now we're ready to complete the whole roach body. Select all the polygons along the center axis and delete them. Then select the points along the center axis and Set The Value to 0 on the x-axis. Then Mirror the object and merge points. Finally, Metaform the model to create the completed roach body, seen in Figure 7.114.

11. Say, now that's a great looking bug! Check out all that detail. Sure, it was a real pain to create, but the results are more than worth the time invested. All we have left to do now is the legs and feelers. Instead of doing a tutorial on modeling them, I've provided them in the Chapter07 folder on the companion CD-ROM, so you can apply them to your model. They are called

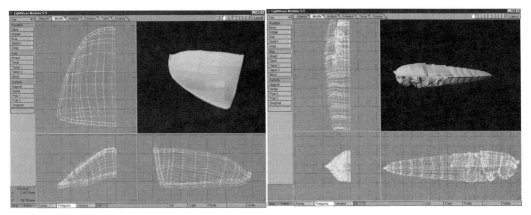

Figure 7.112 The complete rim.   **Figure 7.113** The completed body mass.

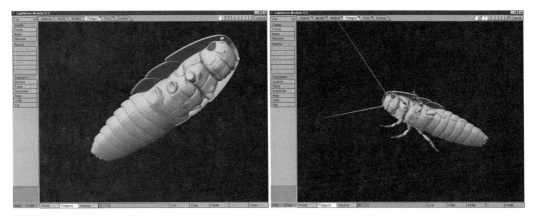

Figure 7.114 The completed roach body.   **Figure 7.115** The completed Madagascar
                                              Hissing roach.

"Legs.lwo" and "Feeler.lwo" We could cover how they were created, but they are truly simple. You can examine the models to see how they were created. It's really a matter of simple shapes, particularly the legs. The feelers were created by making a simple shape, then cloning it several times and tapering the clones.

12. Once you load the legs and feelers, scale them to match your model and you'll have something similar to Figure 7.115.

Well, there you have it. One highly detailed Giant Madagascar Hissing Cockroach. I'll bet you thought this tutorial would never end. It was long, but we covered a lot of ground. Figure 7.116 shows a render of our completed roach model.

The techniques we covered in this tutorial will give you all the tools you need to model any insect you can imagine-or any creature, for that matter. It's really a matter of making liberal use of the Smooth Shift tool, Metaform for smoothing,

Figure 7.116 The rendered roach.

and a whole lot of tweaking. I know this tutorial was long, but it was important to illustrate the amount of work involved when you are creating highly detailed, realistic creatures. It would be great if we could do it in a few clicks of the mouse, but the reality is it takes time and patience. Of course, this isn't all bad since our labor of love is where we get the opportunity to exhibit our skills as a 3D artist. If it was easy, everyone would be doing it, and then we wouldn't be unique.

Wrap Up

Well, that about does it for the modeling part of our exhausting tutorial. As you can see it takes quite a bit of effort and detail to create a realistic insect. It's not difficult work, just extensive and time-consuming. It takes less time with practice, but you will always need a serious commitment of time to create highly detailed creatures, particularly insects. Of course, you can always borrow parts of this critter to aid in the development of other insects since the legs and feelers are quite common, as is the head and even the body. It's always a good idea to borrow parts from existing models to save time. After all, time is money, and we certainly don't want to waste any money.

I hope you enjoyed this tutorial, and I'll see you in the next chapter, where we'll cover detailed surfacing of our Giant Madagascar Hissing Cockroach.

CHAPTER 8

What's Under the Fridge?
Part 2: The Surfacing
(Photoshop and LightWave)

Bill Fleming

COLOR FIGURES ON THE CD-ROM

All the figures from the book are in color on the CD-ROM. This chapter deals heavily with color, so you should refer to the color figures in the Chapter08/Figures folder on the companion CD-ROM before continuing.

Welcome back to fun with roaches. In this, the second part of our "What's Under the Fridge?" tutorial, we'll be surfacing the Giant Madagascar Hissing Cockroach we modeled in the first part. If you haven't already done the modeling tutorial in Chapter 7, "What's Under the Fridge? Part 1," I suggest you do that first, and then proceed with this tutorial.

Insect Surfacing

Insects are some of the easiest creatures to surface since hard surfaces, like exoskeletons, are far easier to mimic in 3D than soft fleshy tissue is. Insects are also less detailed than most soft-tissue creatures. Although they have plenty of chaotic details, the key word is *chaotic*. Organic tissue has more specific details, like wrinkles all over the place, and tissue color changes based on the density of the tissue. Insects have an exoskeleton, so they don't have flesh to be wrinkled or changes in tissue density. Instead, their surfacing is just a matter of chaotic color changes, speckles, and splotches. Of course, we can't simply throw random color changes on the exoskeleton and expect it to look correct. The details do need to be placed properly, according to the physical details of the model, or it just won't look correct. Fortunately, the placement of details is rather simple. Let's take a look at the major surfacing details we can expect to see on an insect, as shown in Figure 8.1.

A. **Body segment coloration.** Probably the most common detail seen on insects is a change in coloration where the segments of the body meet. Quite frequently, this area is much darker than the normal body color, and usually it is an entirely different color. In the case of our Giant Madagascar Hissing Cockroach, this area is black with the occasional beige speck. Most insect surfaces are broken up with speckles and flecks. There is rarely an insect with a solid tone to its body. They are nearly always littered with speckles that break up the color. This is to camouflage the insect in its environment. A solid color never appears in foliage. Plant colors vary widely from both their natural coloration and aging. Therefore, insects need to have similar color changes, so they don't stand out against the environment. Another common segment detail is a ring of color

Figure 8.1 Insect surface details.

around the entire segment, rather than just where segments meet. For example, the shell of a beetle will typically have a dark line running around the entire segment.

B. **Leg coloration.** The legs are generally darker at the ends, and typically, they will have darker areas where the segments meet. The Giant Madagascar Hissing Cockroach has lighter-tone upper legs and completely black lower legs, making them rather simple to surface. One important detail is the irregular line where the light tone meets the dark. A straight line here would be very unnatural. Instead, the line is curved and irregular. There are no clean, straight lines on insects.

C. **Body blotches and speckles.** Most insects have a great deal of speckling on the body, and quite frequently, large blotches of color. This is to camouflage them in their environment. The Giant Madagascar Hissing Cockroach is covered in light speckles set against the darker colors and dark speckles against the lighter tones. It also has a row of large brown splotches running along both sides of the body.

While these three areas don't cover all the surfacing details found on insects, they do encompass most of them. The real key to successful insect surfacing is to include plenty of speckling, darker areas on segment seams, and a well-thought-out pattern of colors. All insects, except those that are completely black, have a rather distinct pattern that identifies them. The patterns are meant to camouflage them in their environment.

When you get down to it, there really is no science to the camouflage-well, to anybody other than someone who studies insects. Normally, the patterns appear somewhat chaotic, but they are actually well-thought-out by Mother Nature. She designs them so the insect will blend into the environment, which means they look rather odd when taken out of their environment. While the patterns don't at first look like they would blend with anything but a tie-dyed shirt, they work amazingly well in their natural environment.

If you are planning to create a fantasy insect, you'll need to seriously consider its environment before you tackle the job of surfacing the critter. If it's a jungle environment, you'll want plenty of bright colors, yes, bright colors. Although we typically think of a jungle as green, there are plenty of flowering plants and fruit-bearing trees where insects love to gather. Therefore we need the insects to blend with these elements. On the other hand, if your insect is a forest dweller, you'll want earth tones because fruit and flowers are scarce in a forest. Typically, the insects reside under ground covers such as dead leaves so they would need to be surfaced with browns and sometimes yellow, since dead leaves yellow.

As you can see, the environment plays a major role in the surfacing of your insects. You'll need to spend a while in your insect's habitat before you tackle the chore of designing the surfacing. Speaking of surfacing, let's get to the task of surfacing our Giant Madagascar Hissing Cockroach.

Defining Surfaces

The first step in surfacing the roach is to define the surfaces for image map application. Fortunately insects surfaces are easy to create because their body parts are segmented, so image map seams are really not a problem. Typically, most insect surfaces can be planar mapped, but you might want to use a cylindrical map if your insect has a round body, like a wasp or bee. In the case of our Giant Madagascar Hissing Cockroach, the body is relatively flat, so a planar map is perfect for all surfaces. Let's define the surfaces for the roach.

EXERCISE: DEFINING THE ROACH SURFACES

1. First, load the roach model into the Modeler. If you haven't already modeled the roach, you can load the "Roach.lwo" object from the Chapter08 folder of the companion CD-ROM.

2. Now select a few polygons on the tail and press the] key, which selects the entire body segment. Next press the W key to bring up the Polygon Statistics window. Select the Eye surface from the drop-down list and then press the - key next to "with Surface" to deselect the eye polygons. Now close the Polygon Statistics window.

3. Next, press the Q key to bring up the Change Surface window and give the selected polygons a surface called "Body." You should now have a unique surface selection for the body. Figure 8.2 shows the portion of the model that should have the Body surface.

4. I have hidden all other surfaces of the model so you can easily see the Body surface. This portion of the model was given a single surface because the details are very redundant. The patterns run down the body along each segment. It would be pointless and require too much effort to create a unique surface for each segment. Let's continue with our surface designation.

5. Hide your Body surface, along with the Eye surface and we'll continue to define surfaces. Next, select the three armor plates over the head, and give them a new surface name of "Armor." Figure 8.3 shows the portion of the model that should have the Armor surface.

6. Now select the leg segments and rename their surface to Legs. Figure 8.4 shows the portion of the model that should have the Legs surface.

7. The legs are a single surface because they are relatively simple and all have similar surfacing. Finally, select the mandibles and feelers, and give them a new surface name called Feelers. Figure 8.5 shows the portion of the model that should have the Feelers surface.

8. The feelers and mandibles are basically pure black, so they can easily be combined into a single surface to make our job easier. The last step is to save the model with a new file name, such as "RoachSurfaced.lwo."

The roach model is now ready to be surfaced. Well, almost ready. Before we continue, we must create painting templates for each surface selection.

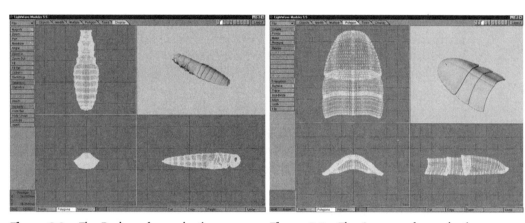

Figure 8.2 The Body surface selection.   **Figure 8.3** The Armor surface selection.

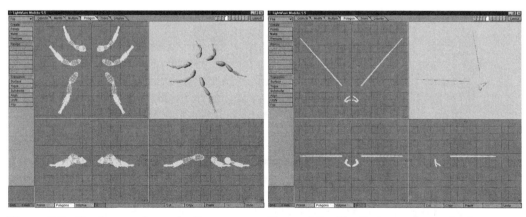

Figure 8.4 The Legs surface selection.   **Figure 8.5** The Feelers surface selection.

Creating Painting Templates

Painting templates is a necessary step in achieving photo-real image map surfacing. Without these rendered templates it is pretty much impossible to get certain details to line up properly. For instance, say you wanted to line up something like the color map for your insect's segments with the actual segments on the 3D model. Guess work isn't going to cut it, so you'll need to have an actual picture of the surface to which you want to apply these details.

Of course, you can't simply load the model and render a template in the hope that it will suffice. When creating renders for use as templates, you never want to use the camera or the perspective view for the actual render because these views will distort your model with perspective. The camera will distort the rendered image based upon the lens zoom factor. To obtain a completely accurate render for a painting template, you'll need to zoom in very tight (at least a setting of 1,000) on your object (as opposed to zooming out) and then pull the camera back until you get a good view of your model. This will flatten out your 3D object, removing the perspective for a perfect painting template.

Why don't we simply grab a screen shot of the wire frame from the naturally Orthographic Modeler viewports? Well, those are fine, but they don't show the depth of the model's surface details, nor are they large enough. We need the painting templates to be large, so we can paint the minute details. You'd have to set your screen resolution to over 2,000 pixels wide to grab a large enough screen grab, and monitors just can't handle that resolution.

Okay, let's create the painting templates for our roach.

EXERCISE: CREATING PAINTING TEMPLATES

1. First, load the "RoachSurfaced.lwo" object from the Chapter08 folder of the companion CD-ROM into Layout. Then rotate the model 90° on the Pitch, so you are looking at the top of the model in the Camera view. Then rotate it 180° on the Heading so you are looking at the belly. We want to render the body template so we see the belly, because that's the view we want to paint. There is no need to render from the top, since the back of the torso will never be seen, but the belly probably will be seen.

2. Now position the camera so the roach fills the screen, as seen in Figure 8.6.

3. Now set the Camera Zoom to 500, then set the Grid Square Size to 50 m. We want to start with a Camera Zoom of 500 so we can control the position of the camera. If we go to 1,000 right off, we'll have a hard time controlling the camera movement. The same applies for the Grid Square size. If we don't enlarge it to 50 m we'll be dragging the mouse forever to move the camera. A larger setting means the camera will move faster.

Figure 8.6 Positioning the camera.

4. The next step is to position the camera so the model can be seen in the viewport. Right now the camera is very close since the zoom is set to 500 m. Before you move the camera disable the x and y movement of the camera. We only want to pull it back.

5. Once you have the roach in view, set the Camera Zoom to 1,000 and the Grid Square Size to 1 m. The smaller Grid Square size will prevent the camera from moving too quickly. Now position the roach so it once again fills the screen.

6. Okay, now we're ready to render some templates. We'll start with the Body template. Of course, we have other surfaces in the way, which we need to remove. To do this we'll simply make them invisible by setting their Transparency to 100%. Of course, we also need to set the Specularity to 0, or we will still see specular highlights. Transparency does not influence specularity. Objects will still be specular even if they are 100% transparent. This was done so we could make glass specular, although it makes it a bit tougher on other surfaces. Start by making the Armor surface invisible, and then render a Sample and copy this surface to all the others except the Body. Then render an image at Print Resolution, with Enhanced Low aliasing and a file name of "BodyTemplate.tga." We use

Figure 8.7 The Body painting template.

the LW_TGA32 file format so we can render an Alpha channel in the final image, giving us an accurate selection of the rendered template. The final render should look something like Figure 8.7.

7. Great, now we have a completed painting template. Next, we'll need to perform the same steps to create the Armor and Legs, but first we need to rotate the model 180° on the Heading, so we shoot the templates from the top, as shown in Figures 8.8 and 8.9.

8. We won't need to create a Feeler painting template since this surface is black and it doesn't need any specific color or bump details.

That's all there is to creating painting templates. Now that we have our painting templates, we are ready to begin painting the image maps, so let's grab our digital brushes and do some painting.

Painting the Image Maps

We'll be painting the "body" surface since it holds the greatest level of detail. All of the other surfaces are rather simple and can be painted using the same

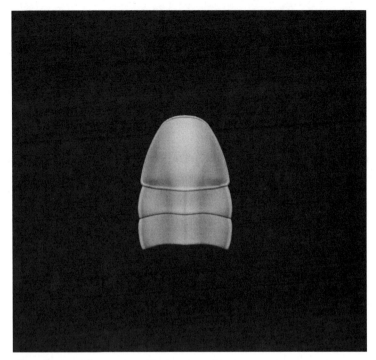

Figure 8.8 The Armor painting template.

Figure 8.9 The Legs painting template.

techniques we are going to use for the body. I'll be covering painting in Photoshop 5 in this tutorial. If you have another paint program or older version of Photoshop, don't worry, the tools are the same in all paint programs, even the low-cost ones like Paintshop Pro.

We'll begin by completing the tail portion of the Body to get a feel for how we add the details, and then we'll finish the torso. Let's begin the exercise.

EXERCISE: PAINTING THE TAIL

1. First, load the "BodyTemplate.tga" image into Photoshop. Then load the Alpha selection, which selects the model. Now cut the model from the image, open a new image, and paste the model into it. This will ensure the template is exactly the same size as our surface.

2. Now create a new Layer named "Base Color," and fill it with RGB, 231, 216, 132, which is the base color of the roach. We will be painting the details on separate layers and combining them with the Base Color layer when we are finished. Deactivate this layer now so it won't block our view of the template beneath it.

3. Now create another layer named "Details." Then select the Airbrush tool with a Brush Size of 27, Pressure of 40% and Color of RGB 0, 0, 0. Then paint a black line along the bottom edge of each segment as shown in Figure 8.10.

4. Next, we continue to add more lines of different colors above the black line. Set the Brush Color to RGB 164, 97, 31 and the Brush Opacity to 20%. Then paint an orange line above the black line, as seen in Figure 8.11.

5. Now set the Brush Color to RGB 208, 165, 110 and paint a faint beige line above the orange line as shown in Figure 8.12.

6. Great, now that concludes the basic colors. Our next step is to create specks, which are quite abundant. To start, set the Brush Color to RGB 101,

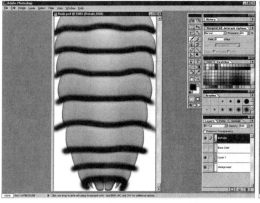 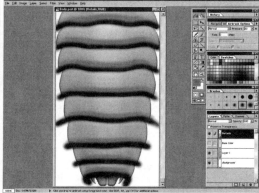

Figure 8.10 Painting the black segment lines.   **Figure 8.11** Creating the orange line.

66, 22 and the Brush Size to 5 pixels, and then paint a grouping of dark brown speckles on either side of the body segments, as seen in Figure 8.13.

7. Now we'll add the horizontal line that divides the tail segments. Set the Brush Size to 5 pixels, the Pressure to 40%, and the color to RGB 163, 106, 45. Then paint a horizontal line down the center of each segment as shown in Figure 8.14.

8. Darken your brush color a bit, and then make another line just beneath the first one with a Brush Size of 3 pixels. This will give the line more character.

9. The next step is to add more color shifting. First activate the Base Color layer so we can see the complete texture. Now set the Brush Size to 27, the Pressure to 15%, and the Color to RGB 213, 169, 97. Then dab the brush along the outside of the segments and then down the middle of the horizontal line, as shown in Figure 8.15.

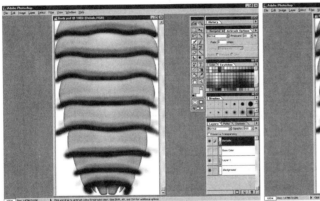

Figure 8.12 Painting the beige line.

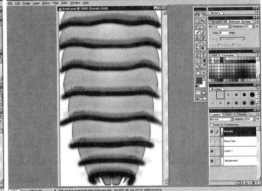

Figure 8.13 Painting the dark speckles.

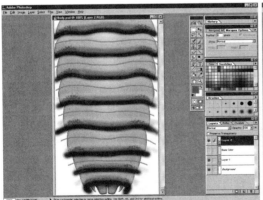
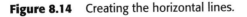

Figure 8.14 Creating the horizontal lines.

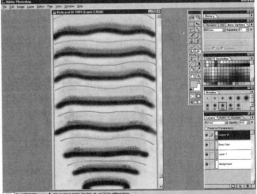

Figure 8.15 Adding color chaos.

10. Now set the Brush Color to RGB 206, 171, 81 and repeat the process of dabbing color. The result should look similar to Figure 8.16.

11. Next we're going to add the row of large splotches down the outside of the segments, which are quite common on insects. First set the Brush Size to 20 pixels, and then set the Color to RGB 144, 88, 28. Now create irregular-shaped splotches on each side of the segments by dabbing the brush several times. Don't use a continuous stroke because it will look unnatural. We want it to be more chaotic. Once you have completed the large splotches, make a tiny one just inside it, as seen in Figure 8.17.

12. Now darken the Brush Color a bit and dab it inside the splotches to darken the center. You never want to use a single shade-ever! Natural creature textures have chaotic color shifting. To create realistic textures we need to add plenty of color shifting. Okay, the next step is very important. We have some rather hard-edged lines on our texture, which just isn't realistic. The black line should have a hard leading edge, but the other lines need to have chaotic edges. You rarely want a hard edge on your creature textures. To fix the problem, set the Brush size to 10 pixels and the Pressure to 15%. Then use the Eyedropper tool to pick the color just above the orange line and then dab the brush along the center of the edge chaotically to rough up the line, as seen in Figure 8.18.

13. As you can see, the lines look a great deal more organic, and therefore more natural. You might also want to repeat the process to rough up the edge of the yellow line just above the orange. Speaking of roughing up the color, let's add more chaos to the lines by creating speckles. Set your Brush size to 5 pixels and the Color to RGB 180, 116, 48. Now drop little flecks of color on the yellowed band just above the orange band, as seen in Figure 8.19.

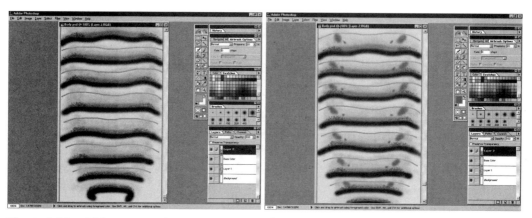

Figure 8.16 Adding more color.   **Figure 8.17** Adding the splotches.

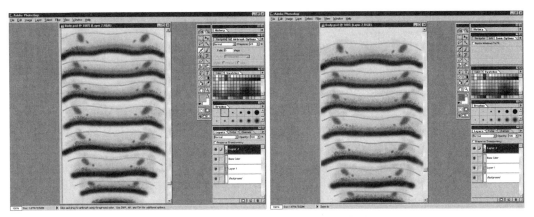

Figure 8.18 Roughing up the lines.   **Figure 8.19** Adding the flecks.

14. Great, now it's time to make the texture appear dirty. Set the Brush size to 61 pixels, the Pressure to 20%, and the Color to RGB 152, 118, 75. Now dab the brush along the outside edge of the segments a bit to darken them. Then cover the light color line of the two lower segments thoroughly and, finally, fill in the area between the spurs at the back with the color, as seen in Figure 8.20.

15. Now that's much better. It's definitely looking dirty. The texture is really taking shape, but I noticed the horizontal lines are too continuous. They need more color chaos. A nice dark line down the center should break it up nicely. Set the Brush Size to 3 pixels, the Pressure to 50%, and the Color to RGB 141, 105, 58. Then draw a line down the center of the horizontal lines, as shown in Figure 8.21.

16. The lines definitely look more natural now. Next we'll finish the tip of the tail by setting the Brush Color to RGB 0, 0, 0 and dabbing the color around

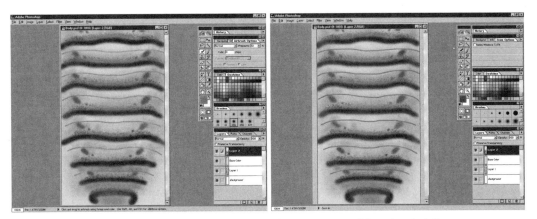

Figure 8.20 Dirtying up the surface.   **Figure 8.21** Adding the dark line.

to darken the segment between the hind spurs and the last segment, as shown in Figure 8.22.

17. Now for the final speckle effect, we'll add some white flecks to the texture along the black and orange lines. Set the Brush Color to RGB 255, 255, 255, the Pressure to 50%, and the Size to 3 pixels. Next, drop little white spots chaotically over the black and orange lines, as seen in Figure 8.23.

18. Very nice, the texture is really taking shape now. We're just about done with the tail. Before we add the last detail, the dark lines around the perimeter of the segments, we'll need to deepen the richness of the texture. It's a little too soft now, which is a common problem with airbrushed textures. The secret is to Burn the texture to deepen the color depth. Select the Burn tool, and set the Brush Size to 50 Pixels and the Pressure to 20%. Then make broad strokes over the darker colors of the texture to make them rich in color, as seen in Figure 8.24.

19. Now we're ready to move on to the last detail, the perimeter lines. We're going to make dark lines around the perimeter of the shell, which is common in most beetles and roaches. First, deselect the Base Color layer. Then select the Airbrush, set the Brush Size to 5, the Pressure to 15%, and the color to RGB 93, 59, 31. Now draw a thin line along the outside edge of the segments, then set the Brush Color to RGB 163, 106, 46 and draw a light line just inside the darker one to add chaos and soften the inside edge. Next select the Burn tool, set the Size to 5 pixels, and darken the very outside edge of the brown line until it's nearly black, as shown in Figure 8.25.

Super, the tail is now complete-well, it's nearly complete, but the last step is to add noise, and we can't do that until the torso is painted. Speaking of the torso, let's take a crack at painting it. It's basically the same techniques we used for the tail, plenty of splotches and speckles to break up the continuous tones.

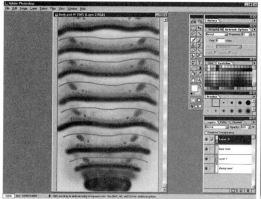
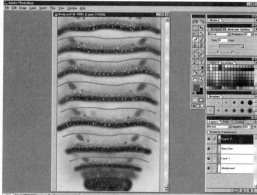

Figure 8.22 Darkening the tip of the tail.   **Figure 8.23** Adding the white flecks.

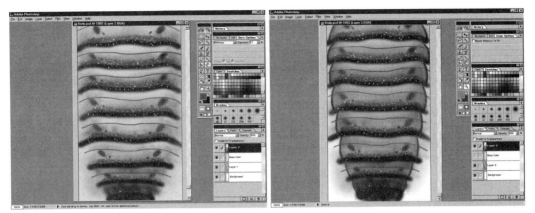

Figure 8.24 Deepening the color depth.   **Figure 8.25** Adding the edge darkness.

EXERCISE: PAINTING THE TORSO

1. We'll begin by adding orange lines along the segment seams. Set the Brush Color to RGB 144, 77, 23, the Pressure to 25%, and the Size to 27 pixels. Now paint strokes along the center of the segment seams, as shown in Figure 8.26.

2. Now we need to add black lines around the major body segments and for most of the head and armor. Set the Brush Color to RGB 0, 0, 0, and paint the black lines seen in Figure 8.27.

3. Now we'll add the light orange lines around the orange and black lines. Set the Brush Color to RGB 196, 147, 78 and paint the lines seen in Figure 8.28.

4. Next we'll add the speckles. Set the Brush Color to RGB 112, 64, 26, the Pressure to 25%, and the Size to 3 pixels. Then paint little speckles around the outside edge of the body segments and around the leg sockets, as seen in Figure 8.29.

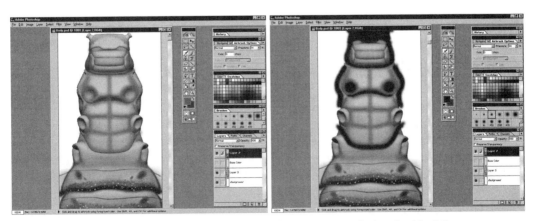

Figure 8.26 Painting the seams.   **Figure 8.27** Painting the black lines.

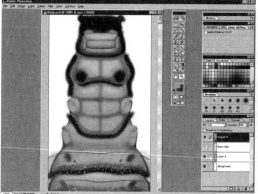

Figure 8.28 Painting the light orange lines.

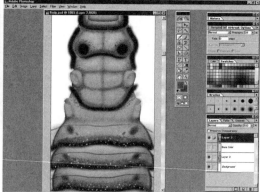

Figure 8.29 Creating the speckles.

5. Now set the Brush Color to RGB 89, 59, 22 and paint more speckles over the ones we just created and then lay down a cluster of dots around the hind leg sockets, as seen in Figure 8.30.

6. That looks good, but we need a greater density in the dark areas around the legs, so set the Brush Size to 15 pixels and drop blotches around the two hind leg sockets, as shown in Figure 8.31.

7. Next, we'll darken the color depth by using the Burn tool. Switch to the Burn tool, and set the Brush Size to 27 and the Pressure to 25%. Now stroke the brush over the darker colors of the torso to deepen the colors, as seen in Figure 8.32.

8. Great, now we're ready for another round of speckles. Set the Brush Color to white and the Size to 3 pixels. Then drop down some speckles over the black lines on the torso. Now set the Brush Color to RGB 216, 175, 112 and

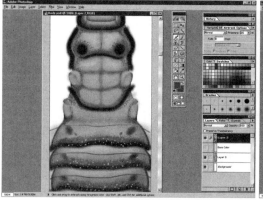

Figure 8.30 More speckles.

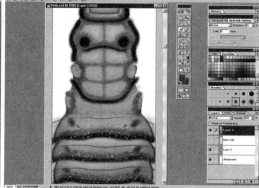

Figure 8.31 Darkening the leg socket speckles.

drop speckles in the center of the body segments to add the color chaos seen in Figure 8.33.

9. Now it's time for a little dirt. Set the Brush Color to RGB 151, 122, 89, and the Size to 64. Now dab the color over the torso body segments as seen in Figure 8.34.

10. That pretty much does it for the torso, well, except for a few details. Before we look at the crowning elements of the torso, let's complete the face of our roach. I won't bother doing a step-by-step of this process since it's rather redundant. Basically, you want to darken the seams, place speckles around the perimeter of the segments, and add speckles in the center to break up the continuous tones. You should have something similar to Figure 8.35 when completed.

11. Okay, now for the crowning elements. Although the texture is looking awesome, we need to break up the lighter lines so they don't appear con-

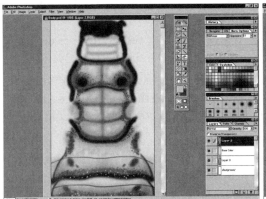

Figure 8.32   Deepening the colors.

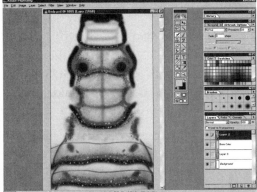

Figure 8.33   Adding more speckles.

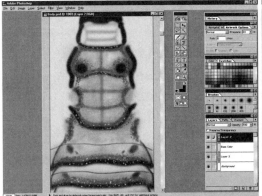

Figure 8.34   Adding the dirt.

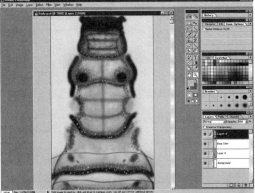

Figure 8.35   The completed face.

tinuous. To do so we'll create many small dots using two colors, RGB 236, 212, 165 and RGB 206, 186, 126. When you have filled the light areas with these speckles, set your Brush Color to 163, 103, 157 and the Brush Size to 15 pixels. Then create several chaotic splotches along the lower segment of the torso, as shown in Figure 8.36.

12. This is a nice detail that helps to break up the lighter tone. Well, that nearly does it for our body texture map. The only thing left to do is break up the softness of the colors. The problem with airbrushed image maps is the soft look of the airbrush. Very few creatures in reality have such "soft" colors. Therefore we need to harden our colors to make them realistic. Fortunately, this is very simply done by adding noise. Select Noise from the Filters menu, and select Monochromatic and Gaussian in the pop-up window. Then set the Amount to 10, as shown in Figure 8.37.

13. As you can see the texture is much harder and more chaotic, which is far more realistic. Of course, we're a bit too grainy, so we need to blend the noise by using a Blur. Select Gaussian Blur from the Filter menu and set the Radius to .4 pixels, as shown in Figure 8.38.

14. Now that's much better and more realistic. Well, it would appear we are done with our body image map, which can be seen in Figure 8.39.

15. It looks great doesn't it? It will look even better once we have it mapped to our model. Now would be an excellent time to save the image file as "Roach-Body.psd." Then create the image map by saving a copy as "BodyColor.iff."

As you can see, creating insect image maps requires a great deal of painting since we need to speckle nearly every pixel of the texture. It's a lot of work, but the payoff is worth it. Speaking of payoff, we should test our image map to see how well it works, but first we'll need to create the bump map so we get the full photorealism effect. Fortunately, this is very simple. We merely need to

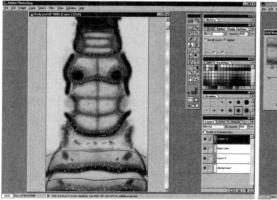

Figure 8.36 Adding more chaos.

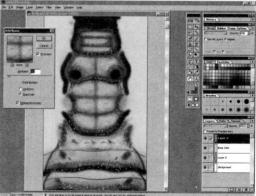

Figure 8.37 Adding noise.

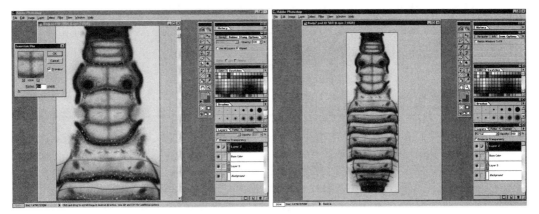

Figure 8.38 Softening the noise.   **Figure 8.39** The completed body image map.

create a bump map that adds little bumps on the surface of the exoskeleton. Let's create the bump map now.

EXERCISE: CREATING THE BUMP MAP

1. Create a new file in PhotoShop that's 300 _ 300 pixels. Then fill it with black. Now set the Brush Color to White, the Brush size to 5 pixels, and the Pressure to 100%. Now scatter white dots and streaks over the image, as shown in Figure 8.40.

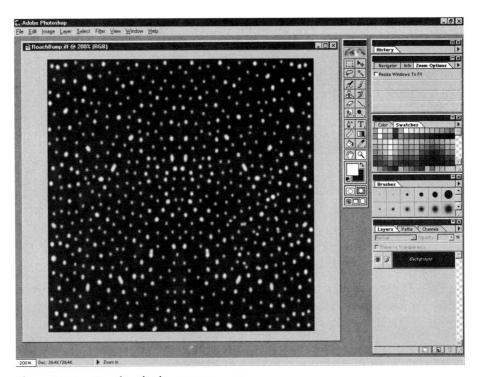

Figure 8.40 Creating the bump map.

2. That's all there is to it. Now save the file as "RoachBump.iff."

Okay, now that we have our color map and bump map, we can get down to the process of surfacing this critter.

Surfacing the Roach

Surfacing the roach is rather simple. We merely have to apply a few image maps, and we're done. If it were an organic, soft-tissue creature, we would have much more work to do, but fortunately insects are rather simple when it comes to applying image maps. Typically, we don't need the extras, such as multiple bump map layers or even a unique Diffusion map. Typically, we can use the color map for the diffusion, since we're making a rather hard and somewhat glossy surface.

Let's surface the body of our roach.

EXERCISE: SURFACING THE BODY

1. First, load the "RoachSurfaced.lwo" model into Layout. Then load your "BodyColor.iff" and "RoachBump.iff" image maps.

2. Now select the Body surface and apply the "BodyColor.iff" image as a planar image map on the y-axis of your Color channel. Be sure to set Automatic Size for the image map.

3. Next, apply the "BodyColor.iff" image as a planar image map on the y-axis for the Diffusion channel. Then set the Opacity to 80%. Since the colors are rather dark, we don't want to use 100% of the image map color for the diffusion or our roach will be very dark.

4. Now set the Specularity to 65%, the Glossiness to 64, and the Reflectivity to 7%. Set the Reflection Options to "Ray Tracing + Spherical Map," and use your favorite reflection map as the image.

5. Next, apply the "RoachBump.iff" image as a Cubic Image Map for the Bump channel and set the size so it spans the width of the roach body. Then make the x, y, and z size the same. Mine is 2 cm, 2 cm, 2 cm.

6. Now add another Bump layer and set it to Fractal Noise with a size of 100 μm, 100 μm, 100 μm. Then set the Amplitude to 25.0 % and the Frequencies to 3.

7. The surfacing of the body is now complete. The last step is to save the model, and then perform a test render. Your model should now look something like Figure 8.41.

Now that's a realistic surface. Notice how the tiny details of the image map really help to make the object realistic. When creating photorealism, it's the

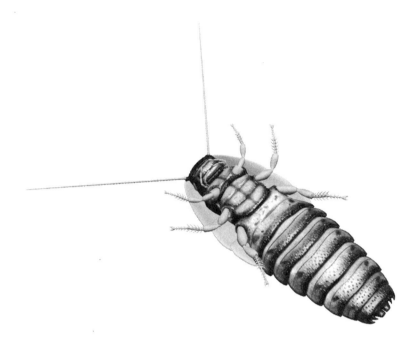

Figure 8.41 The surfaced body.

small details that count most. The roach is well on its way to becoming photo-realistic. All that remains is to surface the legs, armor, eyes, and feelers. We could create the image maps for all these elements, but it would be quite redundant since it's the same technique we used to create the body. Instead, I've provided the image maps in the support file on the companion CD-ROM. They are called "Armor.iff" and "Legs.iff."

If you wish to create these image maps, you can use the ones I provided as a template for the colors and placement of details. The application of the surfacing is identical to the body. The only difference is that there are no image maps for the eyes and feelers. They have all the other surface attributes of the body, but the Color is a simple Black and the Diffusion has no image map but instead is set to 80%.

Once you have completed your image maps and applied them, you should have a completed Giant Madagascar Hissing roach, like the one seen in Figures 8.42 and 8.43.

Not bad! It definitely looks realistic doesn't it? It's amazing what can be accomplished with a bunch of speckles and lines. The real key to creating photorealistic insect image maps is to add a plethora of chaos and fine detail.

Figure 8.42   The top of the roach.

Figure 8.43   The belly of the roach.

Nothing is more unrealistic than a continuous tone. All colors on an insect must be broken up with small details or speckles if they are to appear realistic.

Wrap Up

Well, that does it for our "What's Under the Fridge?" tutorial. As you can see, it can be quite a bit of work to model and surface a realistic insect, but once you are finished you'll have a very cool critter to inhabit your 3D images. Now all you need to do is create a really disgusting kitchen or bathroom scene for your roach, and you're done. Well, this species of insect is more likely to be found in the forest, but they sure do look creepy on linoleum or tile floors. In fact, you can make them even creepier by fitting them with cool accessories, such as a saddle and rider or maybe some military hardware. Once you have a photorealistic insect, you can really mess with your viewer's mind by doing strange things with them.

When Dragons Ruled the Skies (3D Studio Max)

Jerry Potts

For hundreds of millions of years giant winged dragons ruled the skies. Vicious and efficient four-winged hunters who could change direction instantly or could hover in place at will, they saw the coming of the dinosaurs and could have easily avoided the snapping jaws of an annoyed T-rex. How many millions of creatures fled in panic as the shadow of a 24-inch wingspan darkened the skies overhead? Often, it was the last thing these unfortunate creatures would ever see.

These dragons still live, and although they are not as large as their ancestors, they are every bit as capable in the air. Great hunters of the air that have been clocked at over 30 miles per hour—without them, we would be consumed by hoards of mosquitoes, the dragonfly's favorite food.

The Setup

The first thing I do before I start any picture is perhaps the hardest, that is, research. Before you can make anything, you must know that thing inside and out. If you can draw, do so. Drawing forces you to study an object. If not, find pictures of the object or go out into the field and take pictures. While making your scene keep the drawings or pictures in view so you can constantly refer to them. For the dragonfly, I took my sketchpad to the local pond and went home with drawings and a little more respect for this little bug.

I found some great pictures on the Internet, and the local library is also a great resource. Don't skip this part of any project, it may be the most important. If you do not have plenty of reference material at hand while creating your model or while making maps, you will unconsciously generalize or simplify, and the finished product will suffer. I have taken pictures of subjects in the field and I have also made sketches, but it is always the sketches that I turn to first for reference material. I think it may be because a photograph is easy to make and is over in a second, but a sketch forces me to look at each detail of an object. I have to think of the object as a collection of different shapes and how these shapes are connected.

When I looked at the dragonfly, I saw a head, for instance, that was made up of many details. However, when the time came to put it on paper, I was forced to distill the head down to three main shapes or parts to which I could add detail later. This is the same process one uses in any 3D modeling software. Also, the surface of the large eyes of the dragonfly had a great amount of depth, something I did not see in any of the dozens of photos in books or on the net.

I took my completed sketch and scanned it into my computer. If you don't have a scanner, I would highly recommend you get one-not only can you scan sketches and any photo or texture from books, but you can put nearly anything on a flatbed scanner; the prices have come way down, anyway.

Once the image was scanned, I separated it into individual top, side, and leg template images. Then I saved them as JPG images, which you can find in the Chapter09 folder of the companion CD-ROM. They are called "TopTemplate.jpg," "SideTemplate.jpg," and "LegTemplate.jpg"

Now we're ready to load the template images into the backgrounds of our viewports, so we can model the dragonfly proportionally. In Left view port load the "SideTemplate.jpg" image, shown in Figure 9.1, and in Top view load the "TopTemplate.jpg" image seen in Figure 9.2.

Now turn on Aspect Ratio and Match to lock the map to the models when you move and zoom in the viewport. Now is a good time to save the file. I got into the habit of saving often by learning the hard way, after losing hours of work to a lot of computer crashes. Our templates are now loaded and ready to be used. Figure 9.3 shows how your screen should appear with both template images loaded.

We'll be using the leg template later on in the chapter. For now, we only need the top and side templates because we're going to be modeling the body first, and we don't need the distraction of the leg template. Speaking of modeling the body, let's get started.

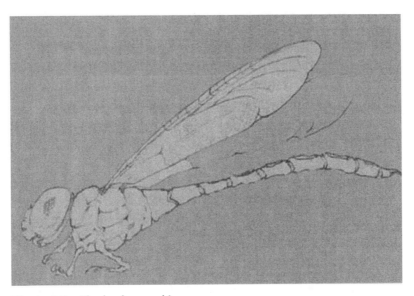

Figure 9.1   The background image.

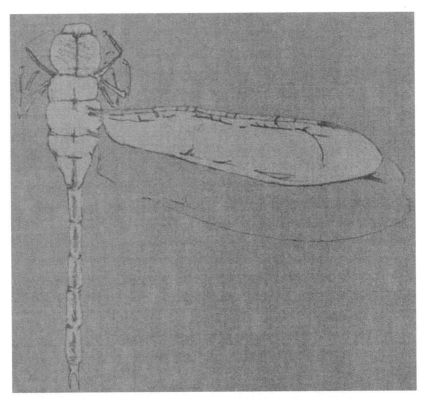

Figure 9.2   The top view image.

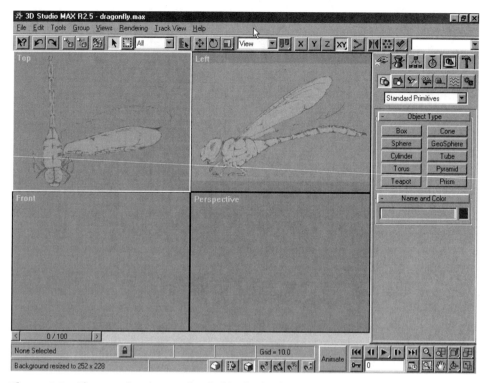

Figure 9.3   The template images loaded in the background.

Modeling the Dragonfly

We'll start the model with the body since it's the center around which all the other objects are applied.

EXERCISE: MODELING THE BODY

1. First, create a box with three width segments roughly the size of the drawing of the main body. Then rename the box and convert it to an Editable Mesh. Renaming objects is a good habit to get into. It may seem like an extra step, but having everything in a scene called Box or Line can be very confusing.

2. With the box collapsed, you can now move the vertices so that they line up with the outline of the main body, as seen in Figure 9.4.

3. Now Mesh Smooth with one iteration, which will give us more vertices to move, and then collapse it to an Editable Mesh. Next, in Sub-Object vertex mode, align the vertices to the template of the insect's body. Take special care to align the third and fifth vertical rows of vertices in both the top and left views with the vertical segments of the body's drawing, as seen in Figure 9.5.

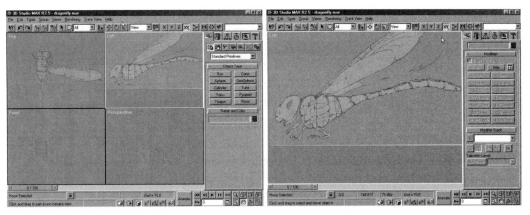

Figure 9.4 Shaping the body.   **Figure 9.5** Aligning the body vertices.

4. Now we will Mesh Smooth our body a third at a time to give it a more segmented look. First, in Sub-Object face mode, select the first third of the body using the third row of vertices as the dividing line and apply Mesh Smooth. Then collapse and repeat the process with the middle and last third of the body. Mesh Smooth the entire body and smooth the result, apply planar UVW mapping coordinates, and collapse it so you have a body like the one in Figure 9.6.

5. Now we're ready to tackle the tail. First, create another box as long and narrow as the drawing of the tail with nine segments running the length of the tail and rename it. Then collapse and move the vertices to align with the outline of the tail. A quick and easy way of doing this is to select an entire vertical row of vertices and scale them larger or smaller as required. Your tail should now look like the one in Figure 9.7.

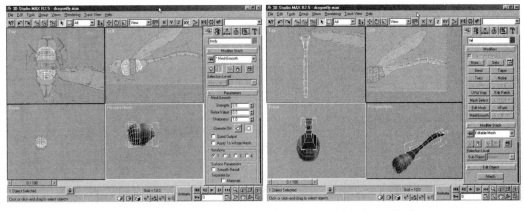

Figure 9.6 The completed body .   **Figure 9.7** The shaped tail.

6. Now it's time to add a little more detail to the tip of the tail. A dragonfly has little spikes at the tip of the tail, which are relatively simple to add using a Mesh Smooth modifier. Select the faces in the first segment of the tail immediately behind the body and apply a Mesh Smooth modifier, Strength 0.3 and Smooth Result with 2 iterations. Next, collapse, then select the remaining faces of the tail and Mesh Smooth them. The tail still looked a little rough for close ups, so add a Mesh Smooth modifier to the entire tail.

7. To make the spikes at the end of the tail, create a cone in the front view with a radius 1 of 3 units, radius 2 of 1 unit, and height of 28 units with 5 height segments and 8 sides. Then apply a Bend modifier with an angle of 25 in the z-axis. Now collapse to an Editable mesh and Mirror in the x-axis with Copy on. Move the cones to the end of the tail and scale to fit. Finally, attach to the tail and apply a planar UVW mapping coordinates then collapse for the completed tail seen in Figure 9.8.

Great, the body of our dragonfly is now complete. The next part we're going to model is the head, which is nothing more than a collection of simple parts as you will soon see. Let's get cracking on the head.

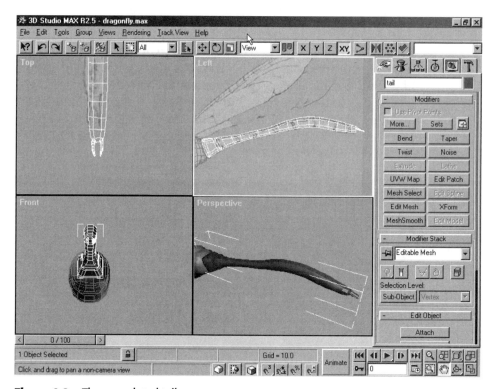

Figure 9.8 The completed tail.

Modeling the Head

The head is a little more complicated than the body and tail. It is made up of three main parts, the base, the eyes, and the mouth. Let's make the base of the head first.

EXERCISE: MODELING THE HEAD

1. Again, start with a box primitive with two width segments and rename it. Collapse it, and in Sub-Object vertex mode move the vertices to align with the head structure, ignoring the shape of the eyes, as seen in Figure 9.9.

2. Now apply a Mesh Smooth modifier with 1 Iteration, collapse it, and again in Sub-Object vertex mode adjust the vertices to fit the head drawing. You'll find we only needed to adjust the vertices on the backside of the head by moving them outward in the top view port. Now apply Mesh Smooth again, give it spherical UVW mapping coordinates, and collapse it. Now let's move on to the eyes.

3. For the eyes, create an Icosa geosphere with the radius of 28 units, 8 segments and rename it "outereye." Then apply a FFD 4 _ 4 _ 4 Box modifier in the top view.

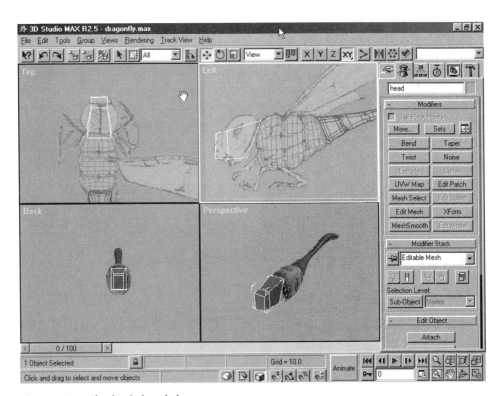

Figure 9.9 The basic head shape.

4. Now select all the control points of the FFD box except for the outside (or left) row, and move them left or toward the outside to narrow the eye slightly. Then in Left View choose the bottom corner row of control points and pull them up toward the center of the eye until it fits the shape of the eye in the z-axis. To give the eye a lot of depth, we will need to create an inner eye with a coloration map applied and an outer transparent layer. We will cover how to map it later in the chapter.

5. While holding down the Shift key, scale down the eye; this will clone a smaller copy of the eye. Scale the clone copy of the eye just a little smaller than the original-you may need to left-click the Scale button to access the scaling unit measurements. Scale the clone at 98% for all three axes or about 2% overall, and then rename it "innereye." Now select both inner and outer eyes and mirror in the z-axis with copy on, to create a duplicate set of eyes seen in Figure 9.10.

6. Next we'll tackle the jaw. The jaw is made up of two claw-like shapes. To make the first create a line outlining the general shape and rename it "jaw," as shown in Figure 9.11.

7. Now extrude the shape 5 units, apply a Mesh Smooth modifier with 1 Iteration, and apply planar UVW mapping coordinates. Then Mirror copy on the x-axis and move the new jaw to align it with the original. Finally, rotate and place it in position as seen in Figure 9.12.

8. Before we move on, we need to create a little detail for the head; namely some antennae. Although dragonflies have very small antennae (if any), it just doesn't seem right to make a bug without antennae. The antennae can be made by creating a three-sided cone, 1 _ 1 _ 20 with 5 height segments so it can bend a little. Now Shift-copy it and move them both to the point where the two eyes meet at the top of the nose.

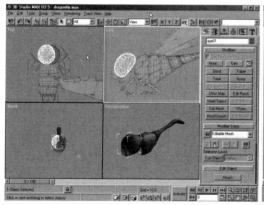 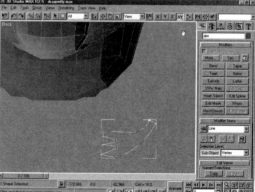

Figure 9.10   The completed eyes.   **Figure 9.11**   The initial jaw line.

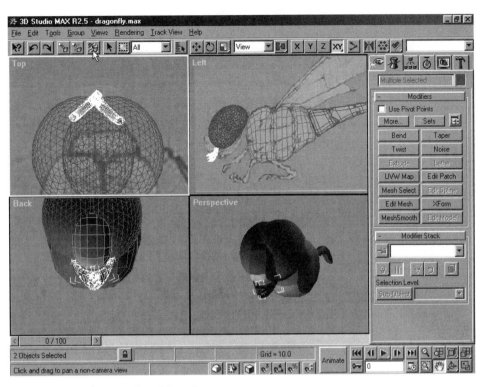

Figure 9.12 The completed jaw shape.

Okay, the head is now complete. The next step is to give this little dragon some legs to stand upon.

Creating the Legs

A dragonfly has six legs, and each one is made up of four segments. The first two legs can be used for catching and grasping its prey during flight. Fortunately, we need to make only one leg. The others can be modified copies of the first. Let's make the legs.

EXERCISE: CREATING THE LEGS

1. For a guide, load the "LegTemplate.jpg," shown in Figure 9.13, into the background of the Left Viewport.

2. Not shown in the drawing is the small section of the leg that joins the leg to the body. This can be made easily with a box twice as high as it is long and wide, with a taper modifier applied to the bottom. Apply a box UVW mapping coordinates and a Mesh Smooth modifier. For the lower sections create a long narrow box with four segments. Then collapse it and align

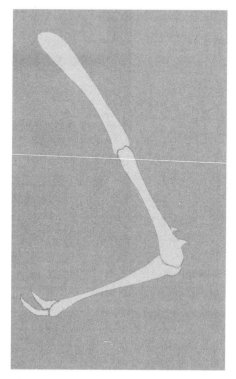

Figure 9.13 The leg template.

the vertices to match the drawing of the upper leg. While holding down the Shift key, select the leg and drag down to create a copy. Repeat these steps until you have three leg segments. Then adjust the vertices to match the drawing as you did with the first segment. Your leg should now look like those in Figure 9.14.

3. To make the spikes on the middle and end sections, select the face that the spikes are to extend from and divide it into two faces by cutting horizontally from the center of each vertical edge of the face. Then in Face Mode, extrude each face three times, uniformly scaling them each time to produce a pair of curved cones like those seen in Figure 9.15.

4. Now rename each segment "upper," "middle," and "lower" leg, respectively. Then Shift-copy move the four shapes twice until you have three copies of the leg. Then apply both a Mesh Smooth and cylindrical UVW mapping coordinates to each segment.

5. Now collapse each segment in the first leg and mirror copy in the x-axis to create the legs on the opposite side. Then adjust the second leg primitive by elongating one or more segments before applying the mesh smooth modifier.

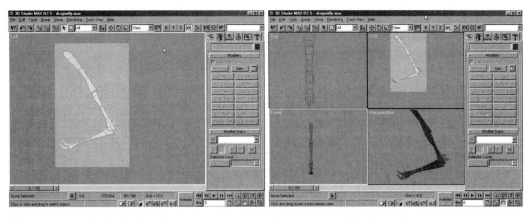

Figure 9.14   The basic leg shape.   **Figure 9.15**   The leg spikes.

6. Now mirror copy as you did for the first leg. Finally, repeat the process for the last leg and adjust all the legs to align with the body, as seen in Figure 9.16.

Now we're really making some progress. The dragonfly has definitely started to take shape. If you plan to animate the dragonfly, you may want to move the

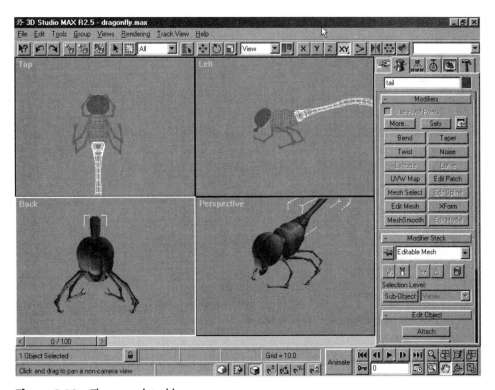

Figure 9.16   The completed legs.

pivot points to the joints of all the leg segments. Now we have one last body part to model, the wings. Let's create them now.

Modeling the Wings

The wing is made in the same way as the jaw, by outlining the shape of the wing, this time using the drawing as a guide then extruding the shape to give it dimension. All four of the wings are not the same The back wings are slightly wider than the front. They also have an intricate web lattice support structure. This will be one case where the texture map is made before the model. Fortunately, I was able to find a photo of both wings, which I used as the basis of all maps.

EXERCISE: MODELING THE WINGS

1. Load the "WingTemplate.jpg" image seen in Figure 9.17, found in the Chapter09 folder on the companion CD-ROM, into the background of the Top Viewport.

2. Then create a line outlining the picture. Now extrude the shape to give it a third dimension, and apply a Mesh smooth modifier. Finally, rename it to "backwing" and collapse it.

3. Now load the "Wing2Template.jpg" image (seen in Figure 9.18) from the Chapter09 folder on the CD-ROM as a background in the top view and repeat the process, this time renaming it to "forewing."

4. Next, move the pivot to the base of each wing to make movement of the wings more natural.

Okay, the wings are now completed and so is our dragonfly model. Of course, before we position the wings, we'll need to apply the mapping, otherwise it won't align properly because the wings will be at an angle, so let's move on to the surfacing portion of this chapter.

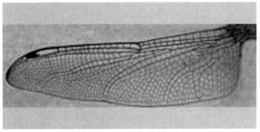

Figure 9.17   The wing template.

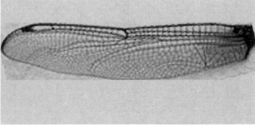

Figure 9.18   The second wing template.

Surfacing the Dragonfly

Mapping is very important, maybe more so than modeling. I know you've probably heard this many times before, especially if you were like me when I first started working in 3D. I was just proud of myself for being capable of producing a 3D model. I wanted to get it out as soon as possible to show people. So, I would slap some basic map or material on it and out it went. Months later, after I had improved my renders, I would look back on these old endeavors, and they always lacked a good set of maps, which made them look rather lame. Now that I'm months older and infinitely wiser, I'll pass this on: Always take the time to create detailed maps; it will be worth the investment when people see your images.

Let's get started surfacing our little dragon. We'll begin with the wings.

Mapping the Wings

The wings have a web-like structure of struts with hundreds of small round and square segments between them. We could have taken the time to draw each one, but we already have a nice set of photos, so why not use them.

EXERCISE: MAPPING THE WINGS

1. We can use our template images for the Diffuse layer of our mapping but we'll need a few more image maps to complete the mapping, such as an Opacity map. We need an opacity map since the areas between the black lines are transparent. To create the Opacity maps, load the template images into your painting program and convert them to grayscale. Then set the Brightness to –14 and the Contrast to +43. This will sharpen the dark lines and darken the areas between a bit so the wing isn't completely transparent, as seen in Figures 9.19 and 9.20.

2. Of course, this isn't the finished Opacity map because the color black represents 90% transparency. If we used these images, we'd have wings with no support structure. But they do make the perfect bump maps, so save the images as "BottomWingBump" and "TopWingBump."

3. To make these images into Opacity maps, we'll need to invert them. Now save the images as "BottomWingOpacity" and "TopWingOpacity." Your completed image maps should look like those seen in Figures 9.21 and 9.22.

4. Now we have our complete set of maps. The next step is to create two materials that are identical, one named "forewing" and the other named

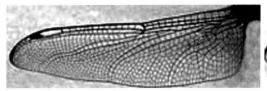

Figure 9.19 The edited bottom wing Opacity map.

Figure 9.20 The edited top wing Opacity map.

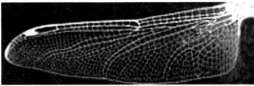

Figure 9.21 The completed bottom wing Opacity map.

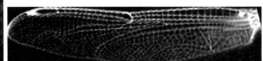

Figure 9.22 The completed top wing Opacity map.

"backwing." To surface the "backwing" material load the "WingTemplate.jpg" image as the Diffuse map, "BottomWingBump" in the Bump channel at 96%, and "BottomWingOpacity" in the Opacity channel at 90%. Now set the Shininess to 22 and Shin strength set to 57.

5. The forewing: material should have "Wing2Template.jpg" in the Diffuse channel, "TopWingBump" in the Bump channel at 96%, and "TopWingOpacity" in Opacity channel at 90%. Now set the Shininess to 22 and Shin strength set to 57.

6. Apply planar mapping coordinates to both wings. You may need to adjust the mapping gizmo a bit to align the Diffuse map.

7. Once both wings look right, you can rotate them into position, with the top wing rotated upward slightly as seen in Figure 9.23.

8. Now mirror-copy the wings to the other side of the body to complete the dragonfly model.

Now we're ready to move on with our surfacing, we'll do the eyes next.

Mapping The Eyes

The eye of a dragonfly has a lot of depth. Layering several maps is a good way of giving a model an appearance of depth, however, for the amount of depth we need here we'll need an inner opaque eye and an outer transparent eye.

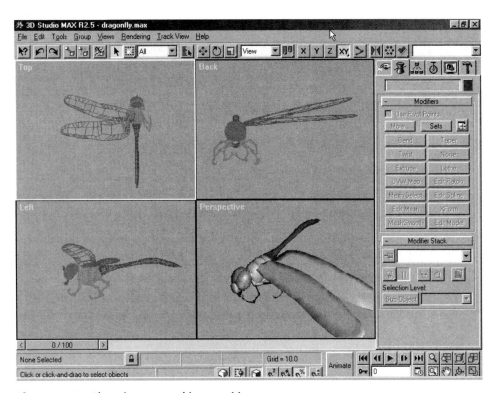

Figure 9.23 The wings rotated into position.

The basic color of the eye is a light green on top, a dark green on bottom with a spotty mixture of the two in the center. In my paint program, I created a layer of light green on top of a layer of dark green and, using the Eraser tool, removed the light green at the bottom to produce the basic pattern. I then used a variety of filters such as one that would rough up the border between the two colors (splatter) and added a little noise and blur to further blend the two together. Finally, I added a little tan and dark brown to offset the colors. The completed image map is shown in Figure 9.24.

Let's begin mapping the eyes.

EXERCISE: MAPPING THE EYES

1. The eye needs a metallic appearance, so change the material to a Metal shading type. Then, in the Diffuse channel, load our map "figure20.tif" and turn both the Shininess and the Shin Strength to 64. Now rename the material "innereye" and apply the same material to both of the inner eyes with a Spherical UVW mapping coordinate.

Figure 9.24 The eye image map.

2. You may need to turn on Show Map in the viewport for the map and adjust the Mapping Gizmo to get the light part of the map to the top of the eye. You can see the inner eyes better by hiding the outer eye in the display floater.

3. The outer eyes must be transparent and shiny, so create a new material called "outereye" and set the Opacity to a value of 30. Then set the Shininess to 49 and Shin Strength of 81. Although not much color will show, some will, so we want to give this material a bit of color. Set the Diffuse color to a gray-blue RGB 63, 96, 120 (HSV 138, 121, 120).

4. The outer eye must also have the multifaceted look of an insect's eye. To get this, we'll need to apply a bump map. Figure 9.25 shows the bump map I created for the eye.

5. This map is easily made by drawing equally spaced diagonal lines onto a transparent layer in your paint program. Then copy this layer on top of the original and rotate it 90°.

6. Load the "EyeBump.jpg" image from the Chapter09 folder on the CD-ROM. Then apply it to the Bump channel of the "outereye" material, and set the value to 90. Then apply this material to each outer eye with a spherical UVW coordinate and rotated the gizmo to align the bump map.

We are now finished with the eyes. Our next task is to surface the body.

Figure 9.25 The outer eye bump map.

Mapping the Body

The body has a more complicated map applied to it. Dark brown lines over a light green background must line up with the valleys of the segments that we carefully modeled. There are many plug-ins that will allow you to paint directly on the model, and they work very well from what I understand. However, this model is relatively simple, so I didn't need to use any fancy plug-ins. I just created a painting template, and used Photoshop to create the image map.

One of the simplest ways to create a painting template is to zoom in on the side of the body in the Left or Right viewports and render it. Then load the rendered image into a paint program and paint directly over it. Figure 9.26 shows the body image map I created.

I painted the body map in much the same way as I did for the eye map using several layers and filters. Let's use this image map to surface the body.

EXERCISE: MAPPING THE BODY

1. To surface the body, create a new material called "body." Then load the "BodyColor.jpg" file from the Chapter09 folder on the CD-ROM and apply it with planar-mapping coordinates to the Diffuse channel.

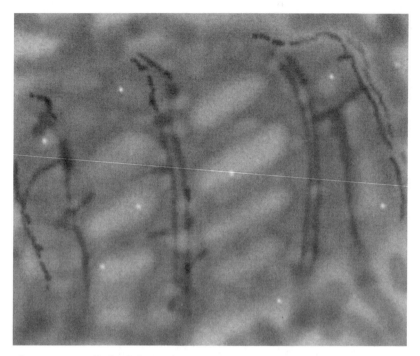

Figure 9.26   The body image map.

2. Now load the "BodyBump.jpg" image from the Chapter09 folder on the CD-ROM and apply it to the Bump channel with a value of 120.

3. The body should be shiny and a little transparent in certain areas, so turn on Shininess and set it to 58, with a Shin Strength of 71.

4. Now load the "BodyBump.jpg" image into the Opacity channels, and set the value to 8%. This will make the body very slightly transparent.

5. Now apply this material to the base of the head and the pair of jaws. You will need to make a few adjustments to their Mapping Gizmos, particularly the nose portion of the head. You want the mapping to tile until the segment line runs horizontally across the nose. You have plenty of freedom with these parts of the dragonfly since they don't have any specific physical details. You basically just want a little chaotic color.

Great, we're almost done surfacing the dragonfly. Let's move on to the tail portion.

Mapping the Tail

The tail was done the same way as the body, by rendering the side viewport and painting a map. The map I created was painted in much the same way as the body by starting with a blue base color. I then added a gradient layer of green on the right side, and then I painted lines on yet another layer for the tail segments. Each layer can then be lightened or made semitransparent to blend with the layers beneath. I added a noise filter to all but the layer with the dark line segments. Figure 9.27 shows the completed tail map.

Let's apply this image map to our tail.

EXERCISE: MAPPING THE TAIL

1. Create a new material named "tail,"and then load the "TailColor.jpg" image from the CD-ROM and apply it to the Diffuse channel as a planar map.

2. Tails of dragonflies often have a metallic sheen, so use a Metal shader here, too, with Shininess at 74 and Shin Strength at 49.

3. Now load the "TailBump.jpg" image from the Chapter 09 folder on the CD-ROM into the Bump channel and set the value to 90%. When making the bump map, I again converted the diffuse map to grayscale, but I didn't want the black spots on top of the tail to be dents, so I removed them from the bump map.

That does it for the tail. The final segment of the dragonfly we need to surface is the legs. Let's get to it.

Mapping the Legs

For the legs, I painted a map that was basically dark brown on each side and light tan in the center, as seen in Figure 9.28.

This was easily done using a light tan for a base and a dark brown gradient layer on top using gradient from the sides to the center, fading to transparency. I flattened the image and then adjusted or replaced some of the color by first selecting a band of color on each side then changing its hue, satura-

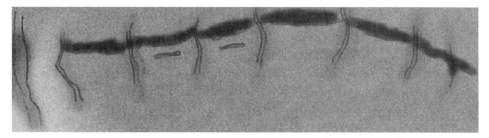

Figure 9.27 The tail map.

Figure 9.28 The leg color map.

tion, and brightness. I then added a new layer and painted some light areas to break it up. I gave this layer an embossed effect, which made the light areas look like bumps.

Let's map the legs now.

EXERCISE: MAPPING THE LEGS

1. First, create a material called "legs." Then load the "LegColor.jpg" file from the Chapter09 folder on the CD-ROM and apply it with planar-mapping coordinates to the Diffuse channel.

2. Now load the "LegBump.jpg" image from the Chapter09 folder on the CD-ROM and apply it to the Bump channel with a value of 120.

3. The legs should be shiny and a little transparent in certain areas so turn on Shininess and set it to 58, with a Shin Strength of 71.

Figure 9.29 The surfaced dragonfly.

4. Now load the "LegBump.jpg" image into the Opacity channels and set the value to 8%. This will make the body very slightly transparent.

5. Next, apply this material to each of the legs, making sure to mirror the mapping coordinates of the images for the legs on the opposite side of the body.

Okay, the legs are now complete, and so is our dragonfly. Figure 9.29 shows a view of the completely surfaced dragonfly in action.

For this final render, I took a stock landscape photo and applied a diagonal motion blur filter to it and used it as the backdrop. I then added a bright light, pale yellow in color to simulate the sun, and two pale gray-blue lights to the side and below for ambient lighting. Be sure to turn on cast-shadows for all lights.

Wrap Up

So now we have a finished dragonfly all set for merging into a detailed pond scene or a scene showing this voracious hunter catching bugs while in flight. I hope you have enjoyed making the dragonfly as much as I did. Of course, the techniques we covered in this tutorial apply to more than just dragonflies. The process of modifying simple boxes and using Mesh Smooth for organic shaping is the foundation for creating nearly every creature or insect you can imagine. You should take some time to experiment with these tools and techniques. You'll be amazed at what you can do with a little creativity.

CHAPTER 10

Stag Party (trueSpace)

Darris Dobbs

I had a hard time settling on exactly which insect I was going to create for this tutorial. I love all of those creepy-crawly critters, and there are so many to choose from. At last, though, I turned to one of my favorites, the Stag Beetle. The beetles are the largest group of insects in the world, with more than 100,000 different types. There are also many kinds of Stag Beetles, and they are distributed all over the world. Figure 10.1 shows the Stag Beetle we'll be creating.

The Stag Beetle gets its name from the long jaws, or pincers of the male, which resemble the antlers of a stag. Stag Beetles are the professional wrestlers of the insect world. They use their formidable pincers to fight other stag beetles over food and the mating rights to lady stag beetles, as well as to defend themselves from predators. In Japan, they are very popular as pets and are sold in nearly every pet store. Even here in the United States, stag beetle collectors and breeders are a fanatical lot, obsessed with these fascinating creatures.

The Stag Beetle really is a remarkable creature. Belonging to the same family as the common June Bug, the lowly Dung Beetle, and the Scarab Beetles (which were worshiped by the ancient Egyptians), they are the heavy armor of the insect world. Think of them as tiny Sherman Tanks. Incredibly strong, they are capable of lifting many hundred times their own weight, and those jaws can give you a pinch that will make you forget your worst St. Patrick's Day experience. The female uses her smaller jaws to bore holes in rotting trees where she deposits her eggs. Relatively long-lived insects, Stag Beetles can live up to five years. Well, that's enough with the Wild Kingdom chit-chat.

Let's get down to our real purpose for being here, which is to build a cool Stag Beetle.

Modeling the Head

The first part of the Stag Beetle, which we will model, is also the most interesting. Stag Beetles have really cool heads. In addition to the massive antler-like jaws, the head has the flowing lines of a '57 Chevy. Let's begin.

EXERCISE: MODELING THE HEAD

1. Our first step is to right-click on the Create Sphere Primitive icon. In the Sphere properties box, enter 16 for latitude and 30 for longitude. Now left-click on the icon to create a sphere. Switch to Top View and rotate the sphere 90° so that the z-axis is now parallel to the ground plane, as seen in Figure 10.2.

Figure 10.1   Two male Stag Beetles face off for combat.

2. Now left-click to open the Deform Object tool, and divide the sphere into six sections along the z-axis. Pull the first section toward the center of the object slightly to create a concavity on that end of the sphere. Then continue deforming the object along the z-axis, as shown in Figure 10.3.

3. Now we need to continue using Deform Object. This time, we will deform along the x-axis, as shown in Figure 10.4. Our objective here is to create a concave surface at the front of the head.

4. Now switch to Left View, delete the current deformation lattice, and create a new one. This time, we will divide the object into nine sections along the z-axis. Deform the head along the z-axis, as illustrated in Figure 10.5.

5. Still in Left View, switch to deforming the object along the y-axis. The head of the Stag Beetle has unusual and very organic lines. It takes quite a

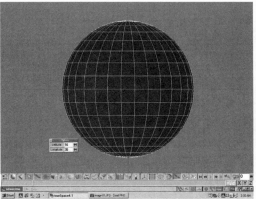

Figure 10.2 Begin by creating a Sphere Primitive.

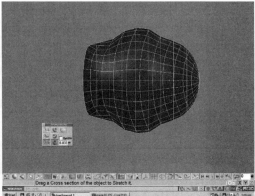

Figure 10.3 Begin deforming the selected Sphere.

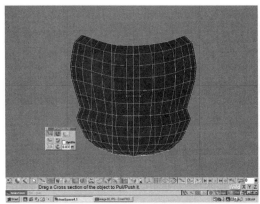

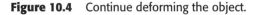

Figure 10.4 Continue deforming the object.

Figure 10.5 Continue to deform the object in the Side View.

bit of tweaking to get the shape right, but you should end up with something similar to Figure 10.6.

6. Now we need to switch to the Front View and deform along the x-axis. Create a new deformation lattice, and deform the object along the x-axis to match the shape shown in Figure 10.7. As you will notice, there is a prominent central ridge along the top of our beetle's head.

7. We now need to do some fine-tuning. Return to Top View and in the Deformation Navigation panel, then select Local Deformation and create a lattice like the one shown in Figure 10.8.

8. In order, select the second, third, and fourth intersections from the top along the center of the object and pull them slightly toward the bottom of the screen, as shown in Figure 10.8. We are creating a sort of dished-in area in the top of the head.

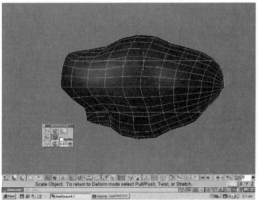 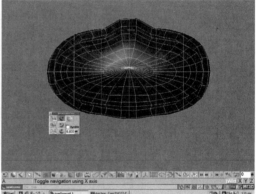

Figure 10.6 Deform the object along the y-axis. **Figure 10.7** Deform along the x-axis.

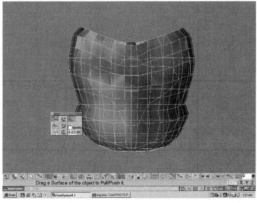 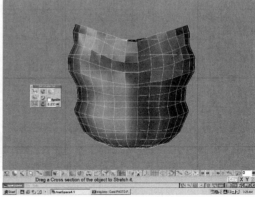

Figure 10.8 Use Local Deformation to fine tune. **Figure 10.9** Deform along the z-axis again.

9. Still in Top View, select Deform Along Z Axis in the Deformation Navigation panel and continue to shape the head, as shown in Figure 10.9. You should see a ridge running along the center of the head and a second bowed ridge perpendicular to it running from side to side.

10. Finally, still in Top View, scale the entire head shorter as shown in Figure 10.10. Also, make the final deformation along the x-axis by squeezing the centerline, bringing the center toward the middle on both ends, as seen in Figure 10.10.

11. Create a new Sphere Primitive with the same properties as the first. Scale it as shown and position it in front of our head object in the Left View, as shown in Figure 10.10. Rotate it 90° so that the z-axis is parallel to the ground. Select Deform Object and begin deforming it along the z-axis, as illustrated in Figure 10.11.

12. Now return to Top View. Use Deform Object to shape the new sphere along the x-axis as illustrated. Position the new sphere so that it is overlapping the head object, as shown in Figure 10.12.

13. Use Boolean Union to join the new object to our head object. This is the front of the beetle's head, which contains its mouth and from which the massive jaws protrude, as seen in Figure 10.13.

14. Now we're finally getting to the fun part. The next step is to create those massive modified jaws. To begin, we will draw a cross section of these pincers using the Polygon tool, as illustrated in Figure 10.14.

15. Once you have drawn the cross section, use the Sweep tool to extrude it once and then position it as shown in Figure 10.15.

16. Open a second window in the Left View. Now use the Sweep tool to continue extruding the polygon into the massive jaw. The final cross section

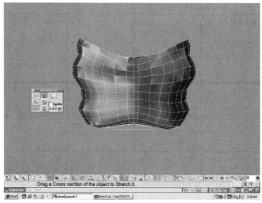

Figure 10.10 A final deformation along the x-axis.

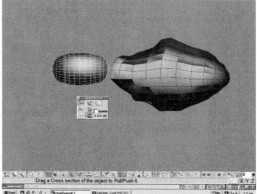

Figure 10.11 Create a second Sphere Primitive.

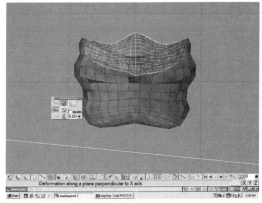

Figure 10.12 Continue deforming along the x-axis.

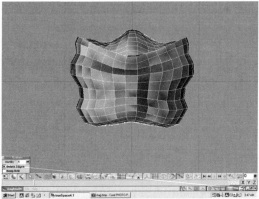

Figure 10.13 Boolean Union the two objects.

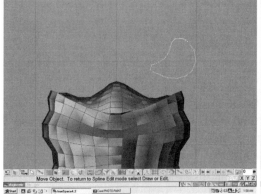

Figure 10.14 Draw the pincer cross section with the Polygon tool.

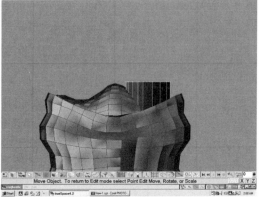

Figure 10.15 Sweep the polygon once and position it.

should be three times as long as it is wide. It is from this face that we will extrude the sharp barbs at the end of the pincers. Figure 10.16 shows the completed jaw.

17. In the Left View, zoom in on the pincer. The first of the sharp, wicked barbs is located just after the first curve. At that point on the left side of the pincer use the Draw Polygon tool to create a roughly round cross-section. Then use the Point Edit:Faces tool while holding down the Control key to select all of the faces inside this round cross section, as shown in Figure 10.17.

18. Return to Top View and sweep the selected faces outward and slightly backward, narrowing each step to create the sharp, inward-hooking barbs. Refer to the illustration in Figure 10.18.

19. Return to Left View and zoom in on the cross section at the end of the pincer. It should be facing you directly. Use the Draw Polygon tool to create a

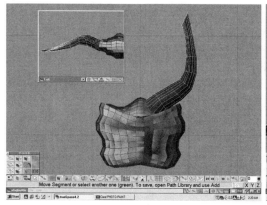
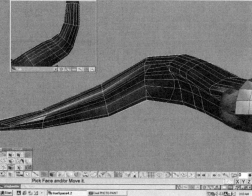

Figure 10.16 Use the Sweep tool to create the jaw.

Figure 10.17 Use Draw Polygon to create a cross section.

vaguely round face at either end of this polygon with two smaller round faces between them as illustrated in Figure 10.19.

20. One at a time, select each of the four faces we have just created and extrude it into a sharp barb, using the Sweep tool. You should now have two large barbs with two smaller barbs between them. Refer to Figure 10.20. Create a copy of the finished jaw. Mirror the copy and position it on the left side of the head.

21. In Left View, select the Sculpt tool and click to position it at the widest point of the head, as shown in Figure 10.20. Switch to Top View and pull the Sculpt tool in toward the center of the head to create a socket for the beetle's eye (see Figure 10.21). Repeat on the opposite side of the head.

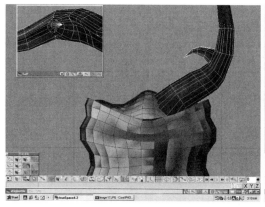
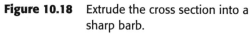
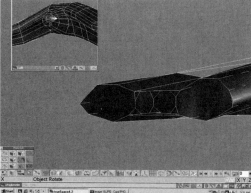

Figure 10.18 Extrude the cross section into a sharp barb.

Figure 10.19 Zoom in on the end cross section.

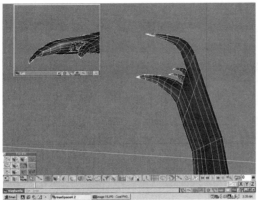 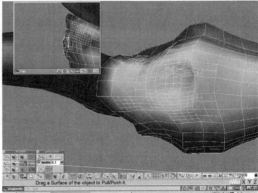

Figure 10.20 Extruding the new faces into barbs.

Figure 10.21 Use the Sculpt tool to create an eye socket.

22. Create a new Sphere Primitive and scale it so that it fits into the socket we just created. Rotate it 90° along the y-axis so that the top of the sphere is now pointing straight out to the side. Finally, position the sphere in the eye socket and repeat on the opposite side (see Figure 10.22).

23. Our next step will be to make our beetle stick his tongue out, but don't be offended-it is like that all the time. Although it is not technically a tongue, we will use another Sphere Primitive to create the visible portion of the mouth. Create a Sphere Primitive, and scale and position it as shown in Figure 10.23.

24. There are two sets of feelers on the Stag Beetle. The first set is located on either side of the mouth. We will build this first. Start with a Sphere Primitive. Deform it along the z-axis as illustrated in Figure 10.24 using Deform Object.

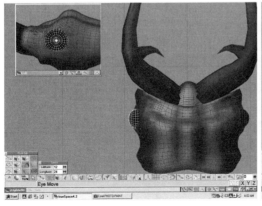 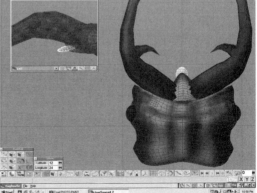

Figure 10.22 Creating new spheres for the eyes.

Figure 10.23 Creating another new sphere for the mouth.

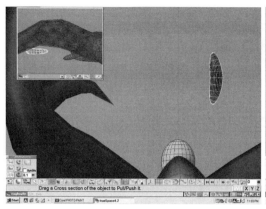 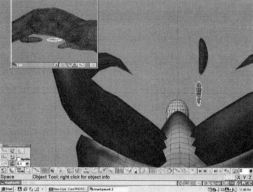

Figure 10.24 Begin building the feelers.

Figure 10.25 Adding a second deformed sphere.

25. Add a second sphere and deform it along the y-axis as well using Deform Object (see Figure 10.25).

26. Create a copy of the currently selected object and move it backwards. Now position and combine the three small, deformed spheres to create a feeler using Boolean Union. Then create a copy of this feeler, mirror the copy, and place it on the other side of the mouth as seen in Figure 10.26. Our Stag Beetle will use these feelers both to sense food and to help move it into the mouth.

27. The second set of feelers is located just in front of and below the eyes. To begin constructing them, select the Regular Polygon tool. Set the number of sides to 6. Create a polygon in Top View. Next, switch to Front View and use Sweep to begin extruding the polygon into the shape shown in Figure 10.27.

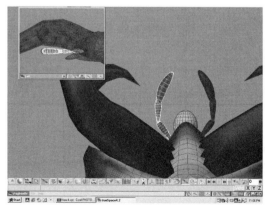 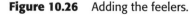 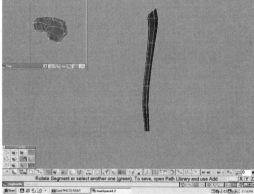

Figure 10.26 Adding the feelers.

Figure 10.27 Use Sweep to begin making the second set of feelers.

28. Rotate the top face counterclockwise approximately 45° and continue sweeping at a right angle, as shown in Figure 10.28. Continue to sweep, scaling and positioning each extrusion to create the segmented portion of the feeler.

29. Beginning at the third segment from the end, select the two faces at the back of the feeler and use Sweep to extrude them back into a lobe shape. These lobes are like sensors at the end of the feeler (see Figure 10.29).

30. We will repeat this process on the remaining two end segments. As you will observe in Figure 10.30, each of the lobes is a slightly different shape. This will complete the feeler.

31. Position the feeler you just created in front of and just below the eye of the beetle. Copy this feeler, mirror the copy, and position it on the opposite side of the head, refer to Figure 10.31.

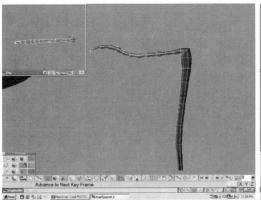

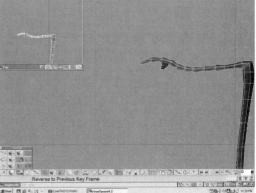

Figure 10.28   Rotate the top face and continue sweeping.

Figure 10.29   Use Sweep to add lobes to the feeler.

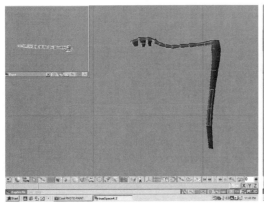

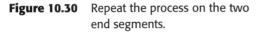

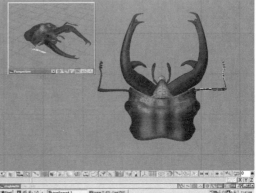

Figure 10.30   Repeat the process on the two end segments.

Figure 10.31   Position the second set of feelers.

Congratulations, you have just finished modeling the head of a Stag Beetle. I think it is appropriate at this time to give our beetle a name. Since he is my beetle, I get to pick the name, and I want to call him Bailey. That's right, he is the beetle Bailey.

Now we're going to tackle the thorax.

Creating the Thorax

Like all insects, beetle bodies are divided into three segments, the head, thorax, and abdomen. Our next objective is to create the thorax. This segment contains the first pair of legs and acts somewhat like a neck connecting the large abdomen and the smaller head. It also houses the respiratory and circulatory organs of the insect. Let's tackle the thorax.

EXERCISE: MODELING THE THORAX

1. Once again, we will begin by creating a Sphere Primitive. And once more, we will rotate the sphere so that the z-axis is parallel to the ground as seen in Figure 10.32.

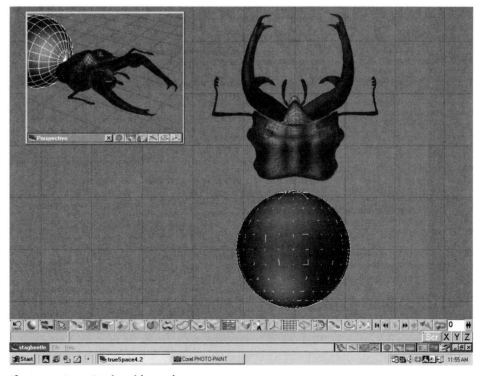

Figure 10.32   Begin with a sphere.

Those of you who have read my tutorials before know that I often begin with a Sphere Primitive whenever I'm going to create an organic object because most organic objects can be created by shaping a simple sphere. Even more useful is a rounded cube, but the only way to create a true rounded cube is by using a third-party plug-in such as the excellent ThermoClay2, which I consider to be an essential tool. I try, however, to avoid using plug-ins in tutorials since not everyone will have access to them.

2. Select Deform Object and click the icon to deform along the z-axis. Create a deformation lattice that divides the sphere into twelve segments and begin deforming the sphere as shown in Figure 10.33. Start by pulling the top and bottom segments inward to flatten the ends of the sphere.

3. Switch to Front View and deform along the x-axis. The outside edges should be scaled down as shown in Figure 10.34.

4. Switch to Top View, create a new deformation lattice like the one shown in Figure 10.35, and continue to deform along the x-axis. Notice the graceful bow developing at the front of the object where the thorax meets the head.

5. Switch to Left View and create another new deformation lattice that divides the thorax into twelve sections along the z-axis. Continue shaping the thorax as shown in Figure 10.36.

6. Switch to Front View and continue deforming, this time along the x-axis as seen in Figure 10.37. I know it seems that we are spending an awful lot of time repeatedly deforming these objects, but that is the secret to creating organic shapes.

7. Now delete the current deformation lattice and create a new one that divides the object into 13 segments along the x-axis. Continue to deform the object along the x-axis as illustrated in Figure 10.38.

8. Then switch to Left View and finish shaping the thorax by using Deform Object along the z-axis. Make certain that the front of the thorax meets neatly with the back of the head (see Figure 10.39).

That's all we are going to do with the thorax at this point. Although the first set of legs attaches at the thorax, we are going to model the legs in a later section.

Now we are going to turn our attention to the abdomen.

Making the Abdomen

The abdomen is the largest part of most insects. It houses the remaining two pairs of legs, as well as the wings. Because we will not be animating this beetle, we are not going to model the actual wings-which are hidden beneath armored wing covers-since they would not be visible anyway.

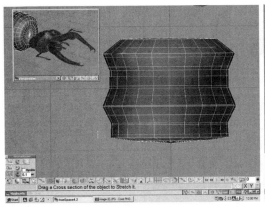

Figure 10.33 Deform the sphere along the z-axis.

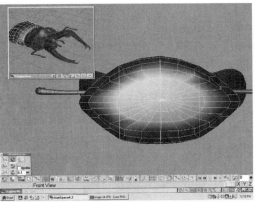

Figure 10.34 Deform along the x-axis.

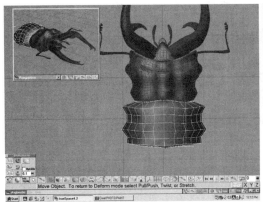

Figure 10.35 Continue deforming along the x-axis.

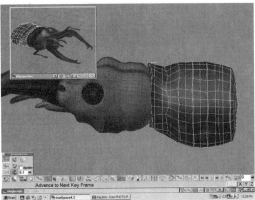

Figure 10.36 Deform along the z-axis.

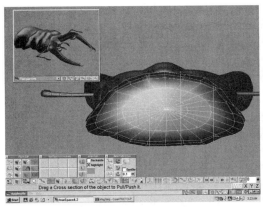

Figure 10.37 Deform along the x-axis in the Front View.

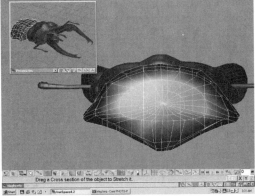

Figure 10.38 Create a new deformation lattice.

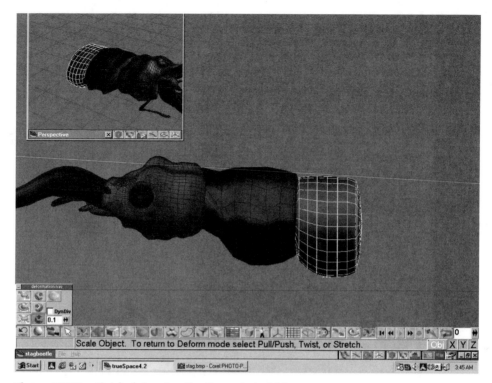

Figure 10.39 Finish deforming the thorax in Left View.

Let's get started on the body.

EXERCISE: MODELING THE BODY

1. Surprise, surprise, we are going to begin building the abdomen by creating a Sphere Primitive, rotating it 90° so that the z-axis is parallel to the ground and deforming it along the z-axis. Are you beginning to see a pattern developing? Refer to Figure 10.40.

2. Once the sphere is properly shaped, we can construct the remainder of the abdomen by making copies of the sphere that are progressively smaller and shaping them as we proceed toward the rear using Deform Object. You will find this is easiest if you open a second window in Left View. Look at Figure 10.41.

3. The next step is to create the wing covers. These are like shutters, or shields, that cover the delicate wings and protect them when the beetle is not in flight. The material that these wing covers and, in fact, the entire exoskeleton of the beetle is constructed of is called "chitin" (pronounced kie-tin). This chitinous exoskeleton is like armor that protects the beetle. It is also what produces the crunchy sound when you step on one.

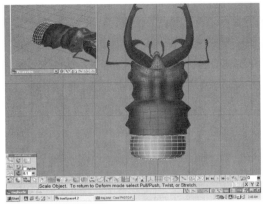 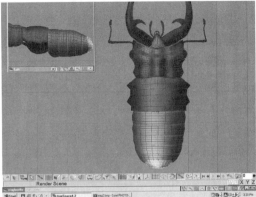

Figure 10.40 Begin by deforming a Sphere Primitive.

Figure 10.41 Build the abdomen with copies of the first sphere.

4. Once again, we begin by creating a Sphere Primitive and rotating it 90° so that the z-axis is parallel to the ground. Scale it to match the illustration in Figure 10.42.

5. Create a copy of the sphere. Scale the copy slightly smaller than the original along all axes as shown in Figure 10.43.

6. Boolean Subtract the smaller sphere from the original sphere. Now, Boolean Subtract a cube from the front of the sphere to leave a hemisphere and then Boolean subtract a second cube (as shown in Figure 10.44) to remove the bottom half of the sphere.

7. Switch to Front View and begin deforming the current object as shown in Figure 10.45. You will see that the object flares out at the bottom. On the beetle this is a sort of narrow skirt or ridge around the edge of the wing covers (see Figure 10.45).

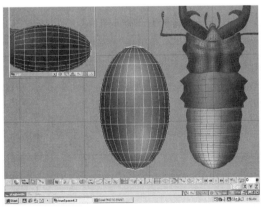  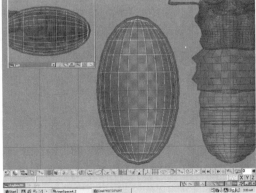

Figure 10.42 Create yet another Sphere Primitive.

Figure 10.43 Create a copy of the sphere and scale it smaller.

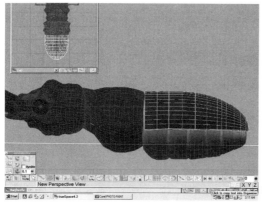

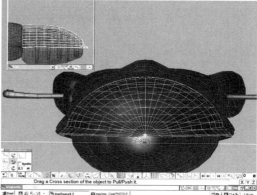

Figure 10.44 Use Boolean Subtraction to cre- **Figure 10.45** Deform along the y-axis in Front
ate the wing cover. View.

8. Use the Polygon tool to draw a shield-shaped polygon in Top View. Then sweep the polygon once and position it as shown with the wide part of the shield where the wing cover object meets the thorax (see Figure 10.46).

9. Next, create a copy of the wing cover object. Right-click on any of the Boolean icons and select Keep Drill. The next step is to Boolean Subtract the shield-shaped object from the wing cover. You should still have an intact wing cover object and the shield-shaped extruded polygon. Next, select the intact wing cover. Deselect Keep Drill in the Boolean panel and perform a Boolean intersection with the extruded shield-shaped polygon. You should now have one wing cover object with a shield-shaped scallop at the top and a smaller object that fits inside the scallop perfectly (see Figure 10.46).

10. Create a Cube Primitive and scale and position it so that it covers just a tiny bit over half of the wing cover object (see Figure 10.47). We are going to use this cube like a knife to divide the wing cover into two halves.

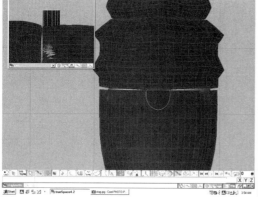

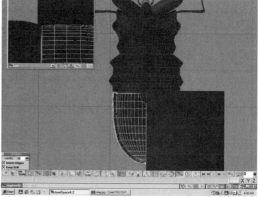

Figure 10.46 Draw and extrude a shield- **Figure 10.47** Create a Cube Primitive that
shaped polygon. overlaps half of the wing cover.

5. Select the wing cover object and Boolean Subtract the cube. Copy what remains, mirror the copy, and position it over the other half of the abdomen.

Great, you now have two wing covers that fit together to protect the abdomen. That's all there is to the abdomen. Now it's time to put legs on this bug.

Adding the Legs

Like all true insects, beetles have three pairs of legs. The first pair is attached to the thorax. The remaining two pairs are attached to the abdomen. Let's make the legs for our beetle.

EXERCISE: MAKING THE LEGS

1. First, Glue all parts of the beetle together if you haven't already. Then click on the Snap to Grid and rotate the entire beetle 180° so that he is now lying on his back, as all beetles are one day destined to. Now position a Sphere Primitive toward the front of the thorax on either side of the ridge that runs down the center. Refer to Figure 10.48.

2. Yeah, yeah, yeah-I know, another Sphere Primitive! I'm as tired of writing it as you are of reading it, but that's the price you pay if you want to be a cool creature creator. And who wouldn't? So, create the stupid sphere and, yes, deform it along the z-axis. But first, for a slight change of pace, this time we are going to rotate the sphere so that it is parallel to the ground but perpendicular to the beetle. If that confuses you, just look at Figure 10.49. Note that in the small Front View window the right end of the sphere is pulled downward. This is the part of the leg that will fit into the socket.

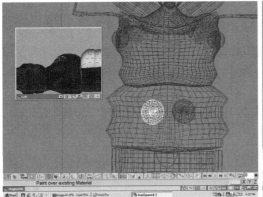
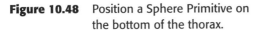
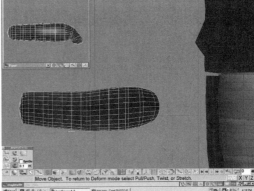

Figure 10.48   Position a Sphere Primitive on the bottom of the thorax.

Figure 10.49   Create another Sphere Primitive.

3. Copy the current object, rotate it 90° clockwise and then revolve it 90° so that the portion that is protruding outwards at the end is now pointing toward the right. Position this object so that the projecting portion is nestled in the end of the previous object. Use Deform Object to deform the other end of this object into a shape similar to the end of a trumpet (see Figure 10.50). Create a copy of this object and set it aside for the moment. Reselect the original.

4. Zoom in on the left edge of the current object, which for all intents and purposes we can think of as the forearm. We are going to create a series of barbs along this forearm in exactly the same way that we created the barbs on the pincers. There are two large barbs toward the front of the forearm, and two smaller barbs farther back. To create them, use the Draw Polygon feature in the point edit tools to create a more or less round shape on the side of the forearm. Select all of the faces inside the round shape and extrude them outward using the Sweep tool. Scale each step smaller and rotate it slightly to create the sharp barbs seen in Figure 10.51.

5. The foremost part of the front legs is actually surprisingly delicate. To create this section, we will use the same process we used on the end of the big feelers. Beginning with a regular polygon with 14 sides, sweep, scaling each step and positioning it to create the segments, as shown in Figure 10.52.

6. The first step is scaled larger, and the next step is the same diameter as the first but moved up slightly. The third step is scaled considerably smaller and brought down even with the previous step, and the process repeated three times. After the fourth segment has been created, begin sweeping

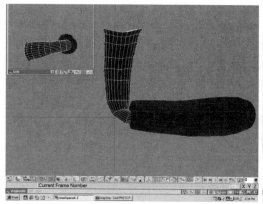

Figure 10.50 Copy the object, rotate it, and deform it.

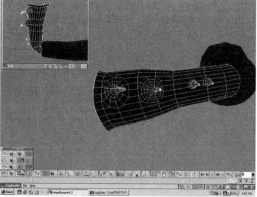

Figure 10.51 Create barbs like we did on the pincers.

the final segment with each step being slightly larger in diameter than the previous one until by the sixth step the diameter is equal to the previous segment. The seventh and final step should be slightly narrower and raised only slightly above the previous one. If you are confused, refer to Figure 10.52.

7. At the end of each foot are two claws. To create the claws, start with a round polygon created using the Regular Polygon tool. Simply sweep this polygon into a claw shape, see Figure 10.53. Position two of these claws at the end of the foot.

8. The last step is to assemble and position all of the legs. Glue all of the parts of the foreleg we just created together if you haven't already done so. Position the leg itself so that it nestles into the sphere we created at the beginning of this section. Next, create a copy of the leg, mirror it and place the copy on the opposite side of the thorax. Glue the sphere to the leg, copy it, and rotate it 180° clockwise so that it is facing rearward. The rear legs are identical to the front legs except that they lack the barbs on the forearm. So, unglue the forearm section and delete it. Now get the corresponding part that we set aside before adding the barbs and substitute it. Now scale and position this rear leg on the abdomen. Create a copy of this leg and move it slightly back, rotating it about 10° clockwise. Glue the two rear legs together, create a copy, mirror it, and position these rear legs on the opposite side of the abdomen. Look at Figure 10.54 for comparison.

That does it for the modeling. Our Stag Beetle is now complete. All that remains is to add a little color to old Bailey's life, so let's get started surfacing him.

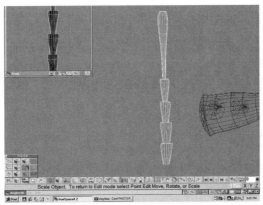

Figure 10.52 Use Sweep to create the fore-most part of the front legs.

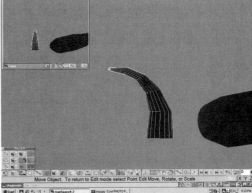

Figure 10.53 Sweep a regular polygon to create the claw.

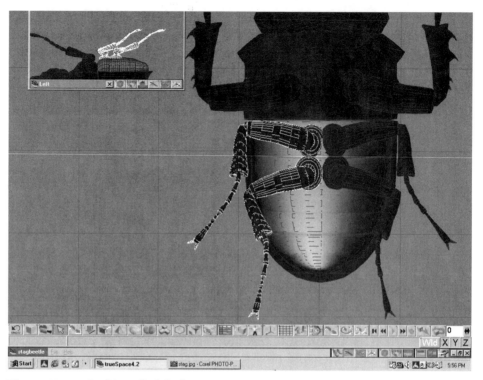

Figure 10.54 Position all of the legs.

Surfacing Bailey

Stag Beetles, although very cool in appearance, are not the most colorful of the beetles by a long shot. Their colors tend toward drab browns and basic black, as shown in Figure 10.55.

But hey, when you've got a classic chassis like that, you don't need a fancy paint job. For a change let's start at the back and work our way forward. The abdomen of the Stag Beetle is a kind of tan or light brown. It tends to be smoother than the rest of the body, somewhat shiny and almost transparent. I selected Plain Color in the color shader and set the values to red 182, blue 110, and green 61. I used no transparency. In the Displacement shader I selected Rough and chose the following settings: scale 1, amplitude 0.02, detail 3, and sharpness 1. I chose the Phong shader, set the Ambience to .1, Diffusion to .77, Shininess to .64, Roughness to 0. The same surface should be applied to the underside of the thorax using the Paint Faces tool.

The next step is to surface the wing covers. Like most beetles, these covers are slightly ridged, or grooved, for added strength. To re-create this characteristic,

Figure 10.55 The final surfaced Stag Beetle.

I used a wood bump map in the Displacement shader. This happened to work out perfectly, and the grain of the wood perfectly followed the contour of the shell. Once in a while, you get lucky. In the Color shader, I chose the solid clouds shader, which I have found useful for a variety of effects. I set the back color to solid black and the clouds color to a dark reddish brown. I set the scale to 3.9 and detail to 6. I again chose the Phong shader, but I lowered the shininess and increased the smoothness slightly.

The upper thorax is our next target. In the Solid Clouds shader, I set the clouds color to an even darker color, leaving the back color as black. I used no transparency. In the Displacement shader, I changed to Wrapped Rough with the following settings: scale .23, amplitude .03, detail 3, and sharpness 0. I used the same material on the head object and the legs.

The eyes of our beetle are shiny black. For the pincers, or jaws, I used the same material that I used on the wing covers. The wood bump map gave them a little grain and texture. The feelers use the same material as the thorax and legs. The visible portion of the mouth is a tan color. I used the Rough displacement shader to try to simulate its fuzzy surface. That's about it for surfacing. Unlike some of his fancy cousins, Bailey is pretty simple as far as coloration.

Wrap Up

This Stag Beetle was a fun project. I've always been fond of these insects, but this is the first time I have actually modeled one. Beetles are such a fascinating group of creatures. Don't overlook the smallest creature when you are looking for a modeling challenge. Some of the most exotic and unusual creatures on earth are living in our backyards. I hope you have enjoyed this tutorial. Happy modeling!

CHAPTER 11

The Postman Butterfly Caterpillar (Strata Studio Pro)

Frank Vitale

O nce again, I get to dive into the wonderfully freaky world of insects. I've always loved the little buggers. One sure-fire way to get me to stop channel surfing is to present me with a program on insects. The diversity of the insect world is just immense. We've categorized at least one million different insect types, each with six legs and an exoskeleton. The fascinating part is we've barely scratched the surface-literally millions upon millions of insects have yet to be discovered. The most difficult part of this project was simply deciding which type of insect to work on. Should I make one up and create, say, an alien insect? Or should I go with one that's alive and well here on earth? Since I like to work from well-documented sources, I decided to construct a well-known terrestrial insect, the quite creepy Postman Butterfly Caterpillar. It's scary looking and as an added bonus, quite poisonous-a great way to keep from getting eaten by birds. Also, this particular caterpillar has many spines and fuzzy patches, a perfect opportunity for me to use the Hair extension in StudioPro.

You might be asking yourself whether a caterpillar is an insect. They have more than six legs and no exoskeleton, so what the heck are they? Well, yes, they are insects and, yes, they only have six legs and, yes, they do have an exoskeleton. The skin of a caterpillar is its exoskeleton. It cannot stretch and must be shed often because they grow very fast. They're voracious eaters, scarfing up vegetation constantly before they finally spin a pupa or chrysalis on their way to Butterfly- or Moth-hood. As for the legs, the six on the front of the body-the ones that look like little daggers-are the only legs. The others are actually just extensions of the body, little nubbies that help them cling to branches as they stuff their chubby little faces. If you must categorize the caterpillar, it is a "nymph," an insect in transition.

So, enough caterpillar facts. I picked this guy because he looks freaky. Constructing him will also allow me to explore a few features of StudioPro that I've not previously explored. One is the Hair extension. I've messed with it before in attempts to create fur and hair and have never had much luck, but I've found that it actually works quite well in many instances. It's great for spikes and patches of hair or fur. Unfortunately, if you want to create a complete head of hair or a furry coat, the hair extension will most likely not cut it. I'll go into the details of this extension later in the tutorial.

Another feature I wanted to mess with was the Bones extension. I've played with this one quite a bit, but I've never used it in a production piece. Here we will use it to deform a mesh, bending the body of the caterpillar into the shape we want. I regret not using this feature more on past projects, since it's a great way to tweak and twist shapes. Bones is more than just a great animation tool, it's also a great modeling tool. Enough babble-on to the tutorial.

Modeling and Organization

Well, as you no doubt already know, the best way to get lost in a project and end up spending five times as much time as is necessary is to fail to properly organize it. StudioPro users around the world use the program for a reason-well, for many reasons. One is its logical layout for keeping your projects organized. Shapes are key. We will create shapes for each of the main parts of the caterpillar such as the body sections, feet, and spines. Working this way will both make our texture mapping easier and simplify our object tweaking.

I'm not going to do much hand-holding in this tutorial, or it will end up being a monster. I won't leave out steps, but it will definitely help if you have a fairly clear understanding of how StudioPro works before tackling this project. If you need a refresher on the basics have a look at Chapter 5, "The Entrance."

The Main Body Section

The body is a relatively simple shape to create. It's really nothing more than nine lumpy segments in a row. Let's get started on the body modeling.

EXERCISE: MODELING THE BODY SEGMENTS

1. The first thing to do is create a new project, and save it with the name "Postman_01.spd." I won't tell you to save often but do-nothing is worse

than losing a few hours work due to a system or software crash, which we all know happens at the most inopportune moments.

2. Now that you have your project, go to the Resource window, click on the Shapes tab, and create a new shape, and name it "Section." Name all shapes-this is what I mean by organization. Within this new shape, we will create one section of the main body. As often as possible I'll be making this project as simple as I can by using primitives. This is a great way to work. There is no need to make more work than necessary. When primitives will work, use them.

3. In this new shape create a sphere. The size is not really important, but the size you create this section will set the precedent for the size of all your other shapes. Now click on the Convert button at the top of your window (box with a sphere in it) and convert the sphere to a Bezier surface, this will allow us to reshape it. Switch the view to Right and Outline and make the x grid active (simply hit the X key, or the Y then X key to make just the x grid active) this should be your view, see Figure 11.1.

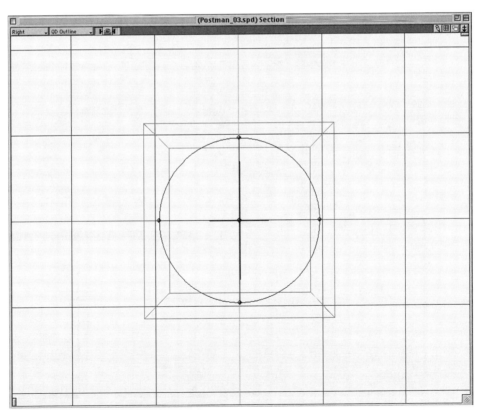

Figure 11.1 The sphere prior to reshaping.

4. Now to reshape the sphere as seen from the right view. Select the sphere and click on the reshape icon at the top of the screen (the white filled arc with the handles). You've now entered reshape mode. When you finish reshaping the object it will look like this, see Figure 11.2.

Notice the reshape tool set included in this figure. As you move the cursor over the different tools, Strata Studio Pro (SSP) displays the tool function in the upper left corner of the screen. I've selected all the nodes on the shape so that you can see the length and angle of the handles, which should aid in the creation of this shape.

When creating shapes such as this, it is best to work in orthographic mode (move the eyeball slider to the far left for orthographic). This is the best way to achieve symmetry. Also, you will need to add a few points to your shape using the Add Point tool (the cursor with the dot). At times, when points are added, more points than are desired get created. If this happens, simply undo and try again in a slightly different area or from a different view.

5. Now that we have our body section, we can build the caterpillar's main body. The single section is complete, so close the shape window and go

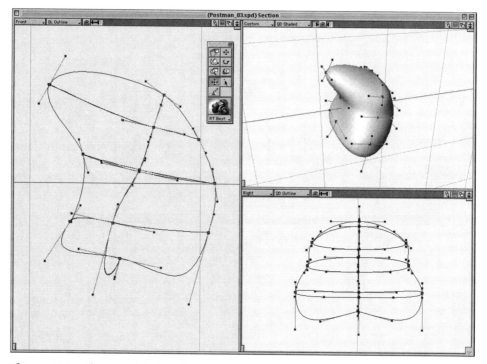

Figure 11.2   The completed section.

back to the main project window. From the shapes tab select the shape called "section" and click Insert. Do this nine times. There, you've just inserted nine instances of the same shape in the exact same place. One by one, click and drag the shapes until you've spaced them as seen in Figure 11.3 (switching to outline view will speed this up greatly).

At this point, we need to think a bit about how we are going to texture map this shape. In this example I'd like to show you another feature that Strata has added recently, called "Burn UV." As you've probably guessed this tool allows you to convert your standard, projection-based mapping to UV mapping. UV mapping is very important in many instances and absolutely required if you want to apply deformations of any kind to an object. If you do not use UV, textures will slide as objects change shape. So, although the main body is still a straight shape, we can texture map it using a cylindrical projection. The map that you use is not important. You can change it later.

6. Make a place holder color map, a grid is a good idea, and build a shader using the grid as your color map. Be sure to name your shader "body main" or something similar. To use the Burn UV tool, your object needs to be a polygonal mesh so group all the sections and convert to polygonal mesh.

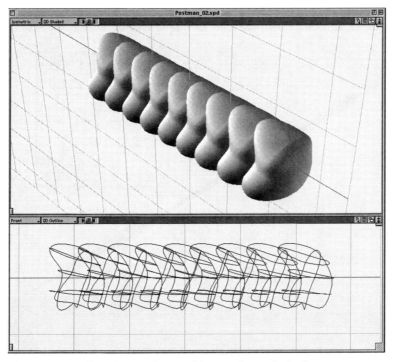

Figure 11.3 The nine sections making up the main body.

7. Now apply the shader using cylindrical as your mapping method. With your object selected, click on the Burn UV button at the top of the screen, it's a small rectangle with a UV in it.

There you have it, the texture is now applied using UV mapping. We will now be able to use bones to deform the object. You might be wondering why we couldn't simply use UV mapping from the get-go. Well, we could have, but then we would have had to build a texture for each shape or use the same one for each shape. Either way, it would not look nearly as good having a noticeable repeat and hard seams. Using one texture will actually help us to hide the seams created by the connecting shapes.

We'll cover texturing a bit more after the model is complete. Right now let's take a look at Bones.

Applying the Bones

Now we get to jump into some fun stuff, using bones to reshape the body. Before we do that, though, I need to talk a bit about bones and how they work. First, have a look at Figure 11.4.

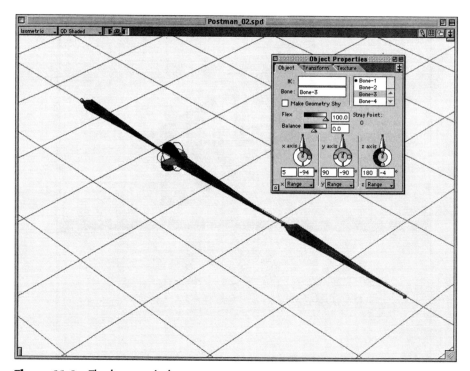

Figure 11.4 The bones window.

After an IK or bones structure is created the Object Properties window reflects its attributes and controls. You can name the IK structure as well as the individual bones. You set the flex and balance for each bone as well as its motion constraints. It's quite intuitive actually. By simply clicking on the little spheres and dragging within the Object Properties window you can set the motion constraints, which are clearly reflected in the object space. The pop-up windows also allow you to set the bone to free or lock. SSP also tells you how many, if any, stray points you have; this will become clear shortly.

Now that you've had a crash course in SSP Bones, we will use them to deform the polygonal mesh.

EXERCISE: ADDING BONES TO THE BODY

1. Expand the mesh in the project window and name it "Body," as shown in Figure 11.5. Never mind the other parts for now, we'll get to them soon. If the name refuses to take, add a space after the word. This usually does the trick.

2. For bones to deform a shape, that shape must be a polygonal mesh. Since we converted the main body to a polygonal mesh to set the texture mapping to UV we're set. Now select the bones tool from the extensions pallet and from a front view click and drag, inserting six bones (see Figure 11.6). Make sure you start from the left, a bit off the left edge of the body, and end a bit off the right side of the body; this will ensure our deformation will work.

3. Notice that bone-1 has a small black dot next to it. This bone represents the entire structure, not a single bone. All other bones fall beneath it in the hierarchy. Now, from the front view click on the IK structure and drag it down so that it falls within the body shape (see Figure 11.7).

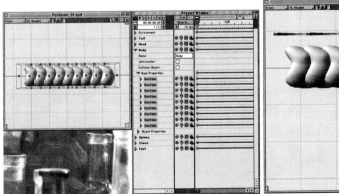

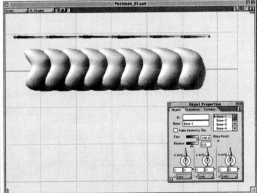

Figure 11.5   The main body and the project window.

Figure 11.6   The six bones and the object properties window.

4. Next we need to attach the IK structure to the polygonal mesh. We will use the Attach tool for this. It's the one that looks like a section of rope at the bottom of the tool bar. Since we are performing a deformation, it is important that you hold down the Option key when attaching the IK structure. This will associate various points on the object to bones within their space. Do this now by clicking on the IK structure-the green bone sticking out of the left side of the body is fine-and dragging to the mesh. The bounding box of the mesh should highlight in red to indicate that the attachment has been made. The name has now changed from body to IK Mesh. You can change it if you like.

5. To reshape the object, select the IK Object in the project window and click the Reshape button. Generally, I'll turn off the mesh at this point to simplify the reshaping process. Reshaping is very simple. Just select the Rotate tool, click on the bone you wish to rotate, and drag. That's all there is to it (see Figure 11.8).

6. The default constraint is full motion in Z, so working from a front view you should be able to get all the adjustments you need without changing any of the settings in the Object Properties window. You'll notice that the Object Properties window shows stray points. In my case it shows 65 stray points. We'll fix this next.

7. Now, in your project window, make your mesh visible again. It should look like Figure 11.9.

8. Everything looks great, with the exception of the stray points that were never associated with the bones when the attachment was made. I don't know why this occurs, but it is very easy to fix. To do so, we will use the Vertex tool, the bone with the blue dot next to it. Whenever you select this

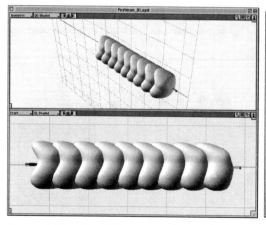

Figure 11.7 The IK Bones positioned in the main body.

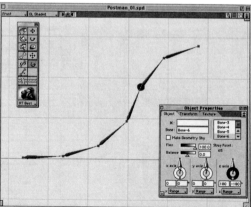

Figure 11.8 The bones rotated into position.

tool, all the vertices are shown either in green, red, or blue. Green would be unassociated with the current bone, red would be associated, and blue would be homeless or stray points (see Figure 11.10). We simply want to single-click on each stray point to associate it with the selected bone.

9. Go through the bones one by one selecting them from the Object Properties window and clicking on the blue stray points to snap them into position. You'll want to switch from Shaded to Point Cloud to see any vertices that are hidden by the shaded view (see Figure 11.11). Also, view the object from different angles to be sure you get all the stray points.

That does it-our main body shape is complete. We rotated the bones only along one axis, the z-axis. As you can see, this is a very powerful way to create complex shapes that can not be created by other means. Bones and IK are generally thought of as animation tools and are great for such. We could use bones to animate the movements of a caterpillar, however, there are some limitations. The other objects that are associated with the caterpillar-the spines, the head, and the feet-would not follow the shape as it is moved about. If we grouped everything and converted it to a mesh, we could deform the entire model only texture mapping would prove to be a major chore; extremely limiting.

Okay, the body model is now complete, the next step is to tackle the detail of the caterpillar's tail.

Creating the Tail

Now we will create the tail end of our caterpillar.

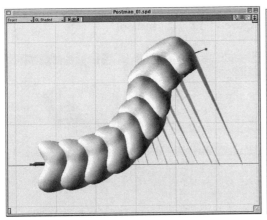

Figure 11.9 The reshaped mesh.

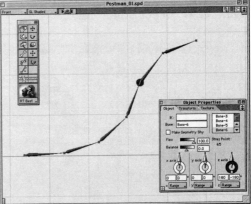

Figure 11.10 The reshaped mesh showing the vertex association.

EXERCISE: CREATING THE TAIL

1. From the Resources window, click on the Shapes tab, create a new shape, and name it "tail." Use the same technique that was used in creating the body section to create the three main sections of the tail. Insert a primitive sphere, convert it to a Bezier surface and reshape it adding points where necessary. See Figures 11.12–11.15 for reference.

2. The last part of the tail to create is the tentacles, or spines, that protrude from the rear end of the caterpillar. These are created by using Path Extrude, converting to a Skin object, repositioning the ribs, and then re-skinning. This is the technique I used to create vegetation such as grass and reeds in the May 1999 cover issue of M3DG. It goes like this.

3. Using the Pen tool create a path (still taking place in the Shape window for "tail") and then create a filled circle, see Figure 11.16.

4. Now, from the Extensions pallet, use the Path Extrude tool, and drag from the circle to the path. This will extrude the shape along the path.

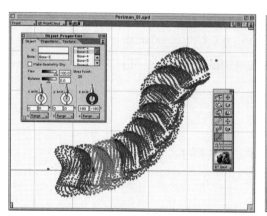

Figure 11.11   A point cloud view.

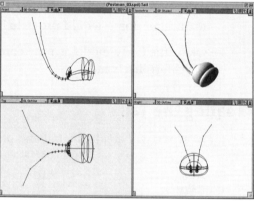

Figure 11.12   Tail section.

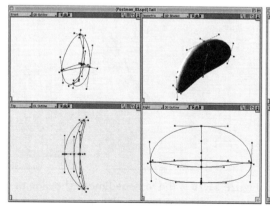

Figure 11.13   Tail section 1.

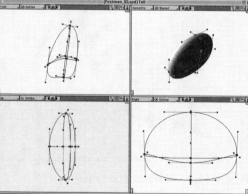

Figure 11.14   Tail section 2.

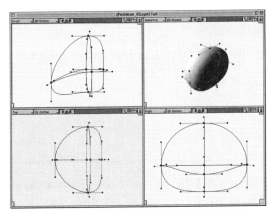

Figure 11.15 Tail section 3.

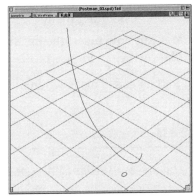

Figure 11.16 Path and circle.

5. Now select the new object and convert it into a Skin object using the Convert button at the top of the screen.

6. Next, use the Unskin tool from the Extensions pallet and click and drag on the object to unskin all the ribs. If you are in shaded view, you might find it difficult to see all the ribs so switch to wireframe.

7. Now select one rib at a time starting from where it attaches to the tail and using the Object Properties window (the Transform tab) select scale, make sure it is locked to Proportional, set it to Percentage and scale down each rib about 10% progressively. What you should end up with is something like that shown in Figure 11.17.

8. Next use the Skin tool to reskin the ribs. Simply click and drag from rib to rib to create the finished object. Duplicate and position the pieces to get something like you see in Figure 11.18, notice also that I've further manipulated the ribs to add more asymmetry to the object, making it more real-

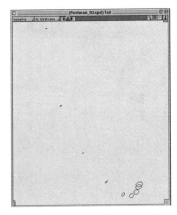

Figure 11.17 Tail protrusion ribs.

Figure 11.18 The finished protrusions.

istic. This is done by moving and rotating the individual ribs just a bit before reskinning them.

9. You can now insert the tail shape into your main window and position it like you see in Figure 11.19.

On to the head. This is where it starts to get creepy.

The Head

I've taken some artistic liberties in this area as I did not have the greatest close-up reference for this area, and all the mouth organs tend to be rather small and tight to the head. I wanted to dramatize this area to make this guy a bit more creepy. If you happen to be an entomologist, please bear with me. This is also one of the areas where I wanted to play with the hair extension as you can see in Figure 11.20.

As you can see, the face is looking quite creepy. That's the great thing about insects, they are really rather frightening. It's a good thing they are small!

EXERCISE: CREATING THE HEAD

1. First, we'll tackle the head and neck regions. For these shapes I used the MetaBall extension. I simply placed spheres of different shapes and sizes

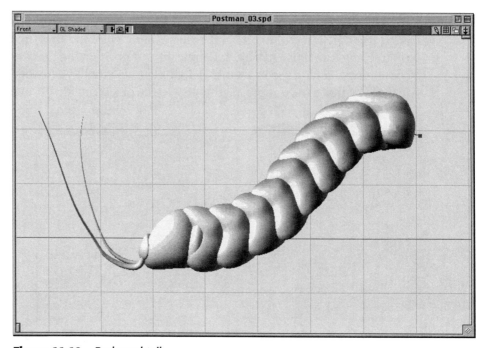

Figure 11.19 Body and tail.

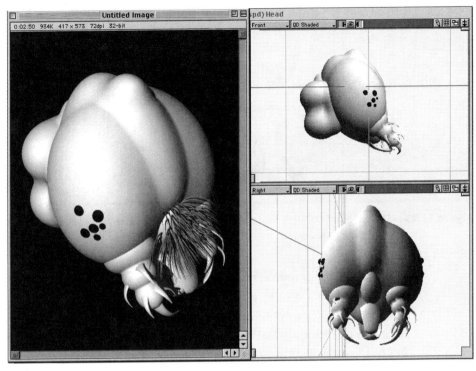

Figure 11.20 Facial hair.

into position and applied the extension. At any time you can unMetaBall the object, move things around, and then reMetaBall it. It's a great, flexible tool (see Figures 11.21–11.24).

2. For the MetaBall tool to work, the spheres must not be in a group. Other than that, there are no real restrictions. The objects must be primitive spheres, you select them all and click on the MetaBall icon on the tool bar

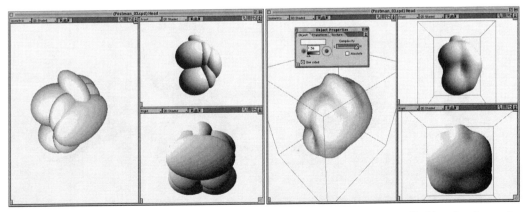

Figure 11.21 The different spheres that make up the neck shape.

Figure 11.22 The MetaBall object for the neck.

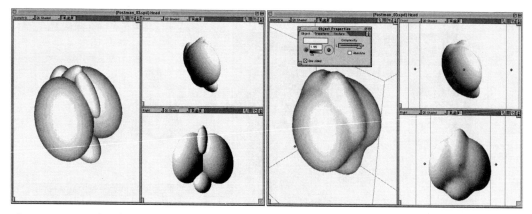

Figure 11.23 The different spheres that make up the head shape.

Figure 11.24 The MetaBall object for the head.

at the top of the screen. The Object Properties window then reflects the attributes of the New MetaBall object.

3. I created the jaws or pinchers in the same way. A MetaBall shape made up of three spheres and then several curving spikes created in the same manner as the protrusions on the tail section. A 2D solid circle is path extruded along a curved path, converted to a Skin object, and then unskinned. The resulting ribs are then scaled down more and more until you reach the end and then reskinned. The finished claw shape is then duplicated several times, scaled, rotated, and positioned in place. There you have it, scary jaws (see Figure 11.25).

4. The beak shape is created similarly, only instead of using a simple 2D solid circle, I used the Pen tool to create a custom shape (see Figure 11.26).

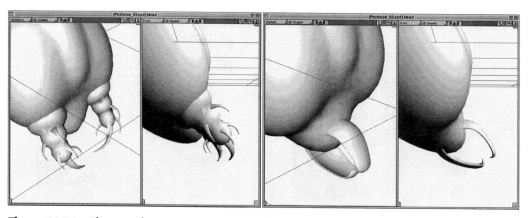

Figure 11.25 The scary jaws.

Figure 11.26 The scary beak.

5. This technique is very simple, and I've found it to be very useful for a number of organic shape types. It's also a technique that is rather application independent.

6. The next features-the eyes-are simply spheres. They have been scaled a bit in z to flatten them and then positioned along the sides of the head. Caterpillars have strange eyes, six on either side of the head. They have evolved to see well up close, that's all they care about, seeing the food they eat. After arranging the eyes on one side of the head, I grouped them and then used the mirror tool to make a copy that mirrors along the z-axis.

7. Select the group you wish to mirror and with the Mirror tool (found on the Extensions pallet) click on the group and drag the cursor around until the axis you wish to mirror across is highlighted in yellow. It's best to work from an isometric view when doing this. After the copy has been made, it is quite easy to move it into position on the other side of the head.

8. Another feature on the head is the patch of fur that appears just above the mouth. This is a feature that I added to draw the attention away from a less than perfect model of the mouth region. A good way to hide a potential error or lack of detail is to simply add additional objects, more detail really just from simple shapes; hair is a great way of doing this. The object used for this patch of hair is a Lathe object. The reason for this is hair will cover all sides of an object, if a sphere is used, we will have to create a great many more hairs than are necessary, ones that will protrude into the face and look quite artificial. So instead, I used a Lathe object that is only lathed around 180° (see Figure 11.27).

9. See Figure 11.28 for a screen capture of the hair dialog box. This is the hair I used for the patch on the face.

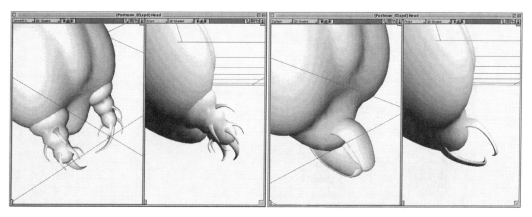

Figure 11.27   The hair patch base.   **Figure 11.28**   The hair dialog box.

10. Hair can be controlled in many ways and with most attributes a grayscale map can be used to affect how the hair behaves. You'll notice that the density of this particular hair is set to 3,000%. I had to play with this a great deal to get the hair density I was after. The render times increase a great deal as you up this number, this is why I don't feel this extension is quite ready for the full-fledged fur-on-a-bear application. All the other controls are great, though, and it turns out to be a truly versatile tool. This extension is accessed throughout the FX tab on the Resource pallet. Hair can be texture mapped by picking a texture from the pull-down menu at the top of the dialog, but the controls are really not there. It's been my experience that it is set to UV and there is no changing it. When working with hair you might notice that all the hairs on your object are drifting in one direction. That is due to two factors: - strength and wind. Yes, StudioPro has wind, and it is set to on as default; it will affect all particle systems. The wind can be turned off from the Environment window, Air tab. Set the intensity to zero (see Figure 11.29).

That about does it for the head. Have another look at Figure 11.20 for the completed head.

Next, we do the legs.

The Legs

The legs are made of three basic parts: the claw, the leg itself, and the bridge section that connects the legs to the body. The bridge section is easy. It is cre-

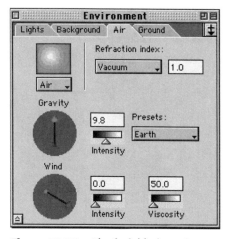

Figure 11.29 The facial hair settings.

ated the same way as the body sections, from a reshaped sphere. The legs are a bit more tricky. Here we used the MetaBall method again, but I've also applied a deformation lattice to them to get just the right shape.

EXERCISE: CREATING THE LEGS

1. First, the MetaBall shape. Create three spheres like those shown in Figure 11.30.

2. Now select all three spheres, and click on the MetaBall tool at the top of the screen (see Figure 11.31).

3. Now for the lattice. You can click and drag a lattice directly into the work space, or you can click directly on an object. When a lattice is inserted this way, it fits perfectly to the object and is automatically attached. Inserting a lattice on its own frees it from its association, and it must then be attached to the object you wish to deform. In this case we are going to apply the lattice directly to the MetaBall object. The tool is simply called Deform, and it is located on the Extensions pallet. Select it and single-click on the MetaBall object. You should now have a lattice attached to your object (see Figure 11.32).

4. A deformation lattice appears in your project window as a separate object, similar to the way an IK chain works. And similar to an IK chain, the deformation lattice needs to be reshaped to affect the object to which it is attached. Now select the lattice in the project window, and click the reshape icon (see Figure 11.33).

5. The tools for reshaping the lattice are quite simple. It's a matter of selecting the points and moving them. That's about it, really. To create the foot shape, you'll want to move the vertices on the lattice like that shown in Figure 11.34.

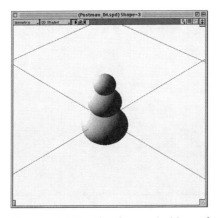

Figure 11.30   The three primitive spheres.

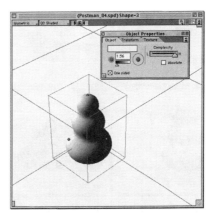

Figure 11.31   Making the spheres MetaBalls.

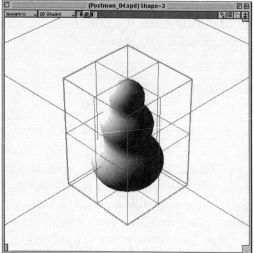

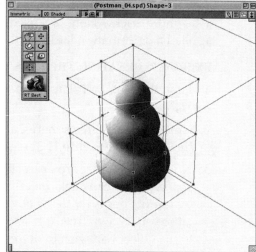

Figure 11.32 The MetaBall object with the lattice.

Figure 11.33 The MetaBall object with the lattice applied and selected for reshape.

6. Next, we'll add the claw and have a completed leg. The claw is made with the Path Extrusion converted to the Skin Shape method. Check out Figure 11.35, and go for it.

7. Additionally, I've added a small sphere to smooth the transition from claw to leg shape. Also, I've rotated the group to be in the position I'll need for integration to the next level. Remember that any manipulation applied to an object on its shape level will be reflected in the main project window. Now create a new shape and name it "Front Claw Complete."

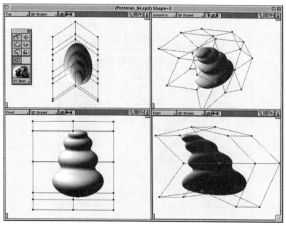
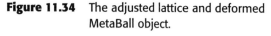

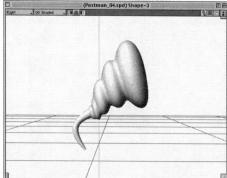

Figure 11.34 The adjusted lattice and deformed MetaBall object.

Figure 11.35 The foot with the claw.

Within this shape, we'll insert two of the leg shapes and create a bridge between the two using the reshape primitive technique (see Figure 11.36).

8. The next set of legs we need to create are the "prolegs," which are not really legs at all but extensions of the body that assist the caterpillar in clinging to and grasping branches as it feeds on leaves. Figure 11.37 shows an exploded view of this proleg section. All of the parts are just reshaped spheres with the exception of the ring, which is a Lathe object.

9. Figures 11.38–11.42 show each shape in detail.

If need be, one could also use either the Deformation Lattice or Bones to further manipulate the legs or the prolegs for modeling or animation. In the case of bones you would need to group the objects and then convert them into a polygonal mesh. If a deformation lattice will do, I would recommend using it instead. With a lattice, you simply need to group the objects in question. This allows you to still texture map the objects separately. Both techniques allow for animation.

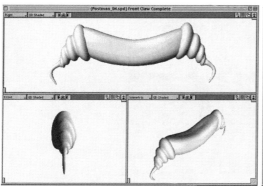

Figure 11.36   The completed front legs.

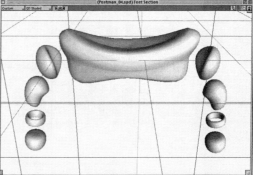

Figure 11.37   Exploded view of prolegs.

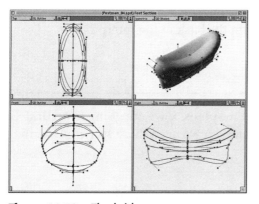

Figure 11.38   The bridge.

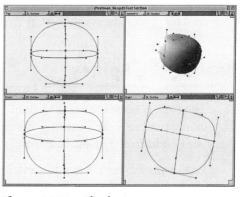

Figure 11.39   The foot.

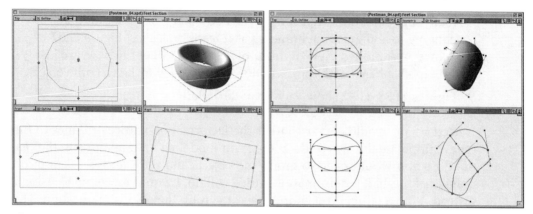

Figure 11.40 Lathe shape for hair.

Figure 11.41 Lower leg section.

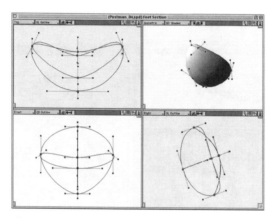

Figure 11.42 Upper leg section

Great, we're almost done modeling this critter. The last step is to create those cool but quite eerie spines that run along the back of the caterpillar.

Creating the Spines

The final objects we need to create are the spines. If we are going to accurately create the Postman Butterfly Caterpillar, then we need these spines. Also, they really add to the creepy factor.

EXERCISE: CREATING THE SPINES

1. Create a new shape and name it "single spike." Within this shape space, create a cone and scale it as you see in Figure 11.43.

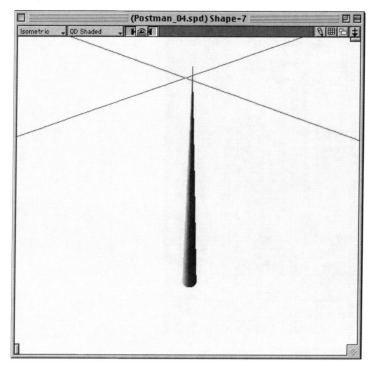

Figure 11.43   The single cone.

2. This cone needs to be very small, as it will act as a hair or spine that appears on the main, much larger spine. Now create another shape and name it "Spine." See Figure 11.44 for a rendering of the finished spine, and then we'll create one.

3. All of the gray portions of this spine are modeled, the pale yellow portions are hair. First, the base shape, as you have likely guessed it, is a MetaBall shape. See Figure 11.45 for its configuration.

4. The spine itself was created using the extrude-along-a-path-convert-to_skin technique we've used on several parts earlier. The small spikes are inserted as shapes and scaled to fit properly. The hair effect we are using has been created similar to the way the patch of hair on the face was created. I've used a Lathe object that is hidden within the base, as I mentioned earlier this helps to cut down on the amount of hairs required, see Figure 11.46.

5. And for the setting on this particular hair shader, see Figure 11.47.

6. Notice how in the hair settings, the preview has a much higher density than our actual shape. This emphasizes the need to preview how the hair looks on the shape you are applying it to.

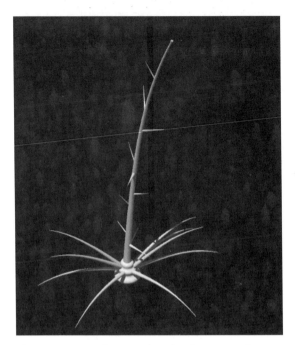

Figure 11.44   The completed poisonous spine.

7. There you have it, all of the parts of the caterpillar have been created. Now assembly is required. Insert the different shapes into the main modeling window arranging them the way you see here in Figure 11.48.

8. You will find it much quicker if you turn the different shapes off when they are not needed. See Figure 11.48 for the completed caterpillar model.

9. The most tedious part will be adding the spines. There are lots of them, and the screen redraws will begin to creep to a crawl. To speed up your assembly, have only one spine turned on at a time. Also, before doing all the rota-

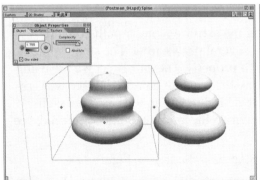

Figure 11.45   The base of the spine.

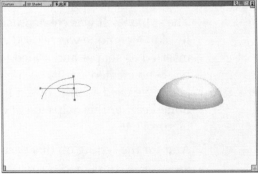

Figure 11.46   Spike hair shape.

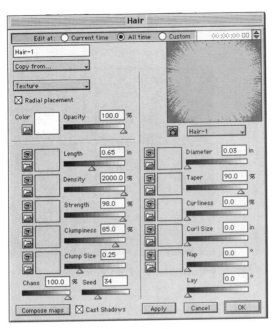

Figure 11.47 Spike hair settings.

tion and transformations, set the view to Point Cloud and move the shapes center point to the bottom, near the base. The center point of any object is a blue dot in the center of the object. To move this point, hold down the Command key, click on it, and drag. Do this in several views to ensure you have it near the base, see Figures 11.49–11.51. This will make rotation of your object much easier.

Figure 11.48 The front view.

Figure 11.49 Top View.

Figure 11.50   Right View.

Figure 11.51   Isometric View.

At last, our creepy caterpillar model is complete. All we have left to do is surface this bug. Although we won't be exploring the surfacing in this tutorial, it's actually quite simple. The body was surfaced with a slightly detailed Cylindrical texture map. The legs were Planar mapped and the head Spherical mapped. The spikes and spots were simple color textures with a little bumpiness added for realism. All of the texture maps were painted in Photoshop and are quite simple. Basically, they were created by using a base green color, and then dabbing splotches of orange in places.

Now that we have completed our modeling tutorial, let's take a minute to explore how I created the elements of my caterpillar scene shown in Figure 11.52.

Let's start with how the other objects were created, and then we'll take a look at the lighting.

Additional Scene Elements

Check out the final render, and you will notice the branch on which our caterpillar rests as well as the vine with all the leaves. The Branch and the vine are simply Path Extruded objects that have been converted to Skin objects, so I could rotate the ribs, creating a twisting effect. The texture maps have been applied using UV, so the pattern follows the shape of the object. The leaves are flat planes that have been converted to Bezier meshes and adjusted to reflect the curvature of the leaf. The leaf shape itself is achieved with a stencil map. See Figures 11.53 and 11.54 for the leaf model and texture maps used for this shape.

Figure 11.52   A complete caterpillar scene.

Figure 11.53   The leaf model.

Figure 11.54   The leaf texture maps.

Notice that one of the maps is a Glow map. Since translucence is not yet an option in StudioPro (not to be confused with transparency) I used a very slight glow to simulate it. This is a subtle effect but one that works well, it brightens the area defined by the glow simulating a slight translucence. Speaking of brightening, let's take a look at the scene-lighting tricks.

Lighting

The lighting for this scene is quite simple, consisting of two spot lights and one global light. The global light has a slight green tint to it and is quite low in intensity. It serves to create a rather ambient green coverage to the scene. The primary light is a spotlight. It has a high intensity, 110% and a slight yellow tint. This light also uses a gel, which simulates light shining through more leaves and vegetation off screen (see Figure 11.55).

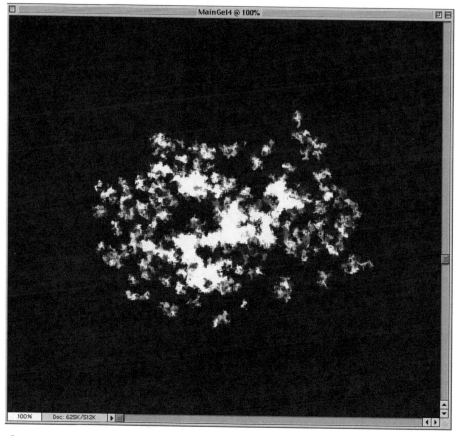

Figure 11.55 The main light gel.

The use of a gel I feel is a very important and under-used effect. To gain realism you need to think not only of your composition and what is in it but also what is out of the field of view and how this might affect your image. The third light is a small spotlight that focuses on the head. The light from the main spot did not illuminate the head sufficiently. The small spot has a slight green tint to it to simulate the idea that the head, which is much shinier, is reflecting green from the leaves.

The final thing to do was add a background, and a simple composite in Photoshop will do. The biggest decision I had to make here was whether to go with a light background or a dark background. A light background made for a more realistic image. All in all, things worked out the way I planned.

Wrap Up

Well, that does it for this tutorial. I hope you enjoyed it. While the representation of the Postman Caterpillar is not exact, it will no doubt make for a beautiful Postman Butterfly. One question that remains is whether insects have memory of past experiences and, if so, do butterflies remember being little grub heads?

The companion CD-ROM contains a variety of support materials for the tutorials in this book. There are 11 folders on the CD-ROM, one for each of the chapters. In these folders you will find support files for the tutorials, which include models and textures. You will also find a folder called "Figures" that has all of the chapter figures in color JPG format so you can see the images in high-resolution color. I highly recommend you take advantage of these figures when reading the chapters.

In addition to the eleven chapter folders, you will find another folder called "M3G." This folder contains three full issues of Mastering 3D Graphics Magazine in HTML format, with more than 20 new tutorials not featured in the text of this book. Below is a complete listing of the tutorials included.

Issue 1 "Digital Botany"

1. Creating Natural Environments
   Bill Fleming
2. Creating Plants and Flowers (LightWave)
   Chris MacDonald
3. A bouquet from an Alien Friend (3D Studio Max)
   Eni Oken
4. Tackling a Thorny Challenge (trueSpace)
   Darris Dobbs
5. The Flowered Bramble (Ray Dream Studio)
   R. Shamms Mortier
6. The Entrance (Strata StudioPro)
   Frank Vitale
7. Digital Botany Creation (Soft F/X Pro)
   Kent Shum

8. Realistic Natural Scenery (Vue d'Esprit 2)

Cécile Laurens

9. Tree Professional version 4

R. Shamms Mortier

10. Modeling Vegetation (Rhinoceros 3D)

Ryan Knope

11. Surfacing—Half the Battle (Photoshop)

Frank Vitale

12. Aging Your 3D Models (Photoshop)

Chris MacDonald

Issue 2 "Creepy Insects"

1. What's Under the Fridge? Part 1 (LightWave)

Bill Fleming

2. Stag Party (trueSpace)

Darris Dobbs

3. Thousands of Legs (Soft FX Pro)

Kent Shum

4. What Hairy Legs You Have! (Animation Master)

Patrick Clarke

5. Searland Ground Wasp (Electric Image)

John Sledd

6. Meet the Little Flyboy (Rhinoceros 3D)

7. Ryan Knope

8. On a Distant Planet... (3D Studio MAX/LightWave)

Nermin Bajagilovic

9. Waterbear; The Indestructible Bug! (RayDream Studio/Poser)

Dave Thomas

10. When Dragons Ruled the Skies (3D Studio MAX)

Jerry Potts

11. Creating a Creepy Insect (Bryce 3D)

R. Shamms Mortier

Issue #3 "Creepy Insects Part 2"

1. What's Under the Fridge? Part 2 (Photoshop/LightWave)
   Bill Fleming
2. The Postman Caterpillar (Strata Studio Pro)
   Frank Vitale
3. Let There Be Light! (LightWave)
   Chris MacDonald
4. An Ant's Life; Modeling and Texturing a Harvester Ant (Electric Image)
   Eric Fernandes
5. Modeling a Mantis (Animation Master)
   Mike Hough
6. Dragonflies: From Basic Model to Naturalistic Scene (Painter 3D/Ray-Dream Studio)
   Janet Glover
7. Toon Insects (Rhinoceros/LightWave)
   Aivaras Grauzinis
8. NURBS Modeling for Insectoid Characters (3D Studio MAX)
   Sergio Muciño
9. Modeling & Texturing a Basic Dragonfly (Cinema 4D)
   Adam Watkins

To view these tutorials load the "index.html" file in your Web browser and follow the menu links.

Software Requirements

You will, of course, need a 3D program to take advantage of the exercise resources found on the CD-ROM. Each chapter title includes the programs being covered in the tutorials so you will know the tools required to complete the chapter.

You will also need a painting program such as Photoshop to open the image files, which are in JPG format. If you don't have Photoshop you can use Fractal Design Painter, Corel's Photopaint, or even Paint Shop Pro.

User Assistance and Information

The software accompanying this book is being provided as is without warranty or support of any kind. Should you require basic installation assistance, or if your media is defective, please call our product support number at (212) 850-6194 weekdays between 9 A.M. and 4 P.M. Eastern Standard Time. Or, we can be reached via email at: wprtusw@wiley.com.

To place additional orders or to request information about other Wiley products, please call (800) 879-4539.

Page references in *italic* type indicate illustrations.
Terms including numbers are indexed as if the number was spelled out.

A

abdomen (Stag Beetle), 264-269
  surfacing, 272
African Giant Millipede, 170
algae, creation in The Entrance,
  126-131
alien plants, 77
  colors, 54-55
  lighting, 75-78
  modeling, 58-61
  painting template creation, 63-65
  plant arrangement, 56-58, 57
  reference material for, 53-54
  secondary plants, 72-75
  texture materials, 65-72
  UV mapping, 61-63
Aliens (movie), insectoid creatures in,
  167, 169
aloe plant, adding to cactus garden,
  94-96, 96
Animation:Master, 167
antennae (dragonflies), 238
Attaphilla fungicola (cockroach
  species), 171

B

back lights, alien plants, 76, 77
bare spots, 7
beetles, 253. *See also* Stag Beetle

Bezier line, 101
Bezier mesh, 101
Blue Spruce, 29
body armor (cockroach)
  creation, 200-201
  painting template, 215
body blotches and speckles, insects,
  207, 209
body (dragonflies), 234-236
  mapping, 247-248
body (Postman Butterfly Caterpillar),
  276-280
  surfacing, 298
body segment coloration, insects,
  208-209
Bones extension (Studio Pro), 275,
  276
bones (Postman Butterfly Caterpillar),
  280-283
bounce lights, The Entrance, 139
box method, with 3D Studio MAX, 58
branches
  creation for alien plants, 58-59
  creation for Christmas tree, 11,
    13-18, 23-27
  creation for The Entrance, 106-107,
    110
  creation for use with Postman
    Butterfly Caterpillar, 298, 299

Bryce, 167
buds
  creation for alien plants, 58-61
  creation in LightWave, 40-42, 45-46,
    48
  texturing, 45-46, 48
  texturing for alien plants, 67-71
bump maps
  cactus garden, 98
  dragonfly eyes, 246
  Giant Madagascar Hissing Cock-
    roach, 225-226
  leaves, 157-162
  Stag Beetle, 273
Burn UV (Studio Pro), 279-280
bushes, 3

C

cactus garden, 79-80, 80
  aloe plant creation, 94-96, 96
  mystery cactus creation, 92-94
  organ pipe cactus creation, 87-89
  prickly pear creation, 80-86, 87
  saguaro cactus creation, 90-92
  texturing, 96-97, 98
caterpillars, 275-276. *See also* Postman
    Butterfly Caterpillar
Cellular material (3D Studio MAX), 66
chaotic details
  insect surfaces, 207
  plant life, 1
Christmas scene, plants and flowers
    in, *34*
Christmas tree, 11-13, *12*, 30
  branch creation, 11, 13-18
  branch group cloning, 23-27
  dressing, 23-31
  pine needle creation, 11, 18-23
Christmas wreath, 29, 30
Cinema 4D, 167
clipping map, 149, 162-163
clover, 8
cockroaches, 171
cockroach (Giant Madagascar Hissing

Cockroach), 170, 171-172, *172,*
    206
body armor creation, 200-201
body armor painting template, *215*
body creation, 179-182
body surfacing, 226-229, 227, 228
bump map creation, 225-226
eye creation, 195-200
feeler creation, 204-205
head armor creation, 201-206
head creation, 193-200
image map painting, 214-226
leg creation, 204-205
leg protusion creation, 182-185
legs painting template, *215*
painting template creation, 212-214
second body segment creation,
    185-187
shoulder segment creation, 192-193
surface definition, 210-211
surface details, 208-209
tail creation, 173-179
tail painting, 216-220
third body segment creation,
    188-192
torso painting, 221-225
coloring
  alien plants, 54-55
  cactus garden, 97
  dragonflies, 243-251
  insect body segments, 208-209
  leaves, 149-154
  natural lights, 137
  plants, 145, 208
  Postman Butterfly Caterpillar, 298
  Stag Beetles, 272-273
Cybermesh plug-in, 102, 128

D

depth of field effects, 134-135, *135*
Desert Warts, 8, 9
digital botany, 99
dragonflies, 231-234, *233, 250*
  antennae creation, 238

body creation, 234-236
body mapping, 247-248
eye creation, 236-237
eye mapping, 244-247
head creation, 237-239
jaw creation, 238-239
leg creation, 239-242
leg mapping, 249-251
tail creation, 235-236
tail mapping, 248-249
wing cover creation, 242
wing cover mapping, 243-244
Dung Beetle, 253

E

Electric Image, 167
Enchanted Goblin Desert, 4, *8*, 8-9
The Entrance, 99-102, *102*, *145*
    camera insertion, 131-135
    grass creation, 113-121
    hillside creation, 121-125, *126*
    lighting, 101, 135-144
    scene arrangement, 131-135
    tree creation, 102-110
    tree texturing, 110-113
    water and algae creation, 126-131
exoskeleton, 167, 207
    caterpillars, 275
Extend Ripples extension (Studio
        Pro), 102, 127-128
EyeCandy 3.0 Jiggle, 151
eyes (dragonflies)
    creation, 237-238
    mapping, 244-247
eyes (Giant Madagascar Hissing Cock-
        roach), 195-200
eyes (Postman Butterfly Caterpillar),
        289
eyes (Stag Beetle), 260
    surfacing, 273

F

FaceScape (3D Studio MAX), 58
feelers (Giant Madagascar Hissing

Cockroach), 204-205
feelers (Stag Beetle), 260-262
surfacing, 273
filler lights
alien plants, 76
The Entrance, 136-137
flat edges, lack of in natural environ-
        ments, 1
flowers, 33-34, *35*, *50*
    alien, 57, 63
    assembly of parts, 49, 50
    bud creation, 40-42
    bud texturing, 45-46, 48
    creating with LightWave, 33-51
    flower creation, 35-39
    leaf creation, 40
    leaf texturing, 47-48, 148-165
    stamen creation, 39
    stamen texturing, 48
    stem creation, 40
    stem texturing, 48
    texturing, 43-49, 148-165
The Fly (movie), insectoid creature in,
        169
fog shader, 141-142
forests, 3
    bare spots, 7
    dense ground cover, 10
    scene with flowers, 50
    texture mapped pine trees, 28
4D Paint, 63
Fractal Painter 5, alien plant texturing,
        69, 78
fringe grass, 5-6

G

gels, 300-301. *See also* lighting
Giant Madagascar Hissing Cockroach,
        See cockroach
global light, Postman Butterfly Cater-
        pillar, 300
Goblin scenes
    The Entrance, 101, *102*
    Unfathomable Crag, 4-8, *5*, *6*

Gradient Designer plug-in, 161
grass
    creation in The Entrance, 113-121
    instancing, 99
grayscale files, 102
Great Goblin Gauntlet, 4
greenery, *See* plants
Gromphadorhina portentosa (Giant
        Madagascar Hissing Cockroach),
        See cockroach
ground cover, 6-8
Grumpy, 4
Guzloader, 5

H
Hair extension (Studio Pro), 275, 276
head armor (Giant Madagascar Hissing
        Cockroach), 201-206
head (dragonflies), 237-239
head (Giant Madagascar Hissing Cock-
        roach), 193-200
head (Postman Butterfly Caterpillar),
        286-290
head (Stag Beetle), 254-263
hillside, creation in The Entrance,
        121-125, *126*
Hollywood movies, insectoid creatures
        in, 167, 169
horror creatures, insect-based, 167

I
Import as 3D Mesh command (Studio
        Pro), 102, 128-129
industrial scenes, natural environ-
        ments contrasted, 1, 3
insects, 167, 275. *See also* cockroach;
        dragonflies; Postman Butterfly
        Caterpillar; Stag Beetle
    chaotic details, 207
    resources for finding, 169-170
    surfacing, 207-210
instancing, 99, 100

J
jaws (dragonflies), 238-239
jaws (Stag Beetle), 257-259
June Bug, 253

L
leafy trees, 31
leaves, 3
    adding as morph targets, 31
    for flowers, 40, 47-48
    instancing, 99
    scanning, 148
    texturing with Photoshop, 47-48,
        149-165
leg coloration, insects, 209
legs (dragonflies), 239-242
    mapping, 249-251
legs (Giant Madagascar Hissing Cock-
        roach), 182-185, 204-205
legs (Postman Butterfly Caterpillar),
        290-294
    surfacing, 298
legs (Stag Beetle), 269-272
lens flare, alien plants, 76, 77
lighting
    alien plants, 75-78
    dragonflies, 251
    The Entrance, 101, 135-144
    Postman Butterfly Caterpillar,
        300-301
LightWave
    Christmas tree creation, 12-31
    cockroach creation, 169-206
    cockroach surfacing, 207-229
    plant and flower creation, 33-51
lilies, *See* flowers
lines, lack of straight in natural envi-
        ronments, 1

M
Macropanesthia rhinocerus (cock-
        roach species), 171

maple trees, 31

Megaloblatta longipennis (cockroch species), 171

MetaBall extension (Studio Pro), 286-288, 291-292

mist shader, 141-142

morph targets, for leaf addition to trees, 31

moss, 8

Mud Goblins, 9

mushrooms, 10

N

natural environments
 challenges of creating, 1, 3-4
 creating, 3-31
 The Entrance, 99-145

O

observation, importance of in viewing natural environments, 1, 3, 10

on-line resources, insects, 170

organ pipe cactus, 87-89

P

painting template
 creation for alien plants, 63-65
 creation for Giant Madagascar Hissing Cockroach, 212-214

Paintshop Pro, 216

parallel light, 135-136

Path Extrude objects (Studio Pro), 102

petals, creating in LightWave, 36-39

Photoshop
 alien plant texturing, 67-71
 cockroach surfacing, 216-229
 dragonfly surfacing, 247
 flower texturing, 38, 43-49
 leaf texturing, 149-165
 Postman Butterfly Caterpillar surfacing, 298
 surfacing overview, 147-149, 166

tree texturing (The Entrance), 110-113

water texturing (The Entrance), 126-131

Photoshop 4 Wow!, 153

pine (Christmas) tree, See Christmas tree

pine needles, on Christmas tree, 11, 18-23

plants. *See also* alien plants; cactus garden; flowers
 chaotic details, 1
 colors, 145, 208
 creating with LightWave, 33-51
 importance in natural environments, 1, 3
 placement in natural environments, 7-8
 when to use, 33-35

point lights, The Entrance, 101

Postman Butterfly Caterpillar, 275-276
 body segment creation, 276-280
 bone creation, 280-283
 head creation, 286-290
 leg creation, 290-294
 lighting, 300-301
 spine creation, 294-298
 surfacing, 298
 tail creation, 283-286

Predator (movie), insectoid creature in, 167, 169

prickly pears, 80-86, *87*

Pro Optic Suite, alien plant lighting, 76

Pumpkinhead (movie), insectoid creature in, 167

R

rain forest, 9-10

random rocks, 7

random weeds, 7

Ray Dream Studio, 2, 167

Rhinoceros 3D, 2, 167

rocks, 7
importance in natural environments, 3
roots, 7

S
saguaro cactus, 90-92
Scarab Beetle, 253
shoulder segment (Giant Madagascar Hissing Cockroach), 192-193
Skin objects (Studio Pro), 101, 102
Soft F/X Pro, 2, 167
Spatter, 151-152
speckling, insect surfaces, 207, 209
specularity maps, leaves, 157, 162
spiders, 169, 170
spines (Postman Butterfly Caterpillar), 294-298
spotlights
The Entrance, 101, 136-138
Postman Butterfly Caterpillar, 300-301
Stag Beetle, 253-254, 254, 273
abdomen creation, 264-269
head creation, 254-263
leg creation, 269-272
surfacing, 272-273
thorax creation, 263-264
stamen, creating in LightWave, 39
texturing, 48
Starship Troopers (movie), insects in, 169
stem, creating in LightWave, 39
texturing, 48
stencil map, 149, 162-163
Strata Studio Pro
The Entrance creation, 99-145
Postman Butterfly Caterpillar creation, 275-301
succulents, 94
surfacing. *See also* texturing
cockroach, 210-229
dragonfly, 243-251
importance of, 147-149, 166
Postman Butterfly Caterpillar, 298
Stag Beetle, 272-273

T
tail (dragonflies)
creation, 235-236
mapping, 248-249
tail (Giant Madagascar Hissing Cockroach)
creation, 173-179
painting, 216-220
tail (Postman Butterfly Caterpillar), 283-286
template, for texture painting, See painting template
texturing. *See also* painting template; surfacing; UV mapping
alien plants, 54, 55, 61-75
cactus garden, 96-97, 98
Christmas tree branches, 24-26
efficient use of, 99
The Entrance tree, 110-113
The Entrance water, 126-131
flowers, 43-49
Postman Butterfly Caterpillar, 298
ThermoClay 2 plug-in, 81
thorax (Stag Beetle), 263-264
surfacing, 273
3D Studio Max
alien plant creation, 53-78
dragonfly creation, 231-251
three-point lighting, alien plants, 76, 77
torso (Giant Madagascar Hissing Cockroach), 221-225
Tree Professional, 2
trees
creation in The Entrance, 102-110
importance in natural environments, 3
leafy, 31
pine (Christmas) tree, 11-31
texturing in The Entrance, 110-113

tree stumps, 3
trueSpace
    cactus garden creation, 79-98
    Stag Beetle creation, 253-274
twigs, 3, 10
    instancing, 99
    on top of Christmas tree, 27-29

U
Unfathomable Crag, 4-8, 5, 6
UV mapping
    alien plants, 61-63, 73
    dragonfly, 236, 239
    The Entrance, 103, 112, 118
    Postman Butterfly Caterpillar, 279-
        280, 298
UV Unwrap (3D Studio MAX), 63-66

V
vegetation, 33
volumetric light, The Entrance, 101,
        140-141
Vue d'Esprit, 2

W
water, creation in The Entrance, 126-
        131
weeds, 3, 7
What's Under the Fridge? tutorial, See
        cockroach
wings (dragonflies), 242
    mapping, 243-244
wings (Stag Beetles), 266-269
    surfacing, 272-273
wolf spider, 170